Brexit

In June 2016 the United Kingdom shocked the world by voting to leave the European Union. As this book reveals, the historic vote for a Brexit marked the culmination of trends in domestic politics and in the UK's relationship with the EU that have been building over many years. Drawing on a wealth of survey evidence collected over more than 10 years, this book explains why a majority of people decided to ignore much of the national and international community and vote for Brexit. Drawing on past research on voting in major referendums in Europe and elsewhere, a team of leading academic experts analyse changes in the UK's party system that were catalysts for the referendum vote, including the rise of the UK Independence Party (UKIP), the dynamics of public opinion during an unforgettable and divisive referendum campaign, the factors that influenced how people voted and the likely economic and political impact of this historic decision.

HAROLD D. CLARKE is Ashbel Smith Professor at the University of Texas, Dallas. His recent books include *Austerity and Political Choice in Britain* (2015) and *Affluence, Austerity and Electoral Change in Britain* (Cambridge, 2013).

MATTHEW GOODWIN is Professor of Political Science at the University of Kent and Senior Visiting Fellow at Chatham House, London. He is the author of four books, including *Revolt on the Right: Explaining Public Support for the Radical Right in Britain* (2014), which was awarded the Paddy Power Political Book of the Year 2015. In early 2016 he authored a report that predicted Brexit. Matthew tweets @GoodwinMJ.

PAUL WHITELEY is a Professor of Government at the University of Essex and is currently the director for the Centre for the Study of Integrity at the University of Essex. He is the author of eighteen academic books including studies of electoral behaviour, party members and citizenship in Britain.

Brexit

Why Britain Voted to Leave the European Union

HAROLD D. CLARKE
University of Texas, Dallas

MATTHEW GOODWIN
University of Kent, Canterbury

PAUL WHITELEY
University of Essex

CAMBRIDGE
UNIVERSITY PRESS

CAMBRIDGE
UNIVERSITY PRESS

University Printing House, Cambridge CB2 8BS, United Kingdom

One Liberty Plaza, 20th Floor, New York, NY 10006, USA

477 Williamstown Road, Port Melbourne, VIC 3207, Australia

314–321, 3rd Floor, Plot 3, Splendor Forum, Jasola District Centre, New Delhi – 110025, India

79 Anson Road, #06-04/06, Singapore 079906

Cambridge University Press is part of the University of Cambridge.

It furthers the University's mission by disseminating knowledge in the pursuit of education, learning, and research at the highest international levels of excellence.

www.cambridge.org
Information on this title: www.cambridge.org/9781107150720

DOI: 10.1017/9781316584408

© Harold D. Clarke, Matthew Goodwin and Paul Whiteley 2017

First published 2017
5th printing 2019

Printed in the United Kingdom by TJ International Ltd. Padstow Cornwall

A catalogue record for this publication is available from the British Library.

ISBN 978-1-107-15072-0 Hardback
ISBN 978-1-316-60504-2 Paperback

Every week we send £350 million to Brussels. I'd rather that we control how to spend that money, and if I had that control I would spend it on the NHS.

Gisela Stuart, 15 April 2016

Theresa May says it's difficult to control immigration as part of the EU. She's wrong – it is not difficult, it's impossible.

Nigel Farage, 29 April 2016

… maybe some point down the line, there might be a UK–US trade agreement, but it's not going to happen any time soon … the UK is going to be in the back of the queue …

Barack Obama, 22 April 2016

I am absolutely convinced that our economic security will be better if we stay in a reformed European Union and it will be seriously at risk if we were to leave.

David Cameron, 15 May 2016

Napoleon, Hitler, various people tried this [unifying Europe], and it ends tragically. The EU is an attempt to do this by different methods.

Boris Johnson, 15 May 2016

As Chancellor, I would have a responsibility to try to restore stability to the public finances and that would mean an emergency Budget where we would have to increase taxes and cut spending … [Q]uitting the EU would mean less money. Billions less. It's a lose-lose situation for British families and we shouldn't risk it.

George Osborne, 15 June 2016

It's a pretty overwhelming case when you have a huge body of economists [that agree] that it's going to cost [the UK], it's going to be negative for income purposes, it's going to reduce trade most likely as a result of uncertainty and those are blatant facts.

Christine Lagarde, 17 June 2016

We know how bad our government is at defending our borders, and within a few years all of these people [Middle East refugees] will have EU passports. We are much less safe as part of this European Union.

Nigel Farage, 22 June 2016

Contents

Figures

Tables

Foreword

Brexit changed everything. Or at least so it seemed. For many amongst what have come to be known as the 'liberal metropolitan elite', it overturned several decades of thinking about what Britain is and where it is headed. 'What have we become?' became a common refrain around middle-class dinner tables.

Obviously, and as ever, reality is slightly more complicated. Britain's decision to leave the European Union revealed as much about how its society had been changing for many years as it did about the impact of the short and bitter referendum campaign itself.

Yet there can be little doubt that the decision that was taken will have profound consequences for the future of the country. Obviously, the nature of its relationship with the European Union will change. As important, however, will be the impact of the decision on our politics.

Already, we see the way in which the Scottish National Party is using Brexit to further its own political and independence-related agendas. There is lingering uncertainty about the future of the UK Independence Party now its central aim has been achieved, and still more over where its voters might go should they decide to withdraw their support. Prime Minister Theresa May clearly has half an eye on these people as she renews her pledge to reduce immigration and bring the country out from under the jurisdiction of the EU's Court. Meanwhile, the Labour Party, largely ineffective within parliament as Her Majesty's Opposition, confronts the danger of haemorrhaging votes at the next election as its leader's popularity rating shows no sign of improving.

In order to understand the way in which politics might develop at this unique moment in our history, it is crucial to have a firm understanding of what has happened to date. And here it is important to understand the importance of careful, detailed, empirically based analysis.

The failure of pollsters accurately to predict not only the Brexit outcome, but also the election of Donald Trump and, 18 months earlier, of a majority Conservative Government in the UK have led many people to conclude that an accurate understanding of contemporary politics is impossible. Yet this is to confuse prediction with explanation. The former has never been simple, and depends, in part, on the ability of pollsters to predict who will vote at all. In contrast, whilst failing to anticipate the outcomes, analysts have proven extremely good at identifying the kinds of choices that people are liable to make.

This book provides an excellent example of the way in which good, clear, methodologically rigorous analysis can further our understanding both of what has happened, and what the implications of these events might be. Following the vote in June, we all knew our country was profoundly divided, but the nature of the divisions and their potential to fundamentally reshape our politics are made abundantly clear in what follows.

Moreover, what the authors have achieved here is to present their findings in a clear and accessible way. Too much academic research is simply impenetrable to non-specialists, meaning that their insights into the social world remain largely undiscovered.

Brexit is too important for that. What follows is of relevance not only to academics but to all those – politicians, journalists, civil servants and 'the public' – who want to understand what has happened and where our politics might be going. I can't think of a better compliment than that.

Anand Menon
Director
The UK in a Changing Europe Initiative
Oxford

Acknowledgements

Brexit: Why Britain Voted to Leave the European Union relies heavily on survey data gathered in two projects. The first are monthly surveys with representative national samples of the British electorate conducted over the period April 2004 to June 2016. These 'Essex Continuous Monitoring Surveys' (ECMS) have generated a wealth of data on the dynamics of the political attitudes and behaviour of the British electorate during a 12-year period when the country was experiencing large-scale economic and social change and major political upheaval. In the latter category, Britain's long-lived political party system was encountering serious stress from several sources, one of the most important of which was the rise of the right-wing populist United Kingdom Independence Party (UKIP). After the 2010 general election, UKIP support increased dramatically, setting in motion a series of events that culminated in the United Kingdom's historic decision in the 23 June 2016 referendum to leave the European Union. The ECMS data provide us with a detailed record of the opinions, beliefs and behaviour of the British electorate as these highly consequential political dynamics unfolded.

The second data set we employ in *Brexit* is the product of a chance encounter between two of the authors, Clarke and Whiteley, and the third, Goodwin, at the September 2014 Elections, Public Opinion and Parties annual conference in Edinburgh. Seated at the same table at the conference banquet, as wine was poured (and consumed!), we talked about the rise of UKIP and the work that we had been doing on the party, as well as earlier studies of party activists in the UK, Canada and the United States that Clarke and Whiteley had undertaken. But UKIP was definitely the focus of attention. All three of us had been using mass survey data to study factors affecting the growing electoral support that UKIP was enjoying. In addition, for his recent book, *Revolt on the Right* (co-authored with Rob Ford), Goodwin had done in-depth interviews with UKIP's leadership and fieldwork observing the party's local organizations and campaign activities.

As the conversation progressed (and more wine was consumed), we agreed that it would be valuable to conduct a large-scale survey of people who had become members of UKIP, using questions that would permit comparisons with data on public attitudes gathered in the ECMS. UKIP generously agreed to permit us to do the member survey, provided us with contact information and, in November 2014, we were in the field. The data gathered via our UKIP party member survey help us to understand the sources of UKIP support and key factors motivating voters to choose the Brexit option in the EU referendum. The analyses in the chapters that follow employ both the ECMS and the UKIP members study data to help us understand the party's rise and its impact on the referendum decision.

We are pleased to have this opportunity to thank those individuals and organizations that made the *Brexit* project possible. First, we thank Anand Menon, Director of The UK in a Changing Europe Initiative, for his interest in our proposal to do the pre- and post-referendum surveys. These surveys are essential for the success of the project and they would not have been possible without generous support from the Initiative. Additional funding for the referendum surveys was provided by the University of Texas at Dallas (UTD) and the University of Essex. At the University of Essex, we particularly wish to thank Lawrence Ezrow, Chair of the Department of Government, for his interest and support. At UTD, we are pleased to acknowledge the encouragement of Vice President Hobson Wildenthal, Dean Denis Dean and Political Science Program Head, Jennifer Holmes.

We also are pleased to acknowledge the Economics and Social Research Council (ESRC) for its generous financial support for the 2005 and 2010 British Election Studies (BES). The monthly ECMS data collections were funded for several years by grant monies from the 2005 and 2010 BES. Major funding for the ECMS also was provided by a grant from the US National Science Foundation (NSF). We especially appreciate the interest in our work shown by NSF Political Science Program Officers, Frank Scioli, Jim Granato and Brian Humes. We also acknowledge ongoing financial support provided by UTD. In addition to assisting with the ECMS surveys, UTD supports the Qualtrics survey platform used for the UKIP members survey.

There are also a large number of people who helped us to develop our knowledge about how to study the important choices that people make in elections, parties, referendums and other democratic political settings. In particular, we wish to thank Robert Ford, Jeff Gill, Ron Johnston, Peter Kellner, Allan Kornberg, Matt Lebo, Larry LeDuc, Mike Lewis-Beck, Helmut Norpoth, Jon Pammett, Jason Reifler, David Sanders, Tom Scotto, Pat Seyd, Randy Stevenson, Marianne Stewart, Guy Whitten and Stan Wong. Also, like many other social scientists, we owe a special debt of gratitude to our colleague and dear friend, the late Allan McCutcheon, who developed valuable tools for studying the dynamics of public attitudes and behaviour and then generously taught us how to use them.

There are also people who assisted us with administrative and technical aspects of the project. At UTD, Cheryl Berry, Political Science Program Assistant, cheerfully kept the paperwork moving smoothly and efficiently, while Karl Ho and Russell Hoffman provided the computing expertise needed to build the *Brexit* website. A very special shout-out is due to Karl for the many hours he spent developing the web survey of UKIP party members. His services are greatly appreciated.

In addition, we are pleased to thank UKIP for permitting us to conduct a rigorous, non-partisan survey of the party's members. In particular, we thank Matthew Richardson, Damian Wilson and Steve Crowther for helping us to field the web and mailback versions of the survey and Nigel Farage for endorsing the project with the membership. Their willingness to assist us made the study possible and we appreciate their co-operation.

Last, but most certainly not least, we are very pleased to acknowledge the assistance of Joe Twyman, Head of Political and Social Research, YouGov, plc. All of the ECMS surveys since April 2004 were conducted by YouGov under Joe's careful supervision. His assistance has been generous, unflagging and invaluable and he is an excellent colleague and great friend. Thanks so much, Joe!

A Note About Data

In this book we draw on a wealth of quantitative survey data to examine public attitudes and the vote for Brexit. Not every reader will be familiar with this kind of data analysis. For this reason, we advise those readers who are unfamiliar with quantitative methods to focus their attention on the text that surrounds the tables and on our write-up of the results, which we have tried to make as accessible as possible.

For those who would like further information about the data that underpins this book – including a description of the variables used in the multivariate analyses, questionnaires, data and a data dictionary for the pre- and post-waves of our EU referendum survey – please visit the following website and click on 'Brexit': www.utdallas.edu/epps/hclarke/. The questionnaires, data and the data dictionary will also be posted on the Harvard Dataverse Archive.

Readers can find further information relating to the book at: www.cambridge.org/gb/academic/subjects/politics-international-relations/british-government-politics-and-policy/brexit-why-britain-voted-leave-european-union?format=PB.

1 | *Brexit Introduced*

On Thursday 23 June 2016, 26.3 million people in the United Kingdom headed to their nearest polling station to cast a vote in a national referendum. Another 7.2 million had already cast their ballot by post. When voters looked at their ballot paper they would have read the following question: 'Should the United Kingdom remain a member of the European Union or leave the European Union?' That this was a question that aroused strong passions in the electorate was reflected in the fact that, at 72.2 per cent, turnout at the referendum reached the highest level of any political contest since the general election in 1992.

The 2016 referendum was not the first time that the people were asked for their view about their country's relationship with continental Europe. In 1975, at the first ever referendum to be held in the United Kingdom, an earlier generation of voters had been asked whether they wanted to stay in what was then called the European Community (the Common Market). In that earlier referendum the people had voted by a margin of two to one to stay in the European Community. Although public support for EC membership seemed commanding, it is important to keep it in perspective, as academics David Butler and Uwe Kitzinger (1996: 279) observed at the time: 'It was unequivocal but it was also unenthusiastic. Support for membership was wide but it did not run deep.' The decision to stay had been influenced by two factors. The first was a stagnating national economy that had left the UK as the 'sick man of Europe', a country that was grappling with what was then called 'the British disease' – a pernicious combination of steep inflation, high unemployment, low productivity and industrial unrest. Not surprisingly, the UK looked at the economies across the Channel with envy. The second factor was a relatively strong and widespread sense of loyalty to the main political parties (Clarke et al. 2004), which were competing in a stable party system, enjoyed support from what was still a largely deferential public and which had collectively recommended that the people vote to stay – which they did.

1

At the referendum in 2016, however, both the result and wider context were entirely different. The country's Conservative Prime Minister, David Cameron, had initially promised to hold the referendum during his so-called 'Bloomberg speech' in January 2013, a move that many interpreted as an attempt to fend off growing pressure from a group of backbench Eurosceptic MPs and the sudden rise of a new Eurosceptic party in national politics, UKIP. The latter was drawing much of its voting strength from disgruntled Conservatives who opposed EU membership (Ford and Goodwin 2014).

Standing in the London headquarters of Bloomberg News, Cameron began his speech by outlining a European continent that looked fundamentally different from that which the UK had looked towards with envy during the 1970s. By 2013, the EU had enlarged from nine countries in the 1970s to 28 member states, some of which had much weaker economies than their West European counterparts. Beginning in 2008, the continent had been hit hard by the Great Recession and a major debt crisis that was especially severe in southern EU member states such as Greece, Spain and Portugal. Unemployment and sovereign debt reached disturbingly high levels, while the continent struggled to revive economic growth, pay down debt and implement necessary reforms. In sharp contrast to the picture that had confronted Prime Minister Harold Wilson in 1975, Cameron now talked of a continent that was blighted by a lack of competitiveness, excessive regulation, a deficit of democratic accountability, and that had taken too many powers away from individual member states.

Cameron, who less than 10 years earlier had warned the Conservative Party that its tendency to 'bang on about Europe' had alienated voters, now committed his party to holding a referendum on the country's EU membership should it form a majority government after the next general election in 2015. When that contest arrived, the Conservative Party asked the electorate for a mandate to negotiate a new settlement with the EU, after which it would hold an 'in or out' referendum. Cameron stated: 'It is time for the British people to have their say. It is time to settle this European question in British politics. I say to the British people: this will be your decision.'[1]

Cameron had always been a gambler. Ever since rising to the top of the Conservative Party in 2005, his political legacy had been defined by a series of gambles – that he could 'modernize' a party that put a premium on tradition; that after the election in 2010 he could successfully lead the first Coalition Government in the country for nearly 70 years; that in 2011 he could convince voters to retain the 'first-past-the-post' electoral system in a national referendum on electoral reform; that in 2014 he could preserve the United Kingdom by winning a referendum on Scottish independence; and in 2015 that he could not only return to power but deliver to Conservatives something they had not had for nearly 20 years, a majority government. By promising a referendum on EU membership, a move that could potentially and profoundly alter the UK's place in the world, the youngest prime minister for nearly 200 years had gambled once again.

Although Cameron would not have known it at the time, by committing the country to a vote on its EU membership he had set himself on a path that would leave him as the third prime minister in post-war Britain who would forever be remembered for only one thing. After Anthony Eden and the Suez crisis in 1956, then Tony Blair and the war in Iraq that began in 2003, Cameron's legacy would soon forever be associated with the result of the 2016 referendum. But all of that was yet to come. At the time of his Bloomberg speech the young leader believed that his lucky streak would continue. As Tim Bale, a leading authority on the Conservative Party, observed:

That belief stemmed, at least in part, from his natural self-confidence: so many of his gambles over the years had paid off, and he was far surer than he should have been that he would be able to extract the kind of eye-catching concessions from other EU member states that would persuade a majority of British voters (if not the diehard sceptics in his own party) that he had achieved a fundamental change in the UK's relationship with 'Brussels'. (Bale 2016)

Cameron placed his bet. It would be his last.

Many expected Cameron to win. During the campaign one 'expert survey' of nearly 600 journalists, academics and pollsters asked them to share their predictions of the result. Overall, some 87 per cent thought that the country would vote to remain in the EU and only 5 per cent predicted a Brexit (the remainder thought that both sides had an equal chance).[2]

This widely held belief that, in the end, people would vote to remain in the EU had, in turn, been driven by an assumption that they would choose the least risky path and side with the status quo. The idea was supported by what we call 'LeDuc's law', a regularity in people's voting behaviour in referendums discovered by Larry LeDuc (2003), a professor of political science at the University of Toronto. After studying referendums around the world, events that are characterized by high stakes and abundant uncertainty about the consequences of the different outcomes, LeDuc noted that while people often expressed support for the 'change option' at the start of the campaign they would increasingly side with the status quo, the less risky option, as the campaign progressed. They would, after a period of indecision, bet on 'the devil they knew'. In the UK, this belief in aversion to risk and bias towards the status quo had been further cultivated by the outcomes of both at the 2011 referendum on changing the electoral system and the 2014 referendum on Scottish independence.

As the country hurtled towards the 2016 referendum this consensus was reflected in an assessment made by *The Economist*'s Intelligence Unit that outlined why the status quo would prevail. One factor was Cameron himself, the nation's newly re-elected leader, who only eight months earlier had won a majority government and was about to throw his full weight behind campaigning for Remain. Then came the voters; while they looked restless, the analysts concluded there was 'little risk' of an anti-establishment backlash. 'Although it is true that anti-establishment feeling is running higher than usual in the UK, and that much of it is directed – albeit in a rather inchoate way – towards Europe, we do not believe that it is strong enough to sway the final result'. In the end, they would side with the status quo. 'As is often the case when a constitutional referendum is held, defending the status quo is easier than arguing for a radical departure from it.'[3]

But the pundits were wrong and David Cameron lost his wager. When the ballots were counted on the night of 23 June, 51.9 per cent of the electorate had voted to leave the EU, a figure that jumped to almost 54 per cent in England. The result sent shockwaves around the world. As we will see in this book, despite being confronted with an avalanche of advice from national and international figures to vote to remain, and apocalyptic warnings about the consequences that would follow a Brexit, a majority voted to leave the EU. By doing so, they chose to reject the recommendations of their prime minister, most of the Cabinet, a large majority of their elected MPs and countless businesses, global political leaders and international organizations, from the World Bank to the International Monetary Fund. As Bogdanor

(2016) observed, the vote marked the first time in the nation's history when the House of Commons would be asked to follow a policy recommendation to which around three-quarters of MPs had been opposed.

All of this underscores the need for research into what led the United Kingdom to vote to leave the European Union. Since the vote there has emerged a lively debate about the drivers of the 'Leave' vote. Some argue that this was driven chiefly by public concerns about a perceived loss of national sovereignty to the EU. Others focus instead on an economically 'left-behind' section of society that saw the 2016 referendum as an opportunity to vent their deep frustration about their relative deprivation. Another view has focused instead on the role of public anxieties over immigration, which in particular since 2004 has moved to the forefront of the issue agenda. As we will see, these debates are also mirrored in academic research that has sought to shed light on the factors that influence public attitudes towards the EU and European integration. One key question that we address in this book concerns the relative importance of these and other explanations for understanding the referendum vote.

Meanwhile, in recent years there has emerged a parallel debate over the role of the populist right party, UKIP, which since 2010 has actively campaigned to mobilize anti-EU and anti-immigration sentiment among the public. The presence of UKIP is another important difference from the context surrounding the 1975 referendum. Far from a fringe movement, the party has been a major contributor to the increasing fragmentation of the UK's party system that has occurred in recent years (see Goodwin and Milazzo 2015; Clarke et al. 2016a). By the time of the 2016 referendum UKIP had attracted a surge of popular support, which we explore in Chapters 5 and 6, replaced the Liberal Democrats as the third most popular party in the polls, won the 2014 European Parliament elections, two parliamentary by-elections in Clacton and then Rochester and Strood, and attracted nearly 4 million votes at the 2015 general election in 2015. But whereas some suggest that UKIP is an important element in the 'Brexit story', others argue that Leave won *despite* the populist right and its divisive leader, Nigel Farage. In the following chapters, we examine in detail the impact of Farage and his party on the politics of the EU referendum and efforts to win a Leave majority.

There are already several books that explore the referendum campaign, including the various personalities and groups that shaped this unique moment in British history.[4] Nor is this the first academic study of Euroscepticism in the UK (see Ford and Goodwin 2014; Goodwin and Milazzo 2015; Clarke et al. 2016a). But it is the first to draw on longitudinal aggregate- and individual-level survey data to examine the drivers of support for leaving the EU in a more holistic fashion, investigating each of several steps that led the country towards voting for a Brexit.

Most of the data on public opinion and political behaviour that we employ in this book were gathered in a lengthy series of representative national surveys conducted virtually every month from April 2004 to the time of the EU referendum in June 2016. It should be noted that the June 2016 survey has a panel design such that respondents were contacted a few days before the referendum and then contacted again right after the balloting so that we could ascertain if they had voted and, if so, whether they had voted Remain or Leave. All of the surveys were conducted online by YouGov, plc. under the direction of the project supervisor, Joe Twyman. Funds for the surveys were provided by a series of research grants from the National Science Foundation (USA) and the Economics and Social Research Council (UK). Major funding for the June 2016 surveys was provided the ESRC's UK in a Changing Europe programme.

The monthly Essex Continuous Monitoring Surveys (ECMS) provide a wealth of information on a wide range of important topics including levels of support among the public for the various political parties, people's feelings about party leaders like Cameron, Jeremy Corbyn and Nigel Farage, perceptions of important problems facing the country and their evaluations of how the Government has performed in key policy delivery areas, such as the economy, the National Health Service, immigration and crime. Other questions tap feelings of whether the country's political and economic systems treat ordinary people equitably and fairly, whether Government is honest and trustworthy, and levels of (dis)satisfaction with how democracy is currently working in the UK. Importantly for this book, each month the surveys also asked people about their attitudes towards the UK's continued membership of the EU, their desired levels of immigration and perceptions of whether Britain or the EU controls the national economy. Taken together, these data provide the information needed to understand the dynamics of public opinion towards the EU and why, in the end, the electorate decided to opt for Brexit.

In addition, we also employ data gathered in a large-scale survey of nearly 15,000 UKIP members. This unique survey was conducted over the period November 2014–January 2015 and contains a number of questions on key topics such as the economy, immigration, the NHS, feelings about various groups in society, perceptions of the behaviour of political and economic elites and the larger political system that are identical to those asked in the monthly surveys of the general public. The ability to compare the men and women who decided to join Nigel Farage's so-called 'People's Army' with the electorate as a whole helps us to understand the bases of UKIP's support and its' appeal (or lack thereof) in wider society.

The remainder of this book is organized as follows. In the first two chapters we 'set the scene' by outlining the referendum campaign. In Chapter 2 we examine the background to the campaign, including the country's mood in the period that preceded the referendum and the role and impact of David Cameron's renegotiation of the terms of EU membership. In Chapter 3, we continue the story of the campaign by examining the competing narratives to voters that were put on offer by the Remain and Leave campaigns and trends in support for the Remain and Leave options in the run-up to the vote.

In Chapter 4 we turn to examine trends in public support for EU membership since 2004. This allows us to show how public attitudes towards this issue have been volatile over a long period of time. Making sense of this volatility and what is behind it is important background information to understanding why the country went on to vote for Brexit. After reviewing recent research on what shapes people's attitudes towards the EU, we put forward a 'valence politics' theory of attitudes towards EU membership, arguing that at root the nation's debate about EU membership has turned on whether membership is seen to have delivered things like economic prosperity, controlled immigration, national and personal security, value for money and, more generally, if the EU is seen as responsive and accountable to people.

In Chapter 5 we explore a development that helped to bring the issues of Europe and also immigration to the forefront of the country's political debate – the rise of UKIP. Several important questions about the party remain unanswered. While UKIP voters have received attention (see Goodwin and Milazzo 2015; Clarke et al. 2016a), there has been almost no research on the men and women who joined the party as members and campaigned at the grassroots for Brexit. What are their social and political backgrounds? What do they believe? What motivates their higher level of commitment to campaigning to leave the EU and how do they compare to the public at large? Contrary to widespread assumptions we show how many rank-and-file members of the populist right party are not radically different from the public at large. Both those who have joined UKIP and those who have not appear deeply concerned about rapacious banks, corporate greed, economic inequality and social injustice and feel they have been economically 'left behind'. UKIP-ers and much of the public at large also share very similar feelings about various minority groups in British society, revealing how the potential for populist revolts in the UK is unlikely to disappear in the short-term.

In Chapter 6, we investigate how UKIP was able to break through during elections to the European Parliament in 2014 and then the general election in 2015. We argue that these two critically important contests 'set the stage' for the historic 2016 vote for Brexit. After examining different theories that seek to account for why populist right parties like UKIP attract support, we investigate the aggregate dynamics of the party's support by drawing on monthly surveys that were undertaken between April 2004 and April 2015, just before the general election. These data allow us to develop an individual-level model to analyse the UKIP vote at the 2014 European Parliament elections and 2015 general election. This allows us to show that while UKIP was propelled into the mainstream by public opposition towards the country's EU membership, there have also been other sources of support for the party. These include the people's negative judgements about how respective Governments have managed the economy, the NHS and immigration, and how the Labour Party was damaged by its perceived incompetence while managing the Great Recession and a surge of immigration that took place during its time in public office. Furthermore, we show how these results provided clear signposts for what was to happen at the 2016 referendum.

In Chapter 7 we study the drivers of support for the Leave vote at the 2016 referendum. Was the decision to leave motivated by instrumental considerations over the perceived costs and benefits of EU membership? Were judgements about adverse economic effects of EU membership concentrated mainly among people who felt they had been 'left behind' by the country's economic transformation? Or was this vote driven more strongly by feelings of national identity and anxiety over perceived threats to the native in-group, from immigration and the free movement of EU nationals? And, also, how influential were 'cues' from individual politicians such as David Cameron, Boris Johnson and Nigel Farage in motivating people to get into the polling booth for Remain or Leave? Drawing on data gathered in our pre- and post-referendum surveys, we show how there was not one 'single' reason for Brexit. Rather, the narrow Leave victory was made possible by a complex and cross-cutting mix of calculations, emotions and cues.

In Chapter 8, we consider the longer-term economic and political consequences of Brexit. Though the full consequences of this momentous decision will not be known for a long time, it is possible to examine some plausible scenarios about what – at a broad level – is likely to happen to the country's economy, society and political system. The analyses demonstrate why, in terms of economic growth, it is hard to discern clear positive effects of membership either in the UK or in many other EU member states, apart from a handful of former 'Warsaw Pact' countries in Central and Eastern Europe. The general conclusion of that chapter is that the adverse effects of Brexit have been exaggerated both by the media and by the UK Treasury.

In Chapter 9, the concluding chapter, we consider three topics that are relevant for understanding the possible futures of the UK and the EU in the post-Brexit era. First, we examine what would have happened if everyone had voted in the EU referendum. In the wake of the referendum, disappointed Remainers claimed that the result did not represent the sentiments of the electorate as a whole. 'If only everyone had voted', some argue, 'then Remain would have won.' Data gathered in our pre- and post-referendum panel survey enable us to assess this claim. The second topic concerns the public mood since the referendum. Have voters suffered from 'Brexit remorse' leading to a groundswell of public opinion to hold a second referendum and give people a chance to undo the decision? A special survey we carried out in the UK, France and Germany in late September 2016 and several opinion polls conducted since the referendum help us to address this question. Third, how do attitudes towards the EU in the UK compare with attitudes elsewhere in Europe? Using our September 2016 survey data and also data from the European Social

Survey, we investigate similarities and differences in the attitudes of the UK, French and German publics towards the EU and the key issue of immigration. We also compare the long-term dynamics of public attitudes towards EU membership in the UK with those in several other EU countries. Chapter 9 concludes with a summary of our major findings and their relevance for understanding the future of the British party system and UK politics more generally in the post-Brexit world.

2 | *Campaign Prologue*

In 2016 two competing camps in British politics went into battle. The outcome between the Remain and Leave forces would not only determine the nature of the country's relationship with the EU but also reshape how the UK interacted with the wider world. In what would become one of the most divisive campaigns in recent political history, the two sides set out to make their case and convince a majority of the electorate that they merited its support. This chapter describes the background to and context of the 2016 referendum campaign, a contest that would dominate British politics and ultimately change the direction of the entire country.

The Public Mood

As the British people celebrated the Christmas of 2015 they knew that a referendum on their country's EU membership was on the horizon. The general mood in the country was reflected in public opinion polls. In terms of the issues that occupied people's minds there was one that stood out more than any other – immigration. When, in their end of year survey, YouGov asked a sample of the electorate to identify the most pressing issues facing Britain 63 per cent selected immigration, putting it well ahead of healthcare (39 per cent) and the economy (33 per cent).[1] Although the British public had long felt anxious about immigration and its impact on the economy and national culture (see McLaren and Johnson 2007; Ford 2010), concern had grown after 2004 when increasing numbers of workers from EU member states in Central and Eastern Europe started to arrive in the country.

By the end of 2015, only a few months before the referendum, the Government revealed that net migration – the difference between the number of people arriving and leaving – had reached a record level of 336,000. Most people felt that this was too much; in fact, 69 per cent of respondents told YouGov that immigration from elsewhere in the EU was 'too high' while only 20 per cent felt it was 'about right'. Worries about high rates of immigration were shared by 93 per cent of voters who said they were planning to vote Leave, 58 per cent who were undecided about how they might vote and 49 per cent who backed Remain.[2] The view that immigration was too high was also notably greater among groups that would also soon play a key role in shaping the result of the referendum, namely pensioners and the working class.

Public anxiety over immigration also was being stimulated by other events. At the end of 2015, the argument that immigration was having negative effects on domestic workers, a view being pushed by UKIP and Nigel Farage, appeared to be legitimized in a widely circulated report by the Bank of England. The analysis suggested that rising immigration could drive down wages for low-skilled British workers, estimating that a 10-percentage-point increase in the proportion of immigrants was associated with a nearly 2 per cent reduction in pay for semi- and unskilled workers in service industries such as care homes, shops and bars.[3] Other events also were keeping immigration in the news. In 2015 a major refugee crisis had erupted on the European continent, sparking both widespread sympathy and mounting anxiety about the number of refugees trying to enter the EU. Between August and October 2015 it was estimated that more than 100,000 people a month entered Europe by sea. Debates about the ability of Western governments to control immigration, secure their borders and protect citizens from terrorism intensified.

The link between security and migration had been underscored by a string of terrorist attacks, including in Paris in November 2015, which resulted in the deaths of 130 people, including 89 at the Bataclan theatre, and injured another 368. The attacks, the deadliest in France since the Second World War, came less than a year after Islamist terrorists had forced their way into the offices of the *Charlie Hebdo* magazine, also in Paris, and killed 11 people. It was later reported that several attackers had passed through Hungary alongside refugees. Two months later, it was widely reported in the media that multiple women at New Year celebrations in Cologne had been sexually assaulted by groups of migrants and asylum-seekers. Shortly afterwards the think-tank Migration Watch appeared in Britain's media, estimating that 4.8 million asylum-seekers could head to Europe and, once they had EU citizenship, as many as half a million could arrive in the UK.[4] Not surprisingly, immigration dominated the political agenda as Britain moved into 2016.

In terms of party politics, meanwhile, Prime Minister David Cameron and the Conservative Party, who had won a surprise majority government seven months earlier, were leading comfortably in the polls. In one early poll in 2016 the Conservatives held a 39 per cent share of the national vote and a commanding 10-point lead over the Labour Party. In September 2015 Labour members had shocked many observers by electing radical left-winger Jeremy Corbyn as their new leader. While the mainly middle-class and well-educated Labour members who had elected Corbyn cheered on their new leader, it was clear that the wider electorate was not impressed.[5]

In the polls Labour was regularly recording less than 30 per cent in voting intentions and Corbyn's leadership ratings were dismal. Although none of the party leaders inspired confidence, Labour's new leader was in a league of his own. At the end of 2015, when YouGov asked a national sample of the electorate whether the party leaders were performing well or badly, David Cameron had a net rating of –6 (meaning that slightly more people felt he was performing badly than well), Tim Farron, the new leader of the Liberal Democrats, scored –13 and Nigel Farage, the leader of UKIP, was on –18. Corbyn, the man who would lead Labour into the referendum with the responsibility of helping to mobilize the Remain vote, scored –32.[6] Yet other opposition parties did not appear to be benefitting. As Britain left 2015 and entered 2016, in the polls the Liberal Democrats and Greens were on single digits, with 6 per cent and 3 per cent, respectively. UKIP was stronger, on 17 per cent, about 4 per cent more than its vote share at the 2015 general election. That said, the party's vote share hid the size of the role that Farage and his party would soon play at the referendum.

The Rival Armies

The contending forces in the referendum campaign were organized into two broad camps. On one side stood those who were fighting to uphold Britain's EU membership – the 'Remainers'. Those who joined the Remain camp came from different political homes but were united by their desire to keep Britain in the EU and silence the Eurosceptics once and for all. Their breadth and diversity was reflected in the composition of the organization that, in April 2016, was designated by the Electoral Commission as the official Remain campaign. Britain Stronger in Europe called on supporters from across the landscape to help Remain win. Its application to become the premier Remain campaign had been accompanied by letters of support from the Labour Party, the Liberal Democrats, Plaid Cymru in Wales and, in Northern Ireland, the Alliance Party, Green Party and the Social Democratic and Labour Party. As its organizers pointed out, Stronger In was supported by parties that had a combined membership of nearly half a million members and, at the last election in 2015, had won more than 12 million votes.

That was not all. Stronger In also could count on a plethora of other groups to spread the word and get out the vote. Although the Conservative Party was officially neutral in the campaign, Stronger In could rely on support from the two largest groups of Conservatives who backed Remain, namely Conservatives In and the Conservative Group for Europe. It could also call upon a wide range of groups that, as their names implied, were focused on mobilizing votes in specific sections of society, such as London First, Friends of the Earth, the European Movement, Lawyers In for Britain, Scientists for EU, Universities UK, Environmentalists for EU, Henna Foundation, City Sikhs, the National Union of Students and the National Association of Women's Organisations.

The diversity of Remainers also was reflected in the backgrounds of key organizers. The executive director, Will Straw, was a former parliamentary candidate for Labour. The director of strategy, Ryan Coetzee, had orchestrated the Liberal Democrat campaign in 2015. Stronger In's pollsters, Andrew Cooper and Stephen Gilbert, had crunched numbers and strategy for Cameron and the Conservatives. The head of the digital team had fulfilled the same role for the Conservative Party, while the head of the policy team had been a senior researcher for Labour. Stronger In's senior board of advisers was similarly diverse and filled with elites who had amassed considerable political experience. They included a former General Secretary of the Trades Union Congress, Conservative MPs, Labour peer Peter Mandelson, Green MP Caroline Lucas, the leader of the Liberal Democrats in the House of Lords and a former leader of Plaid Cymru. Throughout the campaign, many other allies also would make the case for Remain, ranging from the Scottish National

Party and Sinn Fein to civil society groups such as British Influence, Labour In for Britain, Healthier IN the EU, Historians for Britain IN Europe and Students for Europe.

On the other side stood the Eurosceptics, or 'Leavers', an army of activists who ever since their defeat at an earlier referendum in 1975 and in subsequent controversy surrounding the ratification of the Maastricht Treaty in 1992, had been plotting to mobilize a new revolt to extricate Britain from the EU. Although Leavers were often dismissed by the political-economic establishment as a motley collection of wrong-minded trouble-makers – 'mad, swivel-eyed loons' who were obsessively 'banging on about Europe'[7] – they had built a serious army. Like their opponents, Leavers comprised people who, under normal circumstances, often swore allegiance to different movements. Some had been plotting from inside the Conservative Party, rebelling against their leaders and trying to galvanize support for a Brexit on the backbenches in the House of Commons, or from the European Parliament. They included, among others, the so-called 'Awkward Squad' of Conservative Eurosceptics, politicians like Steve Baker, John Baron, Peter Bone, Philip Hollobone, David Nuttall and Daniel Hannan. Others had abandoned the mainstream, frustrated by what they saw as a continual failure by Conservatives to slow European integration and deliver a referendum.

For the latter group, the search for an alternative home had led them to join insurgent outsiders who talked instead about forcing change, including the Referendum Party in the mid 1990s and, later, UKIP. Alongside Nigel Farage, a former Conservative supporter, those who would defect from the Conservatives to UKIP included politicians like Douglas Carswell and Mark Reckless and thousands of Conservative members and voters (see Ford and Goodwin 2014). But among the Leavers there was also a third and smaller group of activists who identified not with right-wing parties but rather the left, who had refused to abandon the Euroscepticism that had dominated Labour in earlier decades. While Conservative and UKIP supporters traced their opposition to EU membership to concerns over a loss of national sovereignty or the issue of immigration, those on the left often argued that the EU had become an 'uber-capitalist' club, that initiatives like the Transatlantic Trade and Investment Partnership (TTIP) threatened efforts to run an independent economic policy and to nationalize public services, that austerity was being unnecessarily imposed on EU member states like Greece or that the EU was undemocratic and indifferent to the plight of ordinary workers.

In April 2016, the Electoral Commission designated Vote Leave as the official Leave campaign. Like its main rival, Stronger In, the organization drew support from across the landscape and in a way that undermined the portrayal of Leavers as bumbling amateurs. As its Chair, Labour MP Gisela Stuart, pointed out, Vote Leave had registered supporters in the Labour Party, Conservative Party, UKIP, Liberal Democrats, Green Party, SNP, Democratic Unionist Party and Ulster Unionist Party. Its backers included eight present or former leaders of political parties and 121 MPs (108 from the Conservative Party, 8 from the DUP, 4 from Labour and 1 from UKIP). These included five serving Cabinet ministers and 10 serving Government ministers. Vote Leave could also call upon 7 members of the European Parliament, 39 members of the House of Lords, 20 members of the devolved parliaments and assemblies and more than 1,500 councillors.[8] Former political heavyweights were also on hand, including two former chancellors of the exchequer, four former secretaries of state, fifteen former Conservative ministers, three former chairmen of the Conservative Party, four former members of Labour Governments, and Lord Owen, one of the founders of the insurgent Social Democratic Party in 1981.

Those who would orchestrate the Vote Leave campaign also had a significant amount of campaign experience, having variously been involved in the referendum campaign in 1975, attempts to oppose ratification of the Maastricht Treaty in 1992, opposition to the Lisbon Treaty and campaigns against Britain joining the euro and regional assemblies. The chief executive of Vote Leave, Matthew Elliott, had previously organized Eurosceptic pressure groups like Business for Britain and the TaxPayers' Alliance and led the successful referendum campaign against the country adopting the Alternative Vote electoral system in 2011. Some of Vote Leave's wealthier supporters had also bankrolled the rise of UKIP. When Vote Leave had applied to become the chief Leave campaign, it claimed to have over 43,000 registered supporters and over 11,000 volunteer activists.

Vote Leave was not the only group that would mobilize the Leave vote, however. A plethora of other movements also were campaigning for a Brexit. Included were groups like Conservatives for Britain, Conservative Voice, the Bow Group, Green Leaves, Liberal Leave, Farmers for Britain, Lawyers for Britain, Muslims for Britain,

Economists for Britain and Students for Britain. Eurosceptics on the left coalesced around groups like Labour Leave, run by a handful of Labour MPs, the Trade Union and Socialist Coalition, Trade Unionists against the European Union and Left Leave, an umbrella group that brought together the Communist Party of Great Britain, the Socialist Workers Party, the Respect Party and the National Union of Rail, Maritime and Transport Workers, among others.[9]

There also were rival groups to Vote Leave that had unsuccessfully petitioned the Electoral Commission to become the official Leave campaign. Grassroots Out (GO) was a cross-party umbrella group that claimed over 700,000 registered supporters and support from a diverse array of Eurosceptic movements including Leave.EU, a platform founded by multimillionaire businessman and prominent UKIP donor Arron Banks. There was also Labour Leave, the Democracy Movement and UKIP, a party that in its own right had over 30,000 members and over 400 grassroots associations. Several prominent Leavers in this broader network, including Banks and Farage, were especially keen that the Leave camp target immigration (e.g. Banks 2016).

In the early months of 2016 these various campaigns, movements and personalities would enter into a fierce battle to win the referendum on continued EU membership. But before the historic political battle began, Prime Minister David Cameron first set out on a quest to negotiate a new settlement between Britain and the EU. He hoped that this new deal would be able to convince a majority of the British electorate to remain in the EU club.

EU Membership Renegotiated

As Britain entered 2016 there was a general assumption across much of the media, business world and financial markets that while the referendum campaign might be close, the people would most likely side with the status quo and vote to remain in the EU. This view had been encouraged by some of the early opinion polls. In the final four months of 2015 there had been no fewer than 40 polls and 31 had put Remain ahead. The position of Remainers looked especially positive in polls that were conducted over the telephone and that, on more than one occasion, put Remain as much as 20 points ahead. The big Remain lead in telephone polls was not novel. As Figure 2.1 shows, in all telephone polls that were conducted between August 2010 and

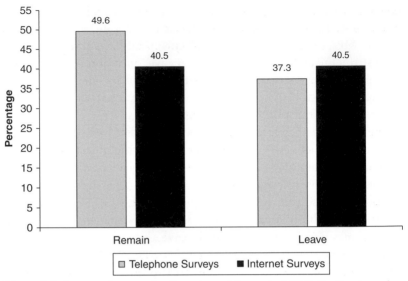

Figure 2.1 Average Support for Remain and Leave in 174 Polls Conducted between 8 August 2010 and 20 February 2016.
Source: en.wikipedia.org/wiki/Opinion_polling_for_the_United_Kingdom_European_Union_membership_referendum.

the official announcement of the referendum on 20 February 2016, Remain averaged 49.6 per cent. This was well ahead of Leave's average share of only 40.5 per cent (the remainder did not know how they would vote). However, the picture was very different in the polls that were conducted online, over the Internet. In these polls the average support for Remain and Leave was a dead heat at 40.5 per cent. This large difference in support for Remain in telephone and internet polls conducted by a variety of reputable survey companies suggested a note of caution. It was not immediately apparent why the two methods of probing public attitudes towards Britain's future relationship with the EU were giving such different answers.

Those who dug a little deeper found other reasons to challenge the conventional wisdom. One important reason was unearthed by Stephen Fisher and Alan Renwick, who examined an array of previous referendums around the world. Although previous research (e.g. LeDuc 2003) had documented that undecided voters were often swayed by risk aversion and opted for the status quo in major referendums, Fisher and Renwick cautioned that electorates do not invariably reject change. They noted that while it was true that a majority had sided with the status quo in the first referendum on the Europe question in 1975, the Alternative Vote electoral system in 2011 and the referendum on independence for Scotland in 2014, there were also examples of the people voting against the existing state of affairs, including at the referendums on devolution in Scotland, Wales and London. Moreover, studying 268 referendums held since 1990 in democracies around the world Fisher and Renwick found that the change option had actually won in 186, or 69 per cent of the time. Although they might hesitate, there were circumstances when electorates were willing to decide against the status quo.[10]

There was also another warning sign for those who assumed that Remain would win. As Britain waved goodbye to 2015, YouGov asked people in six EU member states how they would vote if they were given a referendum on EU membership. Only the British were more likely to say they would leave than remain. The margin was small (41 per cent to 39 per cent) but it was a reminder that the race could be closer than was being suggested by many of the polls.[11] In this regard, while at the end of 2015 telephone polls by firms like Ipsos MORI and ComRes had put Remain ahead by 28 and 24 points respectively (and after undecided voters had been filtered out), online polls by firms like Survation and ICM either had Leave ahead by 2 points or suggested that the race was too close to call.

Aware of these warning signs and cognizant of Britain's tradition of Euroscepticism, David Cameron and his team had decided to try and win over voters by first renegotiating the terms of EU membership. Between June 2015 and February 2016, the Prime Minister and his entourage had tried to carve a new settlement with Britain's partners in Europe that, it was hoped, would convince enough voters that the benefits of remaining in the EU outweighed the costs. That the renegotiation strategy was worth pursuing was reflected in the data. Ever since 2000, the British Social Attitudes (BSA) survey had asked people what they thought the country's long-term policy towards the EU should be. As shown in Figure 2.2, between 2000 and 2015 the percentage that thought Britain should simply leave the EU never surpassed 32 per cent. However, nor was there much support for leaving the relationship as it was or handing further powers to the EU. Crucially for Cameron and his team, the BSA surveys suggested that the most popular view among the electorate was for Britain to remain

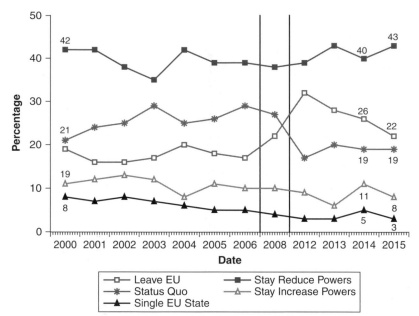

Figure 2.2 Preferred EU Membership Options, British Social Attitudes Surveys, 2000–2015.
Source: British Social Attitudes Surveys.

in a less powerful European Union. In the most recent BSA survey carried out before the 2016 referendum, 43 per cent of respondents felt that Britain should remain in a reformed EU while only 19 per cent backed the status quo, 22 per cent wanted to leave outright and 12 per cent either wanted to give more power to the EU or see a single European government. The message was clear: the people wanted to see some serious reform. They were neither fiercely loyal to the EU nor flagrantly hostile. They were open to remaining in the EU but only if they were convinced that its powers had been reduced. Getting such reform was Cameron's challenge.

Nor was the BSA the only survey to throw light on what the people wanted. That Cameron would likely be victorious if he delivered significant reform was reflected in the findings of a poll that asked people what they wanted from the renegotiation and how they planned to vote in the referendum. People were asked to imagine three scenarios: (1) that Cameron had secured *major change* to Britain's relationship with Europe that included substantial changes to the rules that

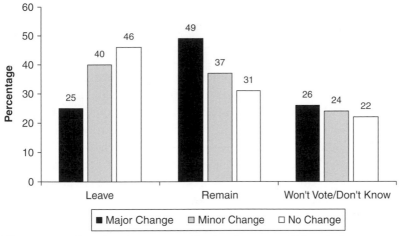

Figure 2.3 Referendum Vote Depending on Outcome of Negotiations to Change UK's Relationship with the EU.
Source: YouGov, 27–28 January 2016.

it has to follow and opt-outs from EU rules in different policy areas; (2) that he had secured *small change* that included guarantees over key issues that protected British interests but without any major change in policy areas the EU has powers in; and (3) that he had *not secured any change* in Britain's relationship with the EU. As shown in Figure 2.3, only when people were told that Cameron had secured *major change* did a plurality voice support for remaining in the EU. In contrast, when confronted with the prospect of only small change or no change at all, more people sided with Leave than Remain. These numbers constituted another warning to Cameron and his team: unless they delivered a renegotiation that was seen by most voters as representing major change, the Prime Minister would most likely lose his latest and potentially last ever gamble in politics.

Exactly what changes did people want to see in their country's relationship with the EU? Surveys of representative samples of the electorate revealed that most people were chiefly concerned with achieving two reforms – reducing the level of immigration from other EU member states, and restricting the amount of welfare benefits that incoming migrants could access. The area where people wanted Cameron to deliver fundamental change was immigration. Such reform would not be easy, however. The so-called 'free movement' of people between

EU states was one of the EU's four 'fundamental freedoms'. To many people in Brussels who were committed to the EU this freedom was simply non-negotiable.

In Britain, the strong public demand for immigration reform was reflected clearly in the data. When the pollsters BMG gave voters a list of things that Cameron was trying to achieve and asked them to choose the objectives they considered 'very important', the two most popular by a wide margin were reducing immigration and curbing welfare for migrants. These were chosen by 52 per cent of voters and were well ahead of cutting red tape (44 per cent) and letting countries overrule EU law (39 per cent). Yet there were also notable differences among different groups in society. Securing the right to reduce immigration was seen as 'very important' for 68 per cent of pensioners but only 24 per cent of 18–24-year-olds. Similarly, reducing the right of EU workers to access welfare benefits was seen as 'very important' among 73 per cent of pensioners but only 26 per cent of the young.[12] Older voters, people who were not only the most likely to support leaving the EU but had also turned out in large numbers at past elections, were especially likely to prioritize immigration reforms.

The centrality of immigration to the renegotiation also was underscored in a similar survey by YouGov, which, at the end of 2015, asked voters to identify up to three areas where they wanted to see change in Britain's relationship with the EU. The two most popular answers, again by a wide margin, were gaining greater control over borders and immigration from the EU (chosen by 52 per cent) and limiting welfare for EU migrants (46 per cent). These were also the most popular answers among those who were planning to vote to remain in the EU, which underlined the extent to which concerns over immigration were widespread. In a distant third and fourth place were giving national parliaments greater powers to block EU policies they opposed (supported by 29 per cent) and having the freedom to establish new trade deals with countries outside of the EU (21 per cent).[13]

Cameron had initially set out four areas where he was seeking reforms in a letter to Donald Tusk, President of the European Council, in early November 2015. First, he outlined proposed reforms in the area of economic governance, asking for legally binding principles that safeguarded the interests of EU member states that were not in the eurozone area.[14] Second, Cameron listed ideas to boost the competitiveness of the EU, calling for it to set a target to cut the regulatory burden on business and do more to fulfil its commitment to the free flow of capital, goods and services. Third, he proposed reforms that were designed to help him tackle perceptions that the EU threatened national sovereignty. These included a legally binding and irreversible opt-out from Britain's obligation to work towards an 'ever closer union', a new mechanism that would allow a group of national parliaments to act together to stop unwanted legislation in the European Parliament and a request for proposals to bolster the role of individual member states, especially in the area of Justice and Home Affairs.

Lastly, regarding the all-important area of immigration, Cameron proposed that any new member states joining the EU in the future would not be able to participate in the principle of free movement until their economies had converged more closely with those of the existing member states. This was a measure that it was hoped would discourage large migration flows from weaker to stronger European states. Cameron also called for a 'crack-down' on the abuse of free movement, including tougher bans for fraudsters and people involved in sham marriages and stronger powers to deport criminals. Consistent with the Conservative Party manifesto in 2015, he had also asked for Britain to be able to restrict in-work benefits and social housing to EU workers who have lived in the country and contributed for four years. Cameron had also requested an end to the practice of EU workers sending child benefit payments that they had received in the UK out of the country, to their countries of origin.

In the shadow of the publication of Cameron's letter there was the inevitable flurry of opinion polls, some of which showed the two camps in a dead heat or had Leave ahead. One poll by Survation, funded by a Eurosceptic group, probed public reaction to Cameron's requests. After being informed that Cameron had *not* demanded a renegotiation of the automatic right of EU citizens to live and work in Britain, voters were asked whether this would make them more or less likely to vote to leave the EU, or if it would make no difference. Although almost 47 per cent of voters said it would make no difference, 31 per cent said it would make them more likely to vote to leave the EU, a figure that increased to nearly 35 per cent among the over-55s and 38 per cent among those who had voted for the Conservative Party in 2015.

This was not the only evidence to suggest that Cameron had not gone far enough. When the same voters were presented with two statements – that the country should limit the number of people coming to the UK from the EU by introducing an Australian-style points-based immigration system, or that the country should not limit the number of people coming to the UK from the EU by introducing such a system – an overwhelming 76 per cent backed restrictions, including 92 per cent of Leave voters, 74 per cent of those who were undecided and 64 per cent of Remain voters.[15] Cameron's reforms, as he was no doubt aware, would be unable to directly limit the number of people coming to live and work in the UK from elsewhere in the EU.

After further negotiations, the details of a draft deal finally emerged in February 2016. By this time the picture in the polls looked decidedly mixed. In the telephone polls Remain continued to hold a commanding lead. But in the online polls the race was still much closer, with both camps close to the 50 per cent mark.[16] The draft deal did include several things that Cameron had requested. There was a clear legal statement that the UK would not be committed to further political integration and confirmation that it had an opt-out from 'ever closer union'. There also was talk of a new 'red-card' mechanism that could potentially allow national parliaments to block EU proposals provided more than 55 per cent of them agreed to do so. In addition, there was a proposal to reduce the amount of red tape although there would be no repatriation of EU social and employment laws.

However, on the crunch issue of immigration Cameron's original requests were not met. It was now proposed that there would be a new mechanism that would allow individual member states that were experiencing very high levels of migration over an extended period of time to limit access of EU nationals to in-work benefits for up to four years, although these restrictions would gradually be phased in during this period. Meanwhile, the practice of EU workers sending child benefit payments that they received in Britain back to their countries of origin would not end outright. Rather, the benefits would be adjusted to take account of the standard of living in their home country. The key reforms to immigration, the most important area where voters wanted to see change, had been watered down.

Sceptical Reactions

It was not long until the Prime Minister's deal attracted criticism. Eurosceptics were quick to point out that Cameron had failed to meet his pledge to ban EU migrants from sending their child benefit back to their countries of origin and that the deal also fell well short of the Conservative Party's promise to achieve a complete ban on in-work benefits for migrants for at least four years. Conservative critics such as David Davis warned that the emergency brake could actually produce a surge of migrants into Britain, while Iain Duncan Smith branded it 'a load of rubbish'. Veteran Eurosceptic John Redwood was similarly dismissive: 'That proposal is an insult to the United Kingdom. It's not a serious offer. We need to take back control of our borders and we need to be able to control our own welfare system.'[17] The country's Eurosceptic newspapers, which would play a key role in mobilizing support for Leave, were also highly critical. 'It stinks', concluded the *Sun*, while the *Daily Mail*'s front page branded the renegotiation 'The Great Delusion!' The latter also claimed that Cameron's measures would only affect around 1 in 10 EU migrants.[18]

Meanwhile, more than a hundred Conservative local councillors who had been angered by the perceived capitulation signed a letter warning Cameron that he risked splitting his party unless he accepted his renegotiation had failed and campaigned alongside Leavers. Even Cameron, while speaking to manufacturing workers after the details of the deal had been released, was forced to concede that the measures would not enable him to meet his promise of returning net migration to the 'tens of thousands'. Speaking in the Commons, Conservative MP Steve Baker claimed that Remainers had been reduced to 'polishing poo'.

More worrying for Cameron was evidence that most voters were unimpressed and clearly felt that the reforms did not go far enough. As we have seen, large numbers of voters were open to Britain remaining in the EU provided that the relationship was significantly reformed and that these reforms included changes to immigration and benefits for migrants. At first glance, when voters were asked about the draft deal most were supportive of the individual proposals. Majorities of at least 6 in 10 supported the idea of a 'red-card' system that would allow national parliaments to block EU proposals, a brake on benefits for migrants, greater protections for countries that were not in the eurozone, cuts to red tape and reductions on the amount of child benefit that EU migrants could send home. But a clear majority felt that the reforms did not go far enough – and this was Cameron's problem. The Prime Minister and his team had misjudged the mood in Europe and would now have to try to sell reforms to a sceptical electorate that clearly wanted more than they were being offered. The Remain camp would have to dress up minor reform as major change. Most voters could see straight through the charade.

High levels of public scepticism were evident in several surveys that were conducted as Cameron's renegotiation drew to a close. The evidence suggested that most people felt that the reforms did not go far enough and represented a bad deal. For example, when YouGov asked people about the package of measures, 38 per cent responded that they represented 'major' or 'significant' change to Britain's relationship with the EU. However, a notably larger 50 per cent of the sample felt that the measures amounted to 'not very much' or 'no real change'. Meanwhile, when asked whether the reforms went far enough, 56 per cent said no and only 17 per cent thought that Cameron had got 'the balance about right' (a further 23 per cent were unsure and 4 per cent judged that the reforms went too far). Overall, based on what they had seen or heard about the agreement, voters were significantly more likely to conclude that Cameron had struck a bad deal (46 per cent) than a good one (22 per cent) – numbers that were corroborated by a similar survey undertaken a few days later.[19]

Public disapproval of the deal extended to the crucial area of immigration. When asked whether the reforms would reduce the number of EU migrants coming to Britain, an outcome that we have already seen was desired by most voters, 54 per cent felt the proposals would 'make no real difference' while only 31 per cent felt that they would lead to reductions. On the idea of an 'emergency brake' there was also widespread scepticism that this would reduce immigration into the UK. According to one survey by Survation only 26 per cent felt that the brake would reduce immigration, while nearly 60 per cent felt that it would make no difference (47 per cent) or would not reduce the level of migration into the country (13 per cent). Similarly, when asked about the proposal to index child benefits to the cost of living in the home countries, 59 per cent said that this would not reduce immigration. Most voters simply did not believe that the reforms would have the desired impact.

These polls also addressed more specific points of concern for Remainers. While the survey by YouGov suggested that nearly one in four Remainers thought that Cameron's deal was a bad one, across half a dozen polls that would follow there was also little evidence that Cameron was bringing his own Conservative Party voters over to Remain. As John Curtice observed, prior to the deal on average 44 per cent of Conservative voters had planned to vote Remain but after the deal only 45 per cent planned to do so.[20] The figure had barely changed at all. Cameron thus seemed to be about to embark on a referendum campaign in which he would be forced to rely far more on support from people who, at the general election less than 12 months earlier, had voted against his Conservative Party. Cameron, quipped John Curtice, looked more like the Leader of the Opposition than the Prime Minister of a majority Conservative Government.

There was another problem, too. The same poll that had followed the announcement of the deal recorded an almost four-point swing to Leave. Once undecided voters had been excluded, this put Leave on 54 per cent and Remain on 44 per cent. It was the largest lead for Leave in any poll since the wording of the referendum question had been confirmed five months earlier – and it had been conducted after Cameron had shown his renegotiation cards. If the aim of the renegotiation had been to provide voters with an offer that they could not refuse, then it had fallen well short. The entire exercise had produced no meaningful surge of support for remaining in the EU. Of the four polls that probed the views of voters before and after the deal, two suggested that public opinion had not moved at all while the other two recorded a notable decline in support for Remain. The backdrop to the referendum campaign was not a propitious one for Cameron and his team, who were about to fire the starting gun for the race that would decide, once and for all, whether Britain was in or out of the EU.

Conclusion: Stage Set

On 20 February 2016 Prime Minister David Cameron announced that the referendum on the UK's continued membership of the European Union would be held on 23 June. In this chapter, we have seen that the contest was likely to be both bitter and sharply contested. Immigration from other EU countries and elsewhere had been a topic of public concern for several years and by early 2016 was seen by most voters as the most pressing issue facing the country. This was decidedly not good news for those who wished to remain in the European Union. Prime Minster Cameron and his colleagues had clearly failed to deliver on their election promise to sharply reduce the number of migrants, giving ammunition to UKIP and other Eurosceptic critics who had repeatedly argued that the only way to control immigration was to leave the EU. The potential for immigration to shape voting in the referendum was significantly enhanced when Cameron failed to strike a deal with Brussels that enabled the UK to opt out of the free movement of labour and then failed again to obtain key reforms that he tried to convince voters would indirectly curb immigration into the country. Public reaction to Cameron's deal was decidedly negative. As we will see in the next chapter, this meant that while Remainers would have to campaign almost exclusively on a narrative that highlighted the claimed economic risks of a Brexit, Leavers would –if they chose to pursue it – have a clear line of attack on immigration.

Organized into rival umbrella organizations, both the Remain and Leave forces had strengths and weaknesses. Led by Prime Minister Cameron, the Remainers would now enjoy the support of much of Britain's political-economic establishment. Although the Conservative Party was deeply divided on EU membership, most of the opposition parties endorsed Remain. However, and as we will see, an important weakness was that Labour Leader Jeremy Corbyn was decidedly lukewarm. A nontrivial fraction of Labour voters were susceptible to UKIP's Eurosceptic appeal and, absent a vigorous campaign by the party leadership, there was a real danger that these people might vote Leave or, at a minimum, abstain.

For its part, Leave was deeply divided between the officially recognized Vote Leave organization and the insurgent Leave.EU group, spearheaded by UKIP leader Nigel Farage and the party's principal financial donor, Arron Banks (Banks 2016). Although this division and the ongoing internecine conflict it provoked were potentially serious liabilities, there also was a strategic upside. Hidden behind the divisions lay a key strength for the Leavers, even if they refused to acknowledge it themselves. As we will see in the next chapter, an awkward coexistence would see the Leavers effectively run a two-pronged campaign to leave the EU, one that sought to appeal to middle-class people who were fearful of being labelled 'racists' for wanting to leave an open-borders

EU and 'straight out of Clacton' populists who were attracted by the politically incorrect team of Farage and Banks voicing a strident anti-immigration message. There was the additional advantage that the establishment-orientated Vote Leave provided a home for ambitious pro-Leave Conservative heavyweights such as Boris Johnson and Michael Gove, who could not to be seen partnering with the toxic UKIP and miscellaneous populists. In Chapter 3 we discuss how the Leave and Remain forces prosecuted their campaigns in the run-up to the 23 June referendum.

3 | *Into Battle*

Shortly after midday on 20 February, after briefing his Cabinet, David Cameron stood outside 10 Downing Street and formally urged the British people to remain in the EU. The Conservative Prime Minister described the vote, to be held on Thursday 23 June, as one of the 'biggest decisions this country will face in our lifetimes'. He then presented the historic choice that faced the people in terms that would dominate the Remain camp's arguments for the next four months. 'Let me be clear', said Cameron, staring into the cameras: 'Leaving Europe would threaten our economic and our national security. Those who want to leave Europe cannot tell you if British businesses would be able to access Europe's free trade single market or if working people's jobs are safe, or how much prices would rise. All they are offering is risk at a time of uncertainty – a leap in the dark ... The choice is in your hands.'

All to Play For

After Cameron had finished, the country quickly divided into two camps. Most of those who had been elected to Parliament shared the Prime Minister's belief that the UK should vote to remain in the EU. Overall, an estimated 479 of 637 MPs who would declare their position before the vote sided with Remain.[1] These included 185 of 329 Conservative MPs, all but 10 of the 232 Labour MPs, all 54 MPs from the Scottish National Party (SNP) and all of the 8 Liberal Democrats. While most of the MPs who campaigned for Leave were Conservative (138 declared for Leave before the vote), 10 represented Labour constituencies, 1 was from UKIP and 8 came from the Democratic Unionist Party.[2] Most of those who were in Cameron's Cabinet also sided with Remain, including Chancellor of the Exchequer George Osborne and Home Secretary Theresa May. As Harold Wilson had done in 1975, before the 2016 referendum Cameron had confirmed that ministers who did not agree with the Government's recommendation to vote

Remain would be free to campaign to leave the EU. In the end, a total of 17 ministers, 6 of whom sat in the Cabinet, joined the campaign to leave the EU. The most prominent included former leader of the Conservatives Iain Duncan Smith, Leader of the Commons Chris Grayling, Justice Minister Michael Gove, Culture Secretary John Whittingdale, Northern Ireland Secretary Theresa Villiers and Minister for Employment Priti Patel. After Cameron had fired the starting gun these Leavers promptly headed to the headquarters of Vote Leave, in Westminster Tower, to pose for the cameras behind a banner that read 'Let's Take Back Control'.[3] The next day, Sunday 21 February, they were joined by former London mayor and Conservative MP Boris Johnson. Standing outside his Islington home, and after what he described as a 'huge amount of heartache', the affable Johnson said that he wanted 'a better deal for the people of his country, to save them money and to take control'. The Leave camp had secured its big beasts.

Leavers, however, were also deeply divided. Many Eurosceptic Conservative MPs were strongly averse to running a campaign focused on immigration and wanted nothing to do with UKIP and its politically incorrect leader, Nigel Farage. Both sentiments were echoed by other prominent groups and individuals, many of whom were well-recognized members of Britain's politico-economic establishment and veterans of past struggles to define Britain's vexed relationship with the EU. These 'respectable Leavers' organized themselves into an umbrella group called Vote Leave.

In opposition was Leave.EU, founded by multi-millionaire insurance magnate and diamond miner Arron Banks, a friend and close confidant of Farage (Banks 2016). Although lacking the depth of political experience and impressive media contacts enjoyed by Vote Leave, Banks's Leave.EU platform, which threw its full weight behind Grassroots Out, was not an amateur operation, as Remainers would learn. Nonetheless, the divisive Banks and the Grassroots Out group were unable to persuade the Electoral Commission to make them the official Leave campaign. On 13 April the Commission announced that Vote Leave was the official leave campaign. The designation was important because it gave the organization the ability to spend up to £7 million, send a free mailshot to voters, make televised broadcasts and access £600,000 in public funds. However, the more overtly populist Leave.EU refused to go away quietly. It would continue to campaign vigorously alongside Grassroots Out, while at the same time continuing to wage internecine conflict with its Vote Leave rivals. Generous infusions of capital and labour by Banks, Farage and their teams – the so-called 'Bad Boys of Brexit' – ensured that the alternative Leave campaign remained visible and influential.

In the days and weeks that followed the formal announcement of the campaign, the Remainers and Leavers set about communicating their core arguments to the electorate. The narratives they articulated to voters were entirely different. Cameron and his team had been directly influenced by their earlier victories in the Scottish independence referendum in 2014 and the 2015 general election, both of which had repeatedly warned voters about the claimed economic risks that would accompany a vote for independence or a Labour Government (so-called 'Project Fear'). In Scotland, Cameron and the 'No' camp had repeatedly warned that a vote for independence would be a 'painful divorce', that there would be 'no going back' and that Scotland's security and economy would be put at risk. A few months later, at the 2015 general election, Cameron recycled many of the same arguments, contending that a Labour Government and Prime Minister Ed Miliband would trigger 'economic chaos' and 'destroy jobs and destroy livelihoods'. As one senior strategist in the Remain camp recalled: '[t]he resonances with the Scottish "No" campaign seemed deep – eerie, sometimes. And both [Scotland and the 2015] campaigns had seemed to show that the genuinely undecided would, however reluctantly, end up coming down in favour of the less-risky option. This meant that even though we knew it was incredibly close going into the final couple of weeks, we still tended to assume the result would be OK.'[4]

This strategic decision was also influenced by research. Long before the culmination of Cameron's renegotiation, between March and July 2015, senior Remain strategists Ryan Coetzee and Andrew Cooper sat down to examine how people were likely to make up their minds in the EU referendum. They undertook a series of focus groups as well as a large segmentation poll that identified the challenge facing Remainers. 'The poll', recalled Cooper, 'left us with the unavoidable conclusion that the Leave argument completely owned immigration and control. If that was the frame for the referendum question, we were going to lose. There was no counter-factual or rebuttal or argument that anyone could come up with on immigration that even slightly dented the Leave lead on the issue of immigration.'[5]

But the research did contain a few glimmers of hope for Remainers. The segmentation analysis of survey data had revealed six groups of voters. While two of these groups were staunchly committed to Leave, and another two to Remain, the remaining two were 'in-play'. However, the two groups that looked as though they might determine the entire contest, described as 'Hearts versus Heads' and the 'Disengaged Middle', were much closer to Leave than Remain in terms of how they saw the world. As Cooper recalled: 'Nearly 80 per cent of them said "my heart says we should leave the EU but my head says leaving the EU is too risky" ... We obviously did a lot of work on what the risks were that they worried about – and they were all about the economy, in one way or another.' This is not to say that these wavering voters did not care about immigration, however. 'To be clear', continued Cooper, who was feeding his research direct into Downing Street, 'the in-play voters who worried about the economy also thought – in common with everyone else – that immigration was too high and should be reduced, that we should get control over immigration back from the EU and that if we did, and cut back the numbers, there would be positive benefits for the UK. But despite thinking this, they still weren't sure – and were sufficiently worried about the economic risks of Brexit to be conflicted, wavering and, at the start of the campaign, grudgingly falling on the Remain side, when forced to take a position.'[6] Will Straw, the executive director of Stronger In, similarly recalled how this led the Remainers to develop a 'defensive campaign script' on immigration. 'This script was the best response that Remain could offer on immigration ... But this was a defensive line while our proactive campaigning focused on making the argument that we were "stronger, safer and better off in Europe than we would be on our own" and that "Leaving is a leap in the dark".'[7]

In the early weeks of 2016 Remainers put into motion their plan to target the 'in-play' voters. The campaign to keep Britain in the EU would focus heavily and relentlessly on a core narrative of economic risk, claiming over and over and over again that leaving the EU would threaten the national economy and people's finances. The message would dominate almost every aspect of the Remain campaign and be assiduously cultivated by an entire cast of prominent politicians, business leaders and spokespersons for international organizations. These Remainers were guided by the assumption that voters would reach their decisions after assessing the costs and benefits of EU membership and that, in the end, they would listen to their head over their heart.

The Leavers, meanwhile, were more divided about their message. Some, like UKIP leader Nigel Farage, had long argued that the campaign should focus on immigration, tapping into the same anxieties that had fuelled the dramatic rise of his party since 2010. Speaking at the party's annual conference in 2015, and in the traditional Labour stronghold of Doncaster, Farage had made clear his belief in the power of the immigration issue to propel Leavers to victory. He had also sent a warning shot to Conservative Eurosceptics who he felt were out of touch with public opinion: 'A lot of people in the Westminster set find that all a bit too difficult, all a bit awkward, not the sort of thing you discuss at dinner in Notting Hill ... Immigration is far and away the biggest issue.'[8]

Others in the Leave camp, however, had very different ideas. Some Eurosceptics who were not aligned to UKIP were certainly aware of the ability of immigration to mobilize support for their cause. In January 2016, for example, Dominic Cummings, the lead strategist for Vote Leave, had taken to social media to suggest publicly that voting to remain in the EU could increase the chance of Cologne-style mass sex attacks on Britain's streets. A few weeks later, Conservative MP Dr Liam Fox, who had helped to launch the rival Grassroots Out network, showed a willingness to press the same button as Farage during a speech on the refugee crisis: 'A million last year, maybe two million this year – they have no idea whether these people are genuine refugees or asylum seekers, or economic migrants, or terrorists operating under the cover of either.'[9] Much of the criticism that had been directed towards Cameron after his renegotiation similarly focused on the immigration question: 'People are not worrying about whether we can pay reduced child benefit or any of the other meaningless things Mr Cameron is asking for', said Conservative MP Peter Bone. 'They are worried about mass immigration of people coming into the continent. Some of those people coming in will be terrorists ... The Prime Minister is fiddling while Rome burns.'[10]

At the same time, many Leavers who did not swear allegiance to UKIP judged that Farage's 'core vote' strategy would fall short of attracting the majority coalition that they needed to cross the 50 per cent mark in a referendum. The Leave campaign, argued Cummings, would need a message that 'aimed far beyond the fraction of the population that already supports UKIP'.[11] Thus, while Farage was rallying his troops in Doncaster, Matthew Elliott, chief executive of 'Vote Leave', maintained that while 'there is no doubt that immigration tops the polls as the No. 1 issue':

However, for a crucial group of voters, roughly 20–25%, their attitude is – 'we don't like the EU, we would like to leave the EU, but we are very worried about the effects on jobs and living standards.' These people are also deeply worried about immigration. However, many of them will not vote to leave unless their fears about living standards are neutralised. If they are neutralised, then they will vote to leave. This does not mean 'they don't care about immigration'. They do care. But they care *more* about their own jobs.[12]

In October 2015, Vote Leave released its launch video. The video told voters that the claimed £350 million a week, or £20 billion each year, that Britain sent to the EU could be better spent on building new, state-of-the-art hospitals, hundreds of new schools, investing in science and research, funding drugs to tackle cancer, building new roads and railways and lowering taxation. Immigration was not mentioned once.

'Stronger In' versus 'Take Back Control'

After deciding to double down on economic risk, the Remainers began to turn the strategy into reality. Even before the conclusion of Cameron's deal, at the beginning of 2016, Mark Carney, the Governor of the Bank of England, sat before the Commons Treasury committee and warned that a vote to leave could result in higher interest rates and capital leaving the country. Carney, whose comments were quickly seized upon by Remainers, was not alone. Countless others issued stark warnings about the economic costs of a Brexit. In Northern Ireland, voters were told that leaving the EU would have a devastating financial impact that would include the loss of billions of pounds' worth of investment funds. In Wales, farmers were urged to remember that their sector had received £240 million from the EU's Common Agricultural Policy and was due to receive a further £300 million before 2020. A world-leading technology company based in Cambridge warned that it would struggle to employ scientists and engineers. The chief executive of a firm that owns British Gas said that a decision to leave would make the energy market less competitive and raise people's gas bills. The Automobile Association (AA) told motorists that their petrol costs would rise and that families would need to find an additional £500 each year. The chair of British Telecom similarly warned that leaving would be a leap into the unknown and a huge risk to invest-ment and jobs. Travel groups forecast that it would bring the era of cheap flights to Europe to an end and herald a return to the time when flying was 'reserved for the elite'.

Financial institutions were especially vocal. The investment bank Goldman Sachs warned that leaving could send sterling crashing by as much as 20 per cent against other major currencies. In a report titled 'Breaking Up is Never Easy, or Cheap', analysts at Credit Suisse predicted that leaving would push Britain into a snap recession, trigger a slump in share prices, house prices and reduce economic growth by up to two points. Another bank, HSBC, wondered publicly whether it would need to move 1,000 jobs to Paris while another, Citi, predicted that the effects of a Brexit would 'be large and painful'. Other banks followed. Deutsche Bank and the Royal Bank of Scotland claimed that leaving the EU would 'slow down' banking and reduce profit-ability due to looser monetary policy and credit losses. Customers of the Clydesdale and Yorkshire Bank were told they would face higher interest rates, while prominent business leaders like the flamboyant Sir Richard Branson remarked it would be a 'sad day' if Britain voted to leave. Senior diplomats warned that leaving the EU might see other European cities such as Frankfurt challenge the dominance of London in the financial markets. Meanwhile, one business group said that a vote to leave would cost London £14 billion a year and 75,000 jobs, an estimate that swirled around the media despite one academic econ-omist pointing out that it was based on 'heroic assumptions'.[13]

Some people did attempt to neutralize these claims. As Cameron's renegotiation concluded, an influential fund manager argued that a British withdrawal would not have a major impact on the fundamen-tals of the economy and could help exporters by reducing the value of sterling. But such voices were quieter and heard less frequently than those offering the case for why a Brexit would be economically damaging. Indeed, according to one survey published during the cam-paign, 87 per cent of more than 100 senior business leaders judged that remaining in the EU would be better for business and 83 per cent supported Remain.[14]

Warnings about major economic risks were accompanied by cautions about threats to security. Foreign Secretary Philip Hammond commented that leaving the EU could lead to 'contagion' across Europe and threaten the very survival of the EU. Cameron went further, warning that such a vote would result in camps of illegal migrants springing up across southern England, that Britain would be more vulnerable to terrorist attacks like those that had erupted in Paris in 2015 and that a Brexit would make it harder for the EU to counter 'dangerous and murderous ideologies'. By the time that Cameron was standing on Downing Street firing the starting gun to the referendum campaign, the effort to frame Leave as a threat to economic stability and national security was well underway.

In the following weeks Remainers gained momentum. A few hours before Cameron had confirmed the referendum date, the *Daily Mail* claimed that his team was set to launch an unprecedented 72-hour propaganda blitz making the case for Remain and warning of the risks that flowed from a vote to leave. However, in reality the so-called blitz would turn into a sustained bombing campaign that would continue for four months as a relentless stream of interventions sought to frame Brexit as a threat to the country's economic future.

The bosses of nearly 40 of the largest companies in the country warned that a vote to leave would deter investment and threaten jobs. A credit rating agency asserted that leaving would threaten Britain's strong credit score, increasing the cost of Government borrowing and imposing economic costs that outweighed any benefits that might arrive after a Brexit. Two organizations that lobby on behalf of businesses told the electorate that 6 out of 10 firms wanted to remain. Former Prime Minister Tony Blair joined the chorus, stating that a vote to leave might trigger the dissolution of the UK. Labour MP Alan Johnson, the head of Labour's Remain campaign, cautioned that exiting the EU would cost 50,000 manufacturing jobs. Against the backdrop of a drop in the value of the pound, which at the end of February reached a seven-year low, HSBC said that leaving would shave another 20 per cent off of the value of sterling, bringing it to its lowest level since 1985. The bank also predicted that inflation would spiral upwards by five points, interest rates would rise and nearly two points would be knocked off economic growth in 2017. A representative from the manufacturing sector darkly counselled that leaving would mark a step into an 'abyss of uncertainty and risk'.

Each day, when voters opened their newspapers and watched the nightly news, they were met by fresh warnings that sought to amplify the risks of leaving. One survey of academic economists suggested that 9 in 10 agreed that leaving would introduce a broad range of risks. The G20, an organization comprising the world's richest nations, said that a Brexit would 'shock' the global economy. 'This isn't some amusing adventure into the unknown', said Chancellor George Osborne. 'A British exit would hurt people's jobs, livelihoods and living standards – it's deadly serious.'[15]

At the end of February, the Government released its own analysis of the effects of leaving the EU and concluded that a decade of uncertainty would hit financial markets, investment and sterling, and that the rights of 2 million expats in other EU states to work, pensions and healthcare could no longer be guaranteed. Arch spin-doctor Peter Mandelson then jumped in, saying that exporters would face trade tariffs of up to 20 per cent. Unsurprisingly, some Leavers were quick to point to the dramatic change of tone:

[I]n a bid to get the whole referendum over and done with as quickly as possible, the government's message changed within a matter of weeks. Cameron went from claiming that the EU needed major changes to saying that if we left the bloc, World War Three would break out, house prices would plummet and millions of people would lose their jobs.[16]

Despite Project Fear's ongoing barrage of dire warnings about the highly negative consequences of Brexit, there were signs that the heavy-handed message was not getting through. In all of the polls conducted by telephone Remain had become used to large leads – in every telephone poll that had been released until 10 March the Remainers had averaged a comfortable lead. However, in mid March a telephone poll released by ORB became the first to put Leave ahead. The lead was only two points (49 per cent to 47 per cent) but it was seen by some as further evidence that the strategy was not resonating. Will Straw recalled how some in the Remain camp were becoming nervous.

Andrew [Cooper]'s strong view was that so long as we keep emphasizing the risks of leaving the economy would trump immigration. Nonetheless, there was a growing unease among some in the campaign, myself and Peter Mandelson in particular, that constantly pivoting back to the economy rather than taking on Leave's arguments about immigration was costing us badly –especially given the daily onslaught on the issue from the tabloids. This was supported by anecdotal evidence from Labour MPs and our focus groups. I argued in various memos that David Cameron should make a major speech, similar to Tony Blair's Dover speech in 2005, or write an article on immigration, to call out Leave's falsehoods. I lost this argument to others in No. 10 who wanted to stick solely to the core script on economic risk.[17]

Aside from leading some to question whether this signalled the beginning of a public backlash against scaremongering by Project Fear, the poll also shed light on another potential problem for Remain. People who supported Leave appeared to be more enthusiastic about the referendum and more committed to turning out to vote. This was consequential – once the ORB poll numbers were adjusted for whether respondents were 'certain to vote', Leave's lead extended from two to fully seven points. In the weeks that followed four additional polls similarly suggested the existence of an 'enthusiasm gap' – two-thirds of Remain supporters but fully three-quarters of Leavers said they were certain to vote.[18] Despite mounting evidence of a possible turnout problem, there was no real change of strategy by Remainers.

As the campaign moved into March the warnings about economic risk continued. This time it was the turn of the British Bankers Association to claim that almost 60 per cent of banks thought that their business would be damaged if Britain left the EU. BlackRock, the world's largest fund manager, warned that a decision to leave would negatively impact on sterling, equities, financial institutions, London's property market and the fashion industry, produce higher unemployment and trigger inflation. Meanwhile, workers at companies such as Rolls-Royce and Siemens received letters from their employers that encouraged them to vote to remain. One letter from Airbus read: 'We all need to keep in the back of our minds that future investments depend very much on the economic environment in which the company operates.'[19] Elsewhere, at a Franco-British summit, French politicians reiterated Cameron's warning that a vote to leave could result in the closure of a camp for migrants in Calais, encouraging the migrants to head to Britain. Mark Carney returned to suggest that leaving posed the 'biggest domestic risk to financial stability', would introduce a period of instability that could 'last a very long time' and lead major financial institutions to relocate outside of Britain.

Cameron was quick to underscore the message, stating in a speech to car workers that Brexit would mean higher mortgage rates, lost jobs and 'hardworking people losing their livelihoods'. The Organisation for Economic Co-operation and Development (OECD) then claimed that leaving would have negative economic consequences for Britain and the world. A French bank joined in, releasing figures purporting to show that a vote to leave would negatively affect British exports and foreign investment. The Confederation of British Industry followed, claiming that leaving would result in a £100 billion shortfall and households would be £3,700 poorer. At the end of March, Health Secretary Jeremy Hunt cautioned that the NHS would face budget cuts, falling standards and an exodus of overseas staff if the people voted for a Brexit.

Meanwhile, Vote Leave had been trying to cultivate its own messages. At the end of March, it released a list of the 50 most dangerous EU criminals, 45 of whom had committed serious offences in the UK, including nine murders and seven rapes. 'We have lost control of our borders and have been unable to prevent dangerous individuals from walking into the UK.'[20] In the same month, Vote Leave released data to support its claim that EU institutions had allocated more than £200 million for 'communications', claiming that the organization was spending more on furthering the EU project than fighting terrorism. Leavers would also release details of expenses that had been claimed by 'Eurocrats' in Brussels, including five-star hotels, private jets and 'pet-friendly' chauffeurs. 'Most families have been hit hard since the financial crisis', said a Vote Leave spokesperson, 'having to tighten their belts to make ends meet. But EU officials are using our money to fund their jollies and exorbitant expense claims.'[21] In Scotland Leavers argued that leaving could secure the long-term future of free university tuition in Scotland, while in Wales they claimed that the steel industry would have a better chance of survival if people voted to leave. 'Instead of handing over £350m [million] a week to Brussels', argued Dr Liam Fox, 'we should be spending that money on local priorities like the Welsh NHS, which has faced a billion pounds of cuts by the Welsh Labour Government since 2011.'[22] From one town to the next, Vote Leave campaigners were delivering similar messages. In Kettering voters were told that while one in four parents could not get their first choice of school locally and there was a shortage of local doctors, Britain was sending £350 million a week to Brussels. In Norfolk a Vote Leave MP claimed that exiting the EU would protect that venerable institution, the British curry house, making it easier for restaurants to get visas for Bangladeshi chefs. Then, in May, Vote Leave attracted publicity after offering voters a chance to win £50 million, the amount it claimed the country paid to the EU each day, should they predict the result of every football match in the 2016 European championships. The competition had been designed to collect data on potential leave voters.

Public Perceptions

As the campaign entered its final hundred days the Remainers stayed committed to their core strategy. As one newspaper observed: 'Mr Cameron's side has shown brutal professional discipline in honing its message to a stark warning of economic loss from Brexit, then hammered that message home with unremitting repetition.'[23] Yet, aside from the headline numbers in some polls there was other evidence to suggest that the strategy was not winning most of the people over. As shown in Table 3.1, when it came to what people thought about the campaign, a YouGov survey suggested that it was Leave, rather than Remain, which held an advantage – slightly larger percentages of the respondents perceived Leave to be honest, positive and 'clear about their case'. In contrast, Remain was seen by larger percentages to be dishonest, negative and to be unclear about its case.

Further insight into public perceptions of how the campaign was being conducted was provided by a YouGov survey conducted in the first week of June. The results showed that neither campaign was judged particularly favourably, but that Leave received slightly higher scores. For example, people were slightly more likely to perceive Leave as more honest (22 per cent) than Remain (20 per cent). In terms of who had made the most negative attacks, 30 per cent said Leave, 33 per cent said Remain. Regarding which side was more realistic, 26 per cent said Leave and 24 per cent said Remain. The widest gap concerned who was doing the most scaremongering – here 41 per cent said Remain, 28 per cent said Leave, with the remainder saying either 'neither' or 'don't know'.[24]

Table 3.1 *Public Perceptions of the Leave and Remain Campaigns*

	5–6 June		17–19 June		20–22 June	
	Leave	Remain	Leave	Remain	Leave	Remain
Honesty						
Mostly honest	22%	19%	26%	22%	24%	22%
Mostly dishonest	42	46	43	46	44	45
Neither/don't know	36	35	31	32	33	33
Tone						
Positive	24%	17%	27%	16%	26%	19%
Negative	49	54	46	58	51	55
Neither/don't know	27	30	27	26	24	26
Clarity						
Clear about their case	30%	25%	34%	27%	34%	29%
Unclear about their case	45	48	41	46	42	46
Neither/don't know	25	27	25	26	24	25

Source: YouGov/*The Times*, 2016.

Such surveys also threw light on whether voters felt that the campaigns understood the concerns of ordinary people. As shown in Figure 3.1, as the race neared its end, 46 per cent judged that Leave understood the concerns of ordinary people 'very' or 'fairly' well. In contrast, only 30 per cent felt that way about Remain. When asked who they thought the respective campaigns represented – the establishment, ordinary people or both equally – a much larger percentage (41 per cent versus 19 per cent) thought that Remain represented the establishment, while Leave were significantly more likely (26 per cent versus 10 per cent) to be seen as representing ordinary people.

Project Fear Doubles Down

Although the Remainers were undoubtedly aware that they were seen in a more negative light, Project Fear remained firmly in place. As

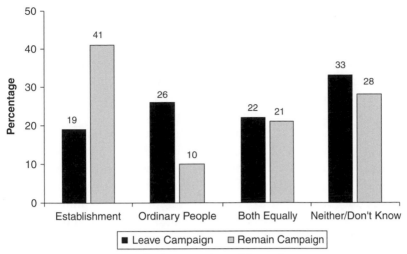

Figure 3.1 Voters' Views of Who Remain and Leave Represent.
Source: YouGov Survey, *Sunday Times*, 16–17 June 2016.

voters made up their minds the chief of the London Stock Exchange warned that leaving the EU would have 'devastating' effects on the economy. The credit rating agency Standard & Poor's projected that Britain would lose the 'AAA' rating that it had enjoyed continuously for nearly four decades. Evidently forgetting that many younger people were anxious to get on the housing ladder, one of the country's biggest mortgage lenders said that a Brexit would lower house prices. In an open letter, 64 Labour council leaders from across the Midlands and North argued that leaving would be disastrous for their local communities. Cameron sent a letter to farmers to warn that they could face trade tariffs of up to 12 per cent and risked 'losing everything'. He also cautioned that the cost of a one-week holiday to Europe could increase by as much as £230 by 2018. The lobbying group TheCityUK said that leaving would cost up to 100,000 jobs in the financial services sector. The International Monetary Fund (IMF) returned to the fray to claim that leaving the EU would 'precipitate a protracted period of uncertainty, leading to financial market volatility and a hit to output'. Other short-term impacts, the IMF speculated, could include falling equity and real estate prices, higher borrowing costs for businesses and households, a decline in foreign investment and the economy shrinking by between 1 and 9 per cent.[25]

In case voters had somehow not encountered the narrative of economic risk, shortly before the official campaign got underway on 15 April the Government distributed a leaflet to every household. As the Leave camp took to the airwaves to argue that the leaflet, which had cost £9.3 million, gave an unfair advantage to Remain, voters were sitting at home reading the dark forecast. The EU, they were told, was Britain's biggest trading partner, the single market attracted hundreds of millions of pounds of investment and more than 3 million jobs in Britain were linked to exports to the EU. Leaving the EU would mean higher prices for household goods, damage living standards, reduce exports, create a decade or more of uncertainty and jeopardize cheap travel and raise roaming charges for mobile phones. Only 2 of the 16 pages were devoted to the benefits of EU membership.[26]

Another avalanche of warnings quickly followed. Former Labour Chancellor of the Exchequer Alistair Darling claimed that a Brexit would leave the country exposed to the same collapse of confidence that had preceded the financial crisis in 2008. Darling returned a few weeks later to state that leaving would land Britain with a £250 billion annual bill for lost trade. Meanwhile, George Osborne repeated his claim that the financial stress of a Brexit would increase the cost of people's mortgages and, for good measure, added that households would be £4,300 a year worse off. His intervention followed a report by the Treasury that forecast that the economy could be 6.2 per cent smaller and £36 billion deeper in debt by 2030 if there was a decision to leave. A lobbying group meanwhile forecast that if the UK voted to leave the EU, northern England would be more 'economically and politically marginalised'.

And so Remain's negative strategy continued. Reports claimed that customs controls after a vote to leave would damage cross-border business between Northern Ireland and the Republic of Ireland. A defence think-tank concluded that Brexit threatened peace in Europe. Writing in *The Times*, eight former US treasury secretaries argued that leaving the EU would damage London's status as a global financial centre, reduce trade flow, boost populist movements across Europe and was a 'risky bet'. They were followed by no less than US President Barack Obama himself. In late April the forty-fourth president flew to London to warn that if the UK voted for a Brexit it would be at the 'back of the queue' when it came to negotiations over a new trade agreement with the United States.

Around the same time, 200 entrepreneurs published an open letter asserting that leaving the EU would stifle small businesses and innovation. The OECD then returned to lecture workers that they would lose the equivalent of one month's pay before 2020 if they voted for Brexit. Cameron, standing alongside a former union leader, similarly argued that ordinary workers would be hit by a 'triple threat' to jobs, wages and prices as well as see unemployment rise to 8 per cent. 'Paid holidays, maternity rights, equal treatment for the millions of people working part-time, protections for agency workers, even equal pay for women at work: all are guaranteed by Europe and all could be at risk if we left.'[27] In the Northeast, workers were told that thousands of jobs in the technology sector were at risk, while in Downing Street the Prime Minister of Japan reminded the British people that more than a thousand companies from his nation invested in the UK and did so mainly because it was a gateway to the EU. No economic threat was left unarticulated.

In May, Cameron launched a new phase of the campaign that was designed to shift attention onto national security. Recalling Europe's violent history, the Prime Minister questioned whether leaving the EU could ensure the continuation of peace and stability. 'The serried rows of white headstones in lovingly-tended Commonwealth war cemeteries stand as silent testament to the price this country has paid to help restore peace and order in Europe. Can we be so sure that peace and stability on our continent are assured beyond any shadow of doubt?' One journalist who had sat listening to the speech wondered aloud why the Prime Minister had decided to hold the referendum if one of the outcomes could be war.

This did not stop others from highlighting threats to national security that would be precipitated by Brexit. Former heads of the security services argued that leaving the EU could undermine the sharing of intelligence and Britain's ability to protect itself. Five former secretary-generals of NATO threw their weight behind Remain, warning that leaving the EU 'would undoubtedly lead to a loss of British influence, undermine NATO and give succour to the West's enemies just when we need to stand shoulder to shoulder across the Euro-Atlantic community against common threats, including on our doorstep'.[28] A seemingly unperturbed Cameron then argued that the only people who would welcome Brexit would be Vladimir Putin and Isis. The President of the European Council, Donald Tusk, then sounded another alarmist note, warning that Brexit could trigger the end of 'Western political civilization'.

Alongside dire warnings about threats to their security, voters continued to be carpet-bombed by a wave of gloomy economic forecasts. As the race neared its final month, one forecast concluded that the national economy would be between 1.5 and 7.8 per cent smaller by 2030, compared to if the people had voted to remain. Trade unions chimed in, saying that working-time protections were under threat. Almost 200 economists signed a letter warning that Brexit would entail 'significant long-term costs' and Mark Carney returned to warn that Brexit could tip the country into recession:

A vote to leave the EU could have material economic effects on the exchange rate, on demand and the economy's supply potential. Households could defer consumption and firms delay investment. Global financial conditions could also tighten, generating negative spillovers to foreign economic activity that, in turn, would dampen demand for UK exports. The consequences could possibly include a technical recession.

After Carney's comments the value of Britain's largest companies slumped to a five-week low. Undeterred, George Osborne elaborated: 'So either families would face lower incomes because inflation would be higher, or the economy would be weaker with a hit to jobs and livelihoods. This is a lose-lose situation for Britain. Either way, we'd be poorer.'[29] IMF Director Christine Lagarde endorsed Carney's remarks and argued that the implications of a leave vote ranged from 'pretty bad to very bad'. As part of a cross-party move Osborne then joined former Labour Shadow Chancellor Ed Balls and former Liberal Democrat Minister Vince Cable to issue a fresh warning. Standing in front of an aeroplane at Stansted airport the three forecast that Brexit would cost £200 million in trade. By mid-May the gloomy predictions were reflected in almost daily headlines that referred to 'substantial damage', 'economic costs' and an impending crash in the stock and housing markets. Commenting on the mountain of doom and gloom, the *Guardian* observed that 'the descent beyond hyperbole into hysteria has been unusually steep over the past week'.[30]

The Final Month

As the campaign entered its final month Remainers continued to double down on their strategy although they also sought to remedy a specific weakness that had become evident in the polls. Ever since Vote Leave had launched their own campaign the Leavers had devoted specific attention to the NHS. Now, polls and focus groups suggested that the message had been cutting through. For example, throughout the campaign YouGov had asked their respondents how leaving the EU might impact on different areas, including the economy, jobs, immigration, Britain's global influence, pensions, terrorism and the NHS. The results, shown in Figure 3.2, reveal how the Remainers held an edge with regard to economic conditions – people tended to believe that both the national economy and their own finances were more likely to be in good shape if the UK remained in the EU. Moreover, Remain's edge on the economy had grown as 2016 had progressed.

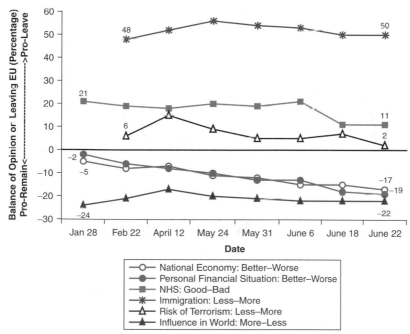

Figure 3.2 Trends in the Balance of Public Opinion on the Consequences of Leaving the EU, 28 January–22 June 2016.
Source: YouGov surveys.

Remain's performance on other issues was less impressive, however. True enough, people tended to believe that the UK's international influence would be greater if the country remained in the EU. However, a huge majority consistently believed that leaving the EU would help the country to control immigration, which as we have seen was a guiding concern for many voters. Leaving the EU also was favoured, but by a much smaller margin, as a way to reduce the risk of terrorism. Finally, as Figure 3.2 indicates, Leave also held an edge on strengthening the NHS – across all of the surveys the percentage of people thinking that leaving the EU would do more to help the NHS was greater than the percentage thinking staying in the EU was a preferable option. The pro-Leave margin on the health service was nontrivial, reaching as high as 21 points and never falling below 18 points until mid June.

Such data reveal how, in terms of political strategy, Vote Leave were right to retain a strong focus on the NHS, a cherished public service that was under immense pressure. At the beginning of 2016 this focus on the NHS had been underlined by healthcare professionals who warned it was being 'bled dry' of resources by 'health tourists' and that progress in tackling major diseases was being hindered by EU directives.[31] Similar interventions would follow. In April, Vote Leave released statistics that claimed to document how immigration was putting pressure on the NHS, causing longer waiting times and a growing deficit: 'What we get back from the EU is a city the size of Newcastle of new immigrants to the UK every year', said Conservative MP Priti Patel: 'Current levels of migration are causing unsustainable pressure on our public services and we can see that the NHS is creaking under the strain.'[32]

The strategy was not lost on the Remainers, some of whom recalled being acutely aware of the impact of Vote Leave's gameplan. Andrew Cooper, who was crunching polling numbers for Remain, noted how his data showed 'in stark terms how the NHS was seen as a clear area of benefit in the event of Brexit'. The Leave camp's advantage on the health service had become abundantly clear in focus groups as well, as Cooper elaborated:

We probed a lot in the focus groups and the ostensible logic was hard to crack: controlling immigration (which most people took to mean more or less stopping immigration, not just winning back the right to control it) would obviously mean less pressure on public services, above all the NHS;

no longer sending a fortune to the EU ... would obviously mean more money for the NHS, which above all seems to most people to need more money. Most people simply refused to accept that the cost/burden to the NHS of immigrants from the EU using its services was a small fraction of what, overall, they contributed in taxes. We tried various different ways of saying that [and] different authoritative sources, but it just felt too counter-intuitive to be true, when set alongside everything else people thought they knew. We found a little bit of traction on the argument that the NHS depends on migrant workers from the EU, though that also annoyed some people. In the end, we fell back on the argument that the only way to sustain the NHS was a strong, growing economy, which would be undermined if we left the EU. I'm not sure there was a better argument available to us, but this obviously put even more pressure on the economic argument.[33]

In the final month of the campaign Stronger In tried to push back. The chief executive of the NHS in England, Simon Stevens, appeared on the BBC's *Andrew Marr Show* to warn against leaving the EU. Referring to Mark Carney's statements, Stevens told viewers that a Brexit-induced recession would be 'very dangerous' for the NHS: 'It has been true for the 68 years of the NHS's history that when the British economy sneezes the NHS catches a cold. This would be a terrible time for that to happen, at just the time that the NHS is going to need that investment.' Stevens also took the opportunity to challenge Conservative MP Penny Mordaunt, who appeared alongside him and reiterated Vote Leave's claim that contributions to the EU could be redirected into the NHS and social care. Stevens looked up data on her local hospital: 'At her local hospital, 80 of the doctors are from the rest of the European Union, 350 nurses in her local hospital are from the EU. If only a proportion of those chose to up sticks and off on the 23 June that would create real problems in hospitals across the country.' Others, including the British Medical Council, would similarly dispute Vote Leave's claims about the NHS.[34]

Under normal circumstances these attempts to prevent the NHS from turning into an area of strength for Leave might have been helped by a proactive Labour Party leader who was firmly committed to campaigning for a Remain vote. Historically, the NHS and Labour were closely linked in the public mind. Shortly after the Second World War, Clement Atlee's Labour Government had founded the NHS as the cornerstone of Britain's welfare state and traditionally Labour had prided itself as the Service's champion. However, Labour's current leader was

the widely unpopular Jeremy Corbyn, who was also a decidedly unenthusiastic participant in the referendum campaign. In March, it had
been reported that Corbyn and his team had removed blogs written
under his name that had criticized the EU, talked of making a 'strong
socialist argument' against the Lisbon Treaty and suggested that the
project had 'always been to create a huge free-market Europe, with
ever-limiting powers for national parliaments'.[35] In the same month,
Labour MPs such as Yvette Cooper and Liz Kendall had publicly
called for Corbyn to campaign more actively and warned Labour not
to 'prevaricate' about EU membership. They had reason to worry.
When, only a few days before the vote, Corbyn was asked on televi-
sion to give the EU a mark out of 10 the Labour leader gave it a 'seven,
or seven and a half'. A few days later, YouGov asked a national sample
whether they knew Labour's position on the referendum. Only 66 per
cent were able to correctly identify that Labour supported remaining
in the EU. One in three thought Labour supported Leave or did not
know where the party stood.[36]

Cameron and Osborne, meanwhile, were still trying to stoke public
fears about risks to the national economy. In a joint letter, the two men,
who had led the country for the past six years and were now fighting for
their political survival, warned that leaving the EU would plunge Britain
into a year-long 'recession of its own making' and could cost between
520,000 and 820,000 jobs. 'With exactly one month to go to the referendum', said Osborne, 'the British people must ask themselves this question: Can we knowingly vote for a recession?' Cameron chimed in: 'As
I stand here in B&Q (a hardware store), it would be a DIY recession.'

Remainers were becoming increasingly frantic. Londoners were
told that by 2018 £7,500 would be wiped off the average value of
homes and reminded that up to 100,000 jobs in financial services were
under threat. The head of the World Bank said that Brexit would hit
the poorest people in the world, while the G7 nations described it as
a 'serious risk' to global growth. The credit ratings agency Standard
& Poor's opined the British people that leaving would threaten sterling's elite status as an international reserve currency. The Institute
for Fiscal Studies reminded voters that there was a 'near consensus'
among economists that leaving would damage the economy and could
prolong austerity measures by two years as the Government struggled
to replace an estimated £20–40 billion in tax revenue. Cameron and
Osborne then turned to Britain's pensioners, who polls suggested were

among the most likely to support Leave. They were warned that leaving the EU could take up to £32,000 from their savings, their retirement income would not stretch as far and social care workers would be in short supply.

As the campaign entered its final phase, Remain's cries of impending disaster reached a climax. The Trades Union Congress claimed that if Britain left, then by 2030 the average weekly wage for workers would be £38 lower. The OECD returned again to forecast that the economy would suffer a 'large negative shock'. 'The weaker UK economy, as well as possible new restrictions after exiting the EU, would lower net migration inflows, adding to the supply-side challenges by reducing the size of the labour force.' The IMF returned once again to the debate, warning that by 2019 Brexit would cost Britain 5.6 per cent of its growth, plunge households into financial peril, lower incomes, trigger inflation and leave the average family at least £240 worse off within a year of the vote. Smokers were told that a packet of cigarettes could rise by £3 as a result of tariffs on tobacco. Consumers were told they would have to pay more for ice cream. Scotland was warned it would sell less Scotch and in the Falklands a politician warned that the islanders could be forced to establish closer ties with Argentina. That Cameron and his team were seen by many as trying to scare voters into supporting Remain was reflected in one question to the Prime Minister, asked by Faisal Islam, political editor of Sky News, during a televised debate. 'What comes first – World War Three or the global Brexit recession?' The audience burst into applause.

George Osborne was not put off and seemed to have found his stride. The Chancellor returned to the airwaves with new figures to support his claim that leaving would increase the annual cost of mortgages by between £920 and £1,470. Osborne also claimed that a Brexit would force him to introduce an emergency budget to increase taxes or cut spending to compensate for the economic costs that would follow. Most people, however, did not buy the claim. When asked whether Osborne's claims were true or false 47 per cent thought they were probably false and only 28 per cent thought they were truthful.[37] Yet the Chancellor continued to practise message discipline. In the days and hours before the vote he would claim that Britain would 'lose control' of its economy if people voted to leave the EU and joined 10 of the largest companies in the country's service sector to argue that 400,000 of their jobs were under threat.

Cameron would also remain firmly on course. Against the back-drop of a further slide in the value of sterling he described a vote to leave as equivalent to 'putting a bomb under our economy'. As the day of reckoning neared, Cameron welcomed further warnings about the economic risks of a Brexit from the chair of the Federal Reserve, chairman of Hitachi and the boss of the World Trade Organization. The Prime Minister cited them all when warning voters that this vote was about 'your wages, your mortgage, your job'.

Others rushed in to try and help push the Remainers over the line in what still looked like a close race. Germany's Finance Minister warned that if Leave won then Britain would not have access to the single market. Others predicted that the London Stock Exchange could fall as much as 20 per cent, wiping £450 billion off share valu-ations. Britain's biggest house builders said that leaving would make it harder and more expensive to build new homes, making it even more difficult for first-time buyers to get on the property ladder. The former boss of the supermarket chain Tesco warned that food prices would have to rise. Analysis by civil servants at the Treasury claimed that northern England would lose 120,000 jobs, house prices would plummet by £20,000 and wages would fall by £710 a year. Ten leaders of Britain's biggest cities warned that leaving would create serious economic dangers. Former Labour Prime Minister Gordon Brown and former Labour leader Neil Kinnock warned that a loss of European structural funds would allow 'Tory Brexiteers' to turn industrial heartlands into 'industrial wastelands'. Spain's Prime Minister also chipped in, warning that the more than 400,000 British citizens living and working in Spain might have to forfeit their right to do so.

The day before the vote, nearly 1,300 of Britain's most senior busi-ness leaders, including more than 50 from the largest companies that collectively employ nearly 2 million people, published a letter in *The Times*. They argued that Brexit would mean more uncertainty, less trade and fewer jobs. As voters prepared to go to the polls, Cameron summarized Remain's core message: 'All the experts seem to be say-ing – the IMF, the ECB, the Bank of England, the Treasury, the Office of Budget Responsibility are all saying – the economy would suffer if we left the European Union and single market, and that is quite a consensus. And if that were to happen it would have a bad effect on the NHS.'[38]

Leavers also ended with a flurry of interventions that were designed to carry them over the line and would, though it was never officially recognized, unite the warring camps. For much of the campaign the unofficial Leave campaign had doubled down on immigration, continuing a strategy that UKIP had deployed since 2010 (Goodwin and Milazzo 2015). Nigel Farage, who despite failing to enter the House of Commons was determined to remain at the forefront of the national debate, had embarked on a tour of the country. Standing aloft a purple double-decker bus the UKIP leader had taken his anti-immigration message through a succession of struggling towns, many of which were controlled by Labour and filled with economically left-behind, white working-class voters – including Dagenham, Dudley, Bolton, Newcastle-upon-Tyne, Gateshead, Blackpool, Leigh, Thanet, Sittingbourne and Nottingham. But by this time Farage was not the only one targeting immigration.

As the official Vote Leave campaign entered the final phase of the campaign it came under fresh attack and not from its main rivals in the Remain camp. The *Daily Telegraph*, a newspaper that backed Leave, published a blistering attack on the campaign, which, it argued, had 'thus far been a disappointment'. Pointing to polls that suggested Conservative Party voters were drifting back to Cameron, the paper asked: 'Where is the positive narrative of how Britain, released from EU bureaucracy and able to strike its own trade deals, might be better off? Where is the relentless reminder that EU membership means uncontrolled European immigration? Where are the warnings that the EU is an inherently unstable economic project that may well be doomed?'[39]

In the little time that remained Vote Leave did change its strategy. As polling day neared, the Leavers began to turn up the volume on the one issue that was dominating the minds of most voters, and that Farage and the unofficial Leave camp had been targeting all along.[40] Immigration was now pushed to the forefront. At the end of May, Vote Leave had already released a new video that suggested Cameron was in favour of Turkey joining the EU. The video had followed a speech by Michael Gove, who claimed that Turkey and four other countries could join the EU as soon as 2020, which could lead to over 5 million extra people entering the country, equivalent to four cities the size of Birmingham. 'The idea', said Gove, 'of asking the NHS to look after a new group of patients equivalent in size to four Birminghams is clearly unsustainable.' He subsequently claimed that to maintain the current levels of funding per person the NHS would need further investment of £4–9 billion per year by 2030 and have to find tens of thousands of new doctors and nurses.[41]

The shift was certainly noted by Remainers like Will Straw, who observed: 'Dominic Cummings could not have been clearer in his various blogs and briefings in 2014 and 2015 that this was not the approach that they hoped to take. But I am convinced that they moved so heavily onto immigration because they had so catastrophically lost the economic argument. In the end, Johnson and Gove were mouthing the words but Farage had written the script.' Shortly afterwards, dismissing George Osborne's warnings as 'an avalanche of scaremongering' and a 'Himalayan snow job of statistics', Michael Gove and Boris Johnson promised that after leaving the EU they would introduce an Australian-style points-based immigration system that would require migrants to speak English and, it was claimed, shorten waiting lists in the NHS. UKIP had been calling for the same system since at least 2015.

Others joined in. Chris Grayling warned that young people would find it even harder to get on the housing ladder if present trends continued. Vote Leave warned that British schools faced an influx of up to 571,000 children from the EU and an increase of up to £1.9 billion in the country's annual education budget if states such as Albania, Macedonia and Turkey joined the EU. Michael Gove then returned to claim that as Justice Secretary he had been unable to stop criminals and terrorists from entering the country.

The strategy continued. Liam Fox claimed that England would have to build a new home every six minutes to cope with the demand caused by mass immigration and that large sections of the countryside would need to be concreted over. Vote Leave seized on news that up to 13,000 foreign criminals were not being deported to claim that each foreign offender who was imprisoned in Britain was costing £36,000 a year to jail and that being in the EU was making it 'more difficult' to deport them. Iain Duncan Smith then attracted publicity after accusing Cameron, his own party leader, of 'deceiving' voters by claiming that workers from other EU countries would have to leave Britain if they could not find a job. The Gove–Johnson double act then promised to invest an additional £5 billion a year into the NHS that would come from cancelling EU membership fees. Vote Leave then claimed that between 2005 and 2014 the cost of EU nationals using Britain's maternity services was over £1.3 billion.

Nigel Farage, meanwhile, who had been focusing almost exclusively on immigration, turned up the volume. He argued that a vote to remain in the EU threatened Britain's security because 'Isis promises to flood the continent with jihadists', and that, as Cummings had been arguing on social media, Cologne-style sex attacks could soon take place across the country. When, at the end of May, more than a dozen illegal Albanian migrants who were trying to get to Britain were rescued off the Kent coast, the UKIP leader warned that unless they were deported the country 'will have drownings and bodies washing up on Kent beaches all summer'.[42] Boris Johnson also returned to the fray to argue that if people voted to remain they might need to contribute billions of pounds to help cover the cost of the refugee crisis. Farage was clearly delighted with the change of strategy. After reiterating a message that he had delivered in towns up and down the country, that the vote was about 'more than money', Farage heralded Vote Leave's shift onto immigration as a 'turning point' in the referendum.[43] Shortly before the vote he would stand in front of a new UKIP poster that appeared to show a line of refugees walking towards Britain. It read: 'Breaking Point – The EU has Failed Us All', with the subtitle 'We Must Break Free of the EU and Take Back Control of Our Borders'. The poster was quickly attacked by Remainers and their media allies as racist propaganda that had been designed to stoke immigration fears.

Although Britain's Eurosceptics had been divided into two warring camps for much of the campaign, in the final days they seemed to converge on the same message. In the final week this was rounded off with Vote Leave releasing a 'Brexit Queen's Speech', detailing six new laws that would be passed by 2020. They included a points-based immigration system and an end to free movement, an end to the European Court's control of Britain's asylum policy, a repeal bill that would cut Britain's ties with treaties that make up the heart of the EU, an end to the European Court of Justice's control over national security, allowing the Government to remove EU citizens whose 'presence is not conducive to the public good', an end to pay-outs under EU law to big businesses, abolishing the 5 per cent rate of VAT on household energy bills and an extra £100 million a week in funding for the NHS, over and above current plans. The question was whether such ideas would be enough.

And the Verdict Is …?

The campaign was over and the country would have to wait for the verdict from the people. What that verdict would be was far from clear. Hundreds of public and private polls had been conducted over the course of the campaign. Figure 3.3 illustrates trends in 103 polls that had been released for public consumption between 8 January and 22 June 2016. As shown, Remainers began the year with a substantial six-point lead among decided voters, a margin that it continued to hold when the referendum was formally announced on 20 February. Thereafter, Remain was always ahead, although be varying margins, until late May, when Leave finally caught up. Leave then moved into the lead, with its margin over Remain reaching as much as four points among decided voters at the end of the first week of June. Then, the race began to tighten again, a trend that continued after the murder of Labour MP Jo Cox on 16 June by a right-wing fanatic. In an act of

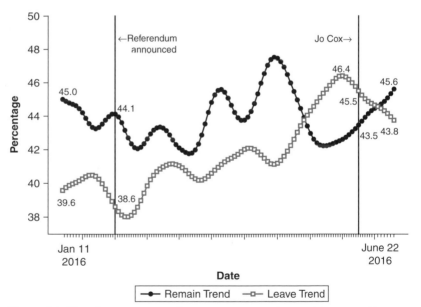

Figure 3.3 Trends in Remain and Leave Vote Intentions, 11 January–22 June 2016.
Note: Trends estimated using the Hodrick–Prescott filter; 103 polls.
Source: en.wikipedia.org/wiki/Opinion_polling_for_the_United_Kingdom_European_Union_membership_referendum.

superb, albeit inadvertent, bad timing, on that same day Nigel Farage unveiled his infamous 'Breaking Point' poster. Following the murder of Jo Cox the rival campaigns were suspended for three days and some commentators stated that the tragic event might create a sympathy vote that would carry the Remainers to victory. In fact, in the final few days before the referendum, and as shown in Figure 3.3, our trend analysis shows that Remain did move slightly ahead in the polls. At the close of the campaign on 22 June, the trend line showed Remain on 45.6 per cent and Leave on 43.8 per cent among decided voters. Allocating survey respondents telling pollsters they were undecided on a proportionate basis, these end-of-campaign trend numbers implied Remain would win by a close 51.0 to 49.0 per cent margin.

The assumption that the undecided should be allocated proportionately is, of course, just that, an assumption. As discussed earlier, research on previous high-stakes referendums (e.g. LeDuc 2003) indicated that, in fact, undecided voters tend to be risk-averse people, many of whom would break for the status quo when forced to choose. But turnout would be very important as well. If, as many observers conjectured, Leave supporters were more highly motivated than those who preferred Remain, Leave might still win even though a majority of the electorate as a whole preferred to stay in the EU.

Regardless of the outcome, the rival campaigns could not be faulted for not trying; both had been remarkably active in pressing their cases with the voters. Besides participating in organized debates, doing copious media interviews and holding multiple rallies and other campaign events, the two sides had reached out directly to millions of people. Altogether, 35 per cent of those who took part in our national post-referendum survey said that they had been contacted about how to vote in the referendum. Given that the total UK electorate exceeds 64 million people, this implies that over 22 million people had been contacted by either or both of the Remain and Leave campaigns. As Figure 3.4 shows, 32 per cent of our survey respondents said they had been contacted either by Britain Stronger in Europe or one of the pro-Remain parties. Leave ran slightly behind, reaching 26 per cent. The parties were less active: 12 per cent of the respondents said they were contacted by Labour, whereas 7 per cent reported that the Conservatives contacted them. None of the other parties reached more than 5 per cent. Although UKIP is included in this latter group, Farage and his key supporters were very active throughout the campaign, working

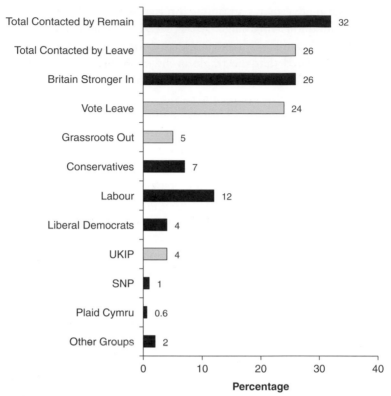

Figure 3.4 Voter Contact by the Remain and Leave Campaigns.
Source: YouGov Post-Referendum Survey.

largely through organizations such as Leave.EU and Grassroots Out.
Farage was not alone – as discussed above, a host of major players
in British politics were deeply involved in the referendum. As voters
went to the polls on 23 June, politicians joined public and pundits in
wondering what the outcome would be. Everyone would soon have
the answer.

Conclusion: Rival Messages Reconsidered

The EU referendum was rightly recognized as a highly consequential
event by the contending Remainers and Leavers. Remain's 'Project Fear'
message to voters was forceful and arrestingly simple – if you choose
to leave the EU, the country, and you personally, will suffer grievous

damage. According to this chilling narrative, it was not that there was a real risk of Brexit hurting the economy, it was a certainty. Moreover, once the decision to go was made, there was no coming back. The harm done would be irreversible. Dozens of 'A-list' domestic and international luminaries, including no less than US President Barack Obama, joined David Cameron and George Osborne in a sustained effort to convince British voters of the economic devastation and loss of international influence that awaited them should they dare to vote Leave. And, if that were not enough, the campaign periodically raised the spectre of a new European war that might result because of the destabilization of the EU that Brexit would precipitate. Cameron and his colleagues used every opportunity to hammer home their very dark message, one that had brought them victory in Scotland and at the 2015 election.

In contrast, Leave's message had a mix of negative and positive themes. As we have seen, Leave's major negative message concerned immigration: as long as Britain remained in the EU, it would be subject to an unceasing flow of immigrants and accompanying cultural, economic and security threats. Since the EU would never abandon the free movement of labour across EU member states, Leavers argued that Brexit was the only option. Stoking fears regarding the consequences of large-scale immigration and linking those threats to EU membership had yielded significant political dividends for UKIP over the past decade. Recognizing its power, Farage and his Leave.EU colleagues made anti-immigration rhetoric the centrepiece of their effort, a strategy that would eventually be shared by Vote Leave in the final weeks of the campaign.

A second message in Leave's campaign had a more positive spin and it concerned the renewal of democracy and the restoration of sovereignty that would ensue when the UK left the EU. These were themes that attracted shire Tory and other middle-class Eurosceptics, and it is likely that many of them would be mortified at being called racists because they had expressed a Farage-style anti-immigrant message. They might approve privately of his ideas, but articulating them publicly as the reason they were voting Leave would never do in polite society. In contrast, sovereignty and democracy were high-minded ideas that had the benefit of providing a politically correct rationale for casting a Leave ballot.

Finally, a third Leave message involved the claim that Britain would have major amounts of cash to invest in the NHS once it left the EU.

Remain had hotly contested this claim as misleading and a blatant falsehood. Nevertheless, the NHS had totemic status in British politics and surveys showed that Leave's claim that exiting the EU would strengthen rather than weaken the NHS resonated with a sizeable portion of the electorate. Linking their various campaign themes, Leave's 'Take Back Control' slogan cleverly covered both the darker and the brighter aspects of its message to the electorate.

In Chapter 7, we demonstrate how the messages of both Remainers and Leavers had strong effects on the choices that the British people made at the historic contest. However, in order to paint the complete picture there are some other tasks to do first. One is to investigate the factors that affected the development of Euroscepticism in the decade that preceded the 2016 referendum. Chapter 4 presents the results of that investigation.

4 | *Attitudes to Brexit Over Time*

In this chapter we take a step back to examine what has shaped public attitudes towards the United Kingdom's membership of the European Union over the last decade and more. Across the continent, the UK has long been seen as the 'awkward partner' of the EU, but how have people thought about their EU membership and what, exactly, has influenced these attitudes?

As we are about to see, one of the most notable characteristics of people's attitudes to EU membership in the UK has been their volatility. Put simply, these attitudes have been far from stable. At different points in time significant majorities of the electorate have approved and then disapproved of their country's EU membership. We need to understand, therefore, what has driven these changes at the aggregate level and then consider what has influenced people's reactions to the EU at the individual level. By doing so, in this chapter we will show how many of these effects were operating for more than a decade before the referendum. In this sense, think of this chapter as a stepping stone to understanding what motivated the actual vote to leave the EU in June 2016 (which we examine in Chapter 7).

We will begin by reviewing past research from across Europe on what drives public attitudes towards the EU and European integration. We then develop and test statistical models at the aggregate and individual level to explain what has shaped people's attitudes towards the EU over a period of more than a decade before the historic vote for a Brexit.

What Drives People's Feelings About the EU?

The 2016 referendum was the second in Britain to ask citizens about their relationship with Europe. The first, held in 1975, asked voters whether they wanted to stay in the European Community and the Common Market, and saw the country endorse continued membership by a margin of two to one (Butler and Kitzinger 1996). In the 41 years between these two referendums a large number of studies have attempted to identify the forces that shape the way in which people think about the EU (e.g. Eichenberg and Dalton 1993; Franklin et al. 1994; Gabel and Whitten 1997; Gabel 1998; Hooghe and Marks 2005, Maier and Rittberger 2008; Armingeon and Ceka 2014). These studies explored a range of factors, including the influence that elites have on mass public opinion (e.g. Steenbergen et al. 2007); the role of political parties in shaping the public's views (Ray 2003); the impact of media coverage of these issues (Vliegenthart et al. 2008); how attitudes towards Europe are shaped by national identities (Carey 2002); and the effects that different policies, particularly in relation to the economy, have on people's views (Gabel and Whitten 1997).

In 2005, Liesbet Hooghe and Gary Marks provided a succinct summary of this research in their influential paper 'Calculation, Community and Cues'. As the title of the paper suggests, Hooghe and Marks argued that three factors shape the way that people think about the EU and European integration.

'Calculations' are about the perceived costs and benefits of being a member of the EU and vary according to who are the 'winners or losers' in this process of European integration. 'Community' refers to the way that people's identities influence the way that they think about the EU. For example, citizens who have more 'exclusive' national identities, who think of themselves as being purely 'British', are significantly more Eurosceptic than those who feel that they have several identities at the same time, such as people who feel both 'British' *and* 'European'. 'Cues', meanwhile, concern how people use their perceptions of different opinion leaders in society, such as politicians, as well as their feelings of loyalty to parties and their ideological beliefs, to form an opinion about the EU. Hooghe and Marks summarize their argument as follows:

Citizens take the economic consequences of market integration into account, both for themselves and their countries. They evaluate European integration in terms of their communal identities and their views towards foreigners and foreign cultures. Further, their attitudes are cued by their ideological placement and by elites and political parties. (Hooghe and Marks 2005: 436–7)

It is helpful to explore the role of calculations, community and cues in more depth. Cost–benefit calculations about EU membership take different forms. Early research stressed the importance of people's objective social characteristics, such as their occupation and level of education (Inglehart 1970; Gabel and Palmer 1995; Anderson and Reichert 1996; Gabel 1998). The argument is that people who work in high-status occupations such as professionals and managers, most of whom are highly educated, possess significant amounts of what economists call human capital. These people are considered to be the 'winners' of European integration; they tend to benefit from lower trade barriers and face no serious competition from the free movement of EU workers that is a founding principle of the EU and so they are more tolerant of this inward migration. Many of these people can get jobs anywhere in the EU (or even the world), given that they have a large and valuable skill set that makes them attractive and flexible in the job market.

In contrast, people in low-status, poorly paid jobs and those with only a few or no educational qualifications find themselves competing with similarly low-skilled workers from other EU countries, such as those who migrated to the UK after 2004 from countries like Latvia, Lithuania and Poland. This serves to limit their access to Britain's domestic labour market and drives down wages, a point raised in a report that was released in 2008 and then updated shortly before the 2016 referendum.[1]

The implication is that high-status individuals who have abundant human capital are likely to support EU integration, whereas those with less human capital, the so-called 'losers' of European integration, or the 'left behind' (Ford and Goodwin 2014), are more likely to feel opposed to this process (Gabel and Palmer 1995). This argument is reinforced by recent research suggesting that human capital, in the form of advanced formal education, has become an increasingly important factor in explaining whether or not people support the EU. Consistent with the arguments above, while the better educated have become more supportive over time the less well educated became less so (Hakhverdian et al. 2013). In addition, there is also evidence to suggest that calculations about the costs and benefits of EU membership have become more important for explaining attitudes to the EU since the Great Recession and the eurozone crisis that followed the 2008 financial meltdown (e.g. Hobolt and Wratil 2015).

Other research has pointed to the important role of economic conditions. One early time series analysis that examined several countries over a five-year period in the 1980s found that national inflation rates negatively affected support for EU integration (Gabel and Whitten 1997). This research also showed that trade relationships between countries within the EU have served to encourage support for integration. However, this study also points out that people's subjective judgements about their surrounding economic conditions were more important predictors of attitudes towards the EU than were objective measures of how the economy was actually performing, such as unemployment and inflation rates. Overall, this finding is consistent with a large body of evidence from studies of how the economy affects political support (Lewis-Beck 1988).

Regarding the second factor, community, a number of studies have demonstrated how national identities can influence people's attitudes towards EU membership. This is partly a matter of identifying with the nation state as the principal focus of political allegiance, but a 'fear of others', such as foreigners, also plays an important role in defining identities (Carey 2002). In the UK, Matthew Goodwin and Caitlin Milazzo (2015) showed how public support for UKIP is partly motivated by feelings of anxiety over the negative effects of immigration, particularly when this is seen to threaten people's identity and culture. Other studies have shown that concerns about national identity are often more important than economic calculations when it comes to shaping public attitudes towards European integration (Hooghe and Marks 2004), a finding that is mirrored in other studies (e.g. Boomgaarden et al. 2011).

However, evidence for how identity influences these attitudes is mixed, since Scottish and Welsh identities have been shown to enhance support for European integration (Haesly 2001). This may help to explain why a majority in Scotland favoured remaining in the EU in the 2016 referendum while a majority in England opted to leave. Similar findings emerge in studies of other EU countries, particularly in Eastern Europe (Maier and Rittberger 2008). If the EU is seen as a guarantor of the integrity of the nation state against outside threats, then patriotism can reinforce support for European integration rather than weaken it. Equally, in a recent laboratory experiment Vossing (2015) showed that individuals with exclusive national identities were more likely to be influenced by elites in forming their attitudes

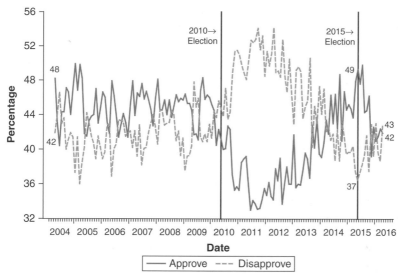

Figure 4.1 Trends in Public Attitudes towards UK Membership of the EU, April 2004–April 2016.
Source: ECMS Surveys, April 2004–April 2016.

to European integration than individuals who held mixed identities, suggesting that these opinions can be volatile and influenced by the specific national context.

To measure public attitudes in the UK about EU membership, our ECMS surveys have asked the following question, each month, since April 2004: 'Overall, do you strongly approve, approve, disapprove, or strongly disapprove of Britain's membership in the European Union?' Figure 4.1 shows trends in approval and disapproval from April 2004 to April 2016, a total of 144 months. Over this 12-year period, on average 44.7 per cent of those who responded approved of membership and 42.9 per cent disapproved. However, these numbers are by no means static, and this close overall balance masks large-scale volatility over time. For instance, approval of EU membership varied from a low of 34.7 per cent in June 2011 to a high of 52.3 per cent in January 2005, and disapproval varied from a low of 34.4 per cent in March 2005 to a high of 53.8 per cent in June 2011. These numbers attest to the ongoing volatility of public attitudes towards EU membership and reveal how these are far from being 'set in stone'.

This volatility clearly presents a problem for explaining EU attitudes with a variable like national identity, which changes rather slowly, if at all, over time.[2] The exception to this is perhaps the 'fear of the other' component of identity, which might change quickly, particularly if it is linked to an event such as the pan-European refugee crisis that erupted in 2015 and flowed from political instability and war in Syria and elsewhere. The implication is that the balance of attitudes towards continuing EU membership, especially in a referendum context, is likely to reflect the operation of factors that are more mutable than deeply rooted historical identities.

The third and final factor that Hooghe and Marks contended shaped public attitudes towards European integration was 'cues'. The basic idea is that when it comes to often complex political issues people rely on their leaders or opinion-makers to provide a 'shortcut', a steer to help them reach a decision. Put another way, some suggest that people will use the images of leaders as a 'fast and frugal' cue, to help them assess which of the parties are most likely to deliver the policies they want (Gigerenzer 2008). These cues, what psychologists call 'heuristics', might include images of party leaders, feelings about various political parties or perhaps advice given by economic and business elites, media pundits or even pop celebrities.

In the early years of the EU, during its formative period, it was argued that cues were especially influential because this was a time when there was a 'permissive consensus' about integration across much of Europe. This meant that voters appeared largely content to leave matters relating to EU integration to elites and generally accepted the decisions that were being made on their behalf (Lindbergh and Scheingold 1970). However, this willingness to abide passively to elite cues diminished over time as integration started to have a bigger impact on the lives of ordinary people.

One particularly important turning point was the Maastricht Treaty of 1992, when the Danes voted against ratifying the treaty in a 1993 referendum and the French came very close to doing so in their own referendum in 1992 (Franklin et al. 1994). This was also a time when more overtly populist and anti-immigration parties were beginning to poll strongly in several European states, including the National Front in France, the Freedom Party of Austria and the Northern League in Italy. Not all of these insurgents opposed the EU, but they often shared a populist anti-establishment strategy that further corroded public trust in governing elites and the political-economic establishment more generally. Such events alerted observers to the fact that the 'permissive consensus' was coming to an end and that ordinary people were poised to become increasingly important players in debates about European integration. Following Maastricht, the 'permissive consensus' gave way to what Hooghe and Marks referred to as a new period of 'constraining dissensus'. From that point political elites faced growing pressure from a sceptical public. '[E]lites, that is, party leaders in positions of authority, must look over their shoulders when negotiating European issues. What they see does not reassure them' (Hooghe and Marks 2009: 5).

The increased role of the public after the Maastricht Treaty focused attention on how voters were behaving in referendum campaigns. In their study of referendums on European integration, Mark Franklin and colleagues showed that contrary to conventional wisdom the people were often influenced less by debates about the future of the EU and more by short-term issues concerning their domestic politics (Franklin et al. 1994). At that time Governments in Denmark and France were relatively unpopular and this played a big role in explaining why the treaty was rejected in the former country and almost rejected in the latter (only 51 per cent of the French supported the treaty). In contrast, the Government of the Irish Republic was relatively popular at the time and the Irish referendum on Maastricht passed easily. Subsequent work confirmed that attitudes towards EU integration are closely tied to issues that animate domestic political controversies at particular points in time (Armingeon and Ceka 2014).

More recent research has focused on the interactions between variables that influence public attitudes to European integration. In their study of the 2005 referendums in France and the Netherlands Steenbergen and colleagues (2007) show how public attitudes did not just reflect the views and debates among elites but how elite opinion and public opinion interacted with each other. Similarly, Ray (2003) showed that parties can influence how voters think about EU integration, but their influence is conditional on levels of elite agreement and how strongly people feel attached to the parties. Simply stated, politicians who are unified and speak with one voice on Europe have a far bigger impact on mass opinions than political elites who are divided – a finding that is especially relevant to the 2016 referendum in the UK. In this chapter and those that follow we will explore the extent to which these findings from elsewhere also hold true in the case of the United Kingdom and its historic referendum.

We have a different, but related take on what is driving public attitudes to the EU from Hooghe and Marks. In our view, performance politics should be at the centre of the stage in explaining how people make up their minds about the EU. As we will show, people in general will support a governing party in their own country or, in the case of the EU, a political system that is delivering what they want. If Governments or the EU are seen to deliver, then they will be successful, but if they fail to do so then the public will withdraw their support. This simple idea – what is known as 'valence politics' – is developed next.

A Valence Politics Theory of Attitudes towards EU Membership

Our central hypothesis is that people's attitudes to EU membership over time can be explained by what is known as the 'valence politics' theory of voting behaviour, which has many links with the ideas discussed above. The valence politics theory of why people vote the way that they do has been used to explain the results of many recent elections, both in the UK and elsewhere (see Clarke et al. 2004, 2009a, 2009b, 2016a; Whiteley et al. 2013). The term 'valence' was introduced by Donald Stokes, one of the authors of *Political Change in Britain* (1969), in his critique of a rival 'spatial model' of party competition that had been advanced by Anthony Downs nearly 60 years ago (Downs 1957; Stokes 1963, 1992).

What did Stokes mean by 'valence'? He argued that valence issues are those on which there is a broad agreement among the people and parties about what the policy should be. In modern democracies, for example, there is a widespread consensus that countries should try to pursue sustainable economic growth and prosperity, that they should protect citizens from crime and terrorism and provide high-quality public services in areas such as healthcare, education and welfare. Although voters agree about the desirability of these policy goals, controversy arises because voters disagree about which party or leader is most likely to deliver them (e.g. Clarke et al. 2004). A good example was the 2015 UK general election, where Labour's defeat can in large part be explained by the facts that many voters blamed Labour for the

Great Recession, which had occurred on its watch, while crediting the Conservatives for the revival of the UK economy, which occurred in the run-up to that contest (Clarke et al. 2016a)

Of course, the issue of EU membership has long been one where such a broad consensus has been lacking. Instead, it has been a deeply divisive issue in UK politics. As Figure 4.1 shows, there has been widespread *disagreement* among people about the desirability of EU membership. This kind of issue was placed centre stage in the analysis of electoral behaviour by Anthony Downs. In his famous book, *An Economic Theory of Democracy* (1957), Downs argued that elections are won by parties that adopt majority positions on issues over which the electorate is divided. People opt for parties they agree with on divisive issues, and so the parties opportunistically change their policy positions to take this on board. Unfortunately, the model has little to say about the origins of attitudes towards divisive issues like Europe that are driven by factors outside of the theory. Downs's spatial model inherited this highly restrictive 'exogeneity' assumption from the field of microeconomics, where consumer preferences are simply assumed to be pre-determined. This is unsatisfactory because accounting for how people reached their views about EU membership is vitally important for understanding the vote for Brexit. In other words, we need to know what has been driving their more general views towards the EU over time before we can turn to the immediate campaign environment of 2016.

Our argument is that these public disagreements about the EU are strongly influenced by valence considerations. At its root, the UK's debate about its EU membership turns on whether being a member of the club has delivered objectives on which there is widespread agreement like economic prosperity, security for citizens, value for money in public spending and, more generally, if the EU is responsive and accountable to the electorate. If voters judge that the EU is promoting prosperity, protecting them from threats to their security, supporting quality public services and enhancing democratic accountability, then they will be more likely to support remaining in the club. But if, on the other hand, people think that the EU is failing to do these things and, worse still, is preventing their own domestic Government in Westminster from doing them, then they will be more likely to want to leave the EU. This places delivery on valence issues at the heart of the debate about Britain's role in the EU.

To develop our theory, we need to consider three explanatory variables: (1) people's evaluations of Government performance on key valence issues like the economy; (2) their images of party leaders; and (3) their feelings of attachment to different parties.

The canonical valence issue is the economy. Successful economic performance is likely to increase support for continued membership of the EU while mismanagement of the economy is likely to reduce support (e.g. Clarke et al. 2004, 2016a). As discussed earlier, voters do not make a clear distinction between the performance of the EU and the performance of the British Government, although, as we shall see, a sizeable minority thinks that the EU bears greater responsibility for Britain's prosperity than the British Government itself. Whatever the sources of successful performance, they will have the effect of increasing support for EU membership since it implies that, by working together, Westminster and Brussels can deliver the things that matter to voters – in this case economic success.

The second valence issue of considerable relevance to debates about EU membership relates to immigration and asylum-seeking. This is a valence issue in the UK because an overwhelming majority of voters think that the British Government should be able to control immigration and there is a consensus that successive British Governments have failed to do so (Clarke et al. 2016a: 66–8). Indeed, academic Lauren McLaren provides evidence to suggest that successive failures by British Governments to show competence on immigration has substantially eroded public trust in the larger political system (McLaren 2012). Immigration was a highly salient issue at the time of the 2016 referendum, as we will discuss in Chapter 7. Nigel Farage, leader of UKIP, repeatedly claimed that the British Government was unable to control immigration because the EU mandates free movement of labour within the member states. The potency of this issue was magnified by German Chancellor Angela Merkel's decision to allow more than a million refugees from the Middle East and Africa to settle in her country and, hence, inside the EU.

In addition to issues, the valence theory emphasizes the importance of voters' images of political leaders. Here, the theory focuses not so much on *what* is delivered or *how* it is being delivered, but rather on *who* is delivering it. Voters will opt for a leader who they think is competent, responsive and trustworthy – a 'safe pair of hands' – and avoid leaders they judge to be not up to the job. Clearly, impressions of the prime minister of the day are likely to provide a simple and powerful heuristic for determining if an incumbent Government can deliver. This was particularly relevant in the context of Prime Minister Cameron's renegotiation of the terms of EU membership. If voters thought that the UK's relationship with the EU needed to be reformed, but lacked confidence that Cameron could accomplish this, then they were more likely to be Eurosceptic.

How strongly people feel attached to parties also plays a crucial role because these attachments are effectively a cumulative 'running tally' of performance evaluations in delivering on the key issues in the past (Fiorina 1981; Clarke et al. 2004; Clarke and McCucheon 2009). If a party delivers successfully and repeatedly on key issues like the economy or immigration then this will cumulatively strengthen people's feelings of attachment to that party and, by extension, make them more willing to accept that party's advice when it comes to questions like whether or not the UK should remain in the EU. In contrast, if a party is seen to perform poorly, this will work to erode such feelings.

In the 2016 referendum, the major parties were arrayed along a single dimension in relation to EU membership. Although UKIP campaigned to leave the EU, the Conservatives were officially neutral, while many of their leading spokespersons were openly divided. Meanwhile, Labour was largely committed to remaining in the EU, but several prominent Labour MPs such as Frank Field and Gisela Stuart campaigned to leave. More generally the party was deeply divided over the leadership of Jeremy Corbyn, who in the past had been Eurosceptic. At the pro-EU end of the spectrum, the Liberal Democrats and the Scottish and Welsh nationalists were strongly committed to membership.[3] All of this means that if people looked to their parties for guidance on how to vote, then while the message sent by smaller parties was clear, this was not true for the two largest parties that have dominated the political landscape for nearly a century.

The valence politics model applies not only to how governing parties and their leaders are performing in relation to key issues like the economy or immigration. It also applies to the political system as a whole in the sense of voters making judgements about whether the system is working well and protecting the interests of citizens and the communities to which they belong (Kornberg and Clarke 1992). In this regard, a prominent theme in the referendum campaign and in debates over the years about the UK's membership of the EU has been the loss of sovereignty to Brussels. There has been a widespread perception that EU membership has meant that the UK's political institutions increasingly lost their ability to govern and make decisions. The result has been a decline in democratic accountability, or what is known as a 'democratic deficit' (e.g. Norris 2011). This is an important aspect of public attitudes to the EU, which will be considered below.

To summarize, we expect to find that public attitudes to EU membership are driven by factors that are central to the valence politics theory, namely how people feel elites have performed on key issues, public images of leaders, how strongly people feel attached to the parties and whether they believe that EU membership has resulted in a loss of sovereignty from the UK to the EU. If this is true, and these factors have been interacting with each other over many years and affecting attitudes towards EU membership, then this is an important first step to making sense of why people voted for a Brexit in 2016.

That these factors are likely to interact has implications for how, statistically, we will test models of EU support. In a standard regression model assumptions have to be made about what drives what, such as the assumption that a person's occupation influences their attitudes and that this does not work in reverse. This example makes perfect sense, since attitudes to the EU are not going to influence a person's occupation and so the latter is described as 'exogenous' – it is determined by factors outside the model. However, in this case all of the predictors interact with each other so we cannot say that people's judgements about the economy influence their attitudes towards the EU but this does not work in reverse. This means that all of the variables are 'endogenous' or determined within the model since they are interacting with each other in a dynamic setting. We have to use a statistical estimation procedure that reflects this fact and this is discussed next.

A Dynamic Model of Attitudes towards EU Membership

We have already seen how British attitudes towards the EU have been very volatile and there are hints in Figure 4.1 that key events may have influenced these dynamics. It is noteworthy that disapproval of EU membership soared, starting in early 2010, and did not return to parity with approval until well into 2013. This upward movement in negative sentiments towards the EU coincided with the start of the eurozone crisis, which involved several member states, such as Greece, Portugal and Ireland, announcing that they would be unable to pay sovereign debts to international organizations such as the IMF and the European Central Bank. The crisis had been building since late 2009 (Desai 2015) and it clearly played a role in influencing public reactions to the EU. It is also noteworthy that EU approval ratings increased substantially after the 2015 general election but started to decline again in the run-up to the referendum.

We can analyse the relationships between the different variables with more precision by employing aggregate time series analyses of our monthly ECMS survey data. These analyses involve examining monthly observations of public attitudes to the EU and other measures derived from the surveys. Aggregate time series methods are also attractive because they enable us to study both short- and long-run relationships among the variables in a statistical model. Regarding long-run relationships, if two or more variables trend together over time in a long-term relationship with each other, they are said to be cointegrated (Enders 2014). If this dynamic equilibrium is disturbed by an external shock such as the eurozone crisis, it will gradually be restored by the cointegrating mechanism the trending variables share. Statistical analyses can estimate the rate at which the equilibrium reasserts itself.

Another attractive feature of time series methods is that they help us to sort out causal relationships between variables. We start by assuming that, for example, attitudes to the UK economy interact in a two-way relationship with attitudes to the EU, but we can test this idea. If two variables are cointegrated, this implies the existence of a flow of influence between them over time that is called 'Granger causality'. This is defined as follows: 'X is said to Granger-cause Y if Y can be better predicted using the histories of both X and Y that it can be by using the history of Y alone' (Giles 2011). The underlying idea is that while observations in the past can influence observations in the future, the future cannot influence the past. So if past observations of the economy influence current attitudes to the EU, but past attitudes to the EU do not influence current economic evaluations, then we can say that the economy 'Granger causes' attitudes to the EU and it does not work in reverse. The approach taken here will be to estimate was is called a Vector Error Correction Model (VECM) to determine if cointegrating relationships exist among the variables of theoretical interest and then to test the variables for Granger causality (e.g. Whiteley, Clarke and Stewart 2016).[4] This model is ideal for estimating relationships in systems in which all variables interact with each other (Juselius 2006; Enders 2014). There are as many equations as there are variables in a VECM, and when a number of time lags are included in the system, the number of parameters that must be estimated grows very rapidly. Given the limited amount of available data, this means that the model specification has to be very sparse. With this point in mind we restrict the specification of the aggregate-level valence politics model to six variables. Later, we will relax this restriction when we specify an individual-level multilevel model of EU attitudes.

Here, we focus on monthly net EU membership approval ratings, that is, the monthly percentage approving membership minus the percentage disapproving. The key valence issues are captured by two variables involving the economy and immigration. The first variable measures the percentage of respondents in the monthly surveys who judged that the Conservative Party was best at managing the economy minus the percentage who thought this about Labour. The second variable is the percentage who concluded that immigration had 'got better' over the previous year minus the percentage who thought that it had 'got worse'.

The leader image variable is measured by the percentage each month who believed that the Conservative leader would make the best prime minister minus the percentage who thought this about the Labour leader. Partisanship is captured by the percentage of Conservative partisans minus the percentage of Labour partisans each month derived from answers to a standard party identification question.[5] These explanatory variables all focus on the two major parties but, in the subsequent individual-level analysis, other parties are considered. Finally, the loss of sovereignty measure is based on responses to the question: 'Which one of the following do you think affects the general economic situation in this country most?' The percentage who thought that the EU controls the UK economy is used in the analysis.

Figure 4.2 shows trends in these variables over the 12-year period from April 2004 to April 2016. All of the variables appear to be trending upwards over time – technically speaking, they are 'non-stationary'. VEC modelling requires that all the variables in a cointegrating system should be non-stationary since one variable cannot be in a dynamic equilibrium relationship with another if the former

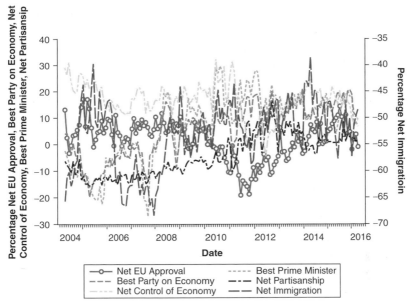

Figure 4.2 Trends in Variables in Valence Politics Model of EU Approval, April 2004–April 2016.
Source: ECMS Surveys, April 2004–April 2016.

is trending upwards or downwards and the latter is stationary, that is, fluctuating around an unchanging mean. We formally test the variables for stationarity (trends) and the results appear in Table 4.1.

These tests indicate that all of the variables of interest are, in fact, non-stationary.[6] There has been a trend change in public attitudes to UK membership of the EU over this period, alongside a growth in support for the Conservative Party relative to Labour in relation to the management of the economy and also in leadership evaluations. These trends accord closely with what is known about the political economy of voting in Britain in the run-up to the 2015 general election (Whiteley et al. 2013; Clarke et al. 2016a).

To determine if these variables are trending *together*, we utilize Johansen tests for identifying cointegrated systems (Johansen 1991; Juselius 2006).[7] Model selection criteria indicate that a lag of one time period is adequate for these tests (see Table 4.2). The Johansen tests (see Table 4.3) indicate that there is one cointegrating relationship in the data.[8] This means that net approval of EU membership, leadership

Table 4.1 *Dickey–Fuller Stationarity Tests of Variables in EU Approval Model, April 2004–April 2016*

	Test Statistic Undifferenced Variable	Test Statistic Differenced Variable
Net Approval of EU Membership (% Approval – % Disapprove)	–1.78	–6.68***
Best Prime Minister (% Conservative Leader – % Labour Leader)	–1.93	–6.14***
Net Partisanship (% Conservative Identification – % Labour Identification)	–.90	–6.77***
Best Party on the Economy (% Conservatives Best – % Labour Best)	–1.58	–5.94***
Net Attitudes towards Immigration (% Immigration Better – % Immigration Worse)	–2.63	–5.08***
EU Controls the British Economy (% Think EU Controls the Economy)	–2.21	–5.34***

Note: *** = $p \leq .001$, rejects null hypothesis of non-stationarity.

Table 4.2 *Tests for Lag Lengths in VEC Model of EU Approval, April 2004–April 2016*

Lags	Log Likelihood	AIC	BIC
0	–2,648.7	37.7	37.8
1	–2,218.4	32.06†	32.9†
2	–2,192.5	32.2	33.8
3	–2,172.2	32.4	34.8

Note: † indicates optimal lag.

evaluations, subjective economic judgements, attitudes towards immigration, partisanship and perceptions of economic sovereignty have all moved together through time in a long-term dynamic equilibrium

Table 4.3 *Johansen Cointegration Tests for Variables in Model of EU Approval*

Maximum Rank	Log Likelihood	Eigenvalue	Trace Statistic
0	–2,285.2	–	114.9
1	–2,259.2	.30	62.9*
2	–2,246.2	.17	37.0
3	–2,239.2	.09	23.1

Note * = $p \leq .05$; N = 144.

with each other. They could all cause each other, but it is also possible that one or more of them could be influencing people's attitudes to the EU without the latter having a reciprocal effect. We investigate this further below.

Table 4.4 contains the estimates of the VEC model for the six variables in the system with change in net approval of EU membership as the dependent variable. Short-run adjustments to shocks appear in the top section of the table and the long-run equilibrium relationships appear in the bottom section. The adjustment coefficient (α) for the cointegrating vector shows how rapidly a deviation from equilibrium caused by a shock to the system is eroded. This coefficient equals –.22, which means that if, for example, there is a shock to the economy, the system will revert back to its long-run trajectory in about five months.[9] The implication is that people's attitudes towards EU membership display only a modest degree of inertia over time. This is consistent with the considerable volatility in EU attitudes observed in Figure 4.1 above.

The short-term coefficients show how each variable reacts when a shock to the system perturbs the long-run equilibrium relationship between EU attitudes and the other variables of interest. For example, if perceptions that the Conservatives are the best party for managing the economy relative to Labour increase by 1 per cent as a consequence of an economic shock, this will reduce net approval of UK membership by –.35 per cent in the short run. In other words, growing perceptions of Conservative economic competence produce a short-term boost in Euroscepticism. All of the short-term variables have statistically significant effects except for partisanship, but this is significant in the cointegrating section

Table 4.4 *VEC Model of Net Approval of EU Membership, April 2004–April 2016*

Predictors	Net Approval of EU Membership
Short-Term Effects	
Best Prime Minister (Δ_{t-1})	.18*
Net Partisanship (Δ_{t-1})	.06
Best Party on the Economy (Δ_{t-1})	−.35***
Net Attitudes to Immigration (Δ_{t-1})	−.21***
EU Controls the Economy (Δ_{t-1})	.25***
Error Correction Adjustment Coefficient	−.22***
Long-Term Cointegrating Effects	
Net Approval of UK Membership of the EU	1.00
Best Prime Minister	1.16***
Net Partisanship	1.79***
Best Party on the Economy	−2.13***
Net Attitudes to Immigration	−.70***
EU Controls the Economy	.29***
Constant	−32.03***
R^2	.22
Test for Residual Autocorrelation	47.4

Note: * = p ≤ .05; ** = p ≤ .01; *** = p ≤ .001, one-tailed test.

of the model (see the bottom section of Table 4.4), so it plays an important long-term role.

The long-term coefficients in Table 4.4 show that, in equilibrium, perceptions of which leader would make the best prime minister have an impact that is 16 per cent larger (1.16) than net approval of EU membership. Partisanship has a bigger impact (1.79) and perceptions of which party is best at managing the economy has the largest impact of all (−2.13).[10]

What are the causal relationships among attitudes towards EU attitudes and the other variables of interest? Cointegration among a set of variables implies that Granger causality exists in the system.[11] In this regard, tests show that all five predictor variables Granger-cause approval of EU membership (see Table 4.5). Economic evaluations,

Table 4.5 *Granger Causality Tests: Net Approval of EU Membership and Valence Politics Variables*

Dependent Variable	Excluded Lagged Predictors	X² Test Statistic Excluding Predictors	Probability Level for Test
Net Approval of EU Membership	Best Party on the Economy	5.70**	.05
Net Approval of EU Membership	Best Leader as Prime Minister	5.29*	.07
Net Approval of EU Membership	Net Party Identification	6.54**	.04
Net Approval of EU Membership	Net Attitudes to Immigration	5.00*	.08
Net Approval of EU Membership	EU Controls the Economy	8.46***	.01
Best Party on the Economy	Net Approval of EU Membership	1.00	.61
Best Leader as Prime Minister	Net Approval of EU Membership	1.56	.46
Net Party Identification	Net Approval of EU Membership	1.11	.57
Net Attitudes to Immigration	Net Approval of EU Membership	2.59	.27
EU Controls the Economy	Net Approval of EU Membership	4.03	.13

Note: $* = p \leq .10$; $** = p \leq .05$; $*** = p \leq .01$.

partisanship and perceptions of EU control of the economy have the strongest effects, while immigration and leadership evaluations have slightly weaker effects. These tests are presented in the top five rows of the table and the remaining rows contain tests for reciprocal causation in the system. The latter show that there is no evidence that approval ratings of EU membership Granger-cause any of the other variables in the VEC model. We started by assuming that all of them interact with each other, but this statistical evidence suggests that the valence measures influence attitudes to the EU rather than vice versa.

This finding is consistent with the argument that valence politics considerations do much to drive people's attitudes towards EU membership, and it fits well with the argument that attitudes to European integration are influenced by 'calculations, communities and cues'. Cost–benefit calculations are linked to policy performance, identities are invoked from the alleged threat posed by mass immigration and a perceived loss of sovereignty to Brussels, and cues from voters' images of their political leaders and parties also have important effects. All of these are part of the mix of factors affecting people's attitudes towards the EU.

The earlier discussion indicated that the specification of the cointegrating system had to be sparse because of the demands it makes on the data. As a result, the time series model does not take into account other factors that might influence attitudes towards the EU. These include the influence of people's attachments to minor parties, images of the leaders of these parties and the effects of having different parties in government. Studying the influence of these factors is important, given that the Liberal Democrats and Scottish Nationalists were the most Europhile parties during the referendum and UKIP was the most Eurosceptic. In addition, it will be useful to consider whether people's individual characteristics, such as age and gender, might help to explain their reactions to EU membership. In the next section we develop a model that examines the effects of these variables at the individual level, while simultaneously taking into account the aggregate-level contextual conditions that vary over time.

Explaining Individual-Level Attitudes towards EU Membership

This section discusses multilevel models of attitudes to EU membership that utilize a richer specification than the time series model above. The approach taken is to examine the influence of different parties and leaders and other issues, alongside the variables that we have already examined.[12] We replace the net leader image variable we used in the time series models with 11-point affect scales ranging from 'strongly dislike' = 0 to 'strongly like' = 10 to measure attitudes towards the Labour, Conservative and Liberal Democrat leaders. These scales provide convenient summary measures of how people feel about various leaders and they correlate strongly with judgements voters make about leader traits such as competence, honesty, responsiveness and trustworthiness (Clarke et al. 2009a).

Measures of partisanship are specified for the Conservatives, Labour, the Liberal Democrats and UKIP. As discussed above, these variables summarize cumulative evaluations of the performance of various parties over time and are relevant for explaining voters' attitudes towards EU membership. In addition, there are two issue indicators that focus specifically on the EU. The first is a dummy variable that is scored 1 for individuals who think that the EU is the most important issue facing the country and 0 for everyone else. This variable enables us to study how the salience of the EU issue affects attitudes towards membership. The second variable was used in the time series analyses and it taps perceptions that the EU controls the British economy. This is the indicator of the perceived loss of sovereignty discussed earlier. A third dummy variable that relates to economic policy-making is scored 1 if someone believes that no party effectively controls the British economy and 0 otherwise.

The key valence issue in the time series modelling was the economy, and here its effects are captured by three variables. The first taps retrospective evaluations of the state of the economy over the past year. The second is retrospective evaluations of personal finances, again over a one-year time horizon. Numerous studies have shown that these judgements about national and personal economic conditions influence voting in general elections (see, e.g. Clarke et al. 2009a; Lewis-Beck et al. 2013) and the expectation is that they should have significant effects on attitudes towards EU membership. The third variable measures affective reactions to economic conditions. This variable is based on a question that asks survey respondents to choose words such as 'afraid', 'confident', 'happy' and 'uneasy' to describe their feelings about the state of the economy. Such affective reactions have been shown to exert significant effects on political attitudes and voting behaviour independently of calculations of costs and benefits (e.g. Marcus et al. 2000; Neuman et al. 2007).

Two other explanatory variables involve reactions to immigration and perceptions of the performance of the NHS. The first of these captures public evaluations of the competence of governments in managing immigration, but it also touches on the 'fear of others' dimension of identity discussed earlier. The second variable measures evaluations of the delivery of a very important public service. Immigration and the performance of the NHS are highly salient issues and they played prominent roles in the 2015 general election (Clarke et al. 2016a).

Finally, the model includes measures of occupational status, education, age, gender and the country of residence (England, Scotland, Wales). As well as acting as statistical controls, these variables permit us to investigate the impact of socio-demographic characteristics on attitudes towards EU membership. This is an interesting question given the findings discussed elsewhere in this book that high-status and well-educated people tend to support remaining in the EU, whereas low-status and poorly educated individuals are more likely to support leaving the organization.

The multilevel modelling approach we use enables us to examine the impact of aggregate-level variables measured over time on individual-level attitudes to the European Union (Hox 2002; Raudenbush and Bryk 2002). In particular, it allows us to study the contextual effects of objective economic conditions such as unemployment and inflation rates alongside the individual-level subjective economic variables described above.[13]

In addition to the aggregate economic variables, two election-related variables are included in the model to assess the impact of the European parliamentary and general elections that occurred over this period. Elections are likely to increase the salience of the EU as an issue during the campaigns and this has the capacity to influence support for UK membership. These election variables are scored 1 at the time of the elections and 0 otherwise. A third dummy variable covers the period of the Coalition Government from May 2010 up to May 2015 and this is designed to discover whether attitudes towards EU membership were influenced by the change of government that occurred after the 2010 general election. Coefficients for the individual-level model estimated without the aggregate variables appear in the second column of Table 4.6. These coefficients indicate that someone who thinks that Europe is the most important issue facing the country is much less likely to approve of UK membership than people in general.[14] Moreover, individuals who identify with the Conservatives are less likely to approve of EU membership than those who identify with either Labour or the Liberal Democrats. And, as expected, identifying with UKIP has a very strong negative impact on EU approval. Images of party leaders are relevant as well. People who rate the Conservative party leader highly are more likely to be Eurosceptic, whereas those who rate the Labour and Liberal Democrat leaders highly are likely to be Europhiles. The effects associated with the Labour and Liberal

Table 4.6 *Multilevel Ordinal Logit Model of Attitudes towards EU Membership*

	Individual-Level Model	Multilevel Model
Aggregate-Level Predictors		
Change in Retail Price Index	–	–.02***
Unemployment Rate	–	–.04***
Coalition Government Dummy Variable	–	–.06**
European Elections Dummy Variable	–	–.02
General Elections Dummy Variable	–	–.38***
Individual-Level Predictors		
Europe the Most Important Issue	–1.03***	–1.03***
Conservative Partisanship	–.05**	–.05**
Labour Partisanship	.27***	.27***
Liberal Democrat Partisanship	.55***	.56***
UKIP Partisanship	–1.58***	–1.58***
Conservative Leader Evaluations	–.06***	–.06***
Labour Leader Evaluations	.10***	.10***
Liberal Democrat Leader Evaluations	.10***	.10***
Retrospective Personal Financial Performance	.11***	.11***
Retrospective National Economic Performance	.04***	.04***
Affective Economic Evaluations	.06***	.06***
Evaluations of Immigration in Britain	.49***	.49***
Evaluations of the National Health Service	.14***	14***
Perceptions that the EU Controls the UK Economy	–.98***	–.98***
Perceptions that No One Controls the UK Economy	–.10***	–.09***
Socio-Demographics		
Occupational Status	.34***	.34***
Age	–.01***	–.01***
Male	.25***	.25***
University Graduate	.53***	.53***
Lives in Wales	.06**	.06**
Lives in Scotland	.19***	.19***
Aggregate Pseudo R^2	–	.33

Note: * = p ≤ .05; ** = p ≤ .01; *** = p ≤ .001, one-tailed test.

Democrat leaders are approximately the same strength, while the negative effect of images of the Conservative leader is slightly weaker.

The results also show that economic evaluations have significant positive effects on support for EU membership. Those who are optimistic about economic conditions are more supportive of EU membership than those who are pessimistic. In this regard it appears that people's evaluations of their personal financial circumstances are more important than judgements about the national economy.[15] In addition, emotional responses to economic conditions exert significant effects, with people reporting positive feelings about the economy being more supportive of the EU than those reporting negative ones. Overall, these findings support the idea that cognitive and emotional reactions to economic conditions both influence attitudes towards EU membership.

Additionally, we see that evaluations of immigration and the state of the NHS affect how people feel about EU membership. Once again, positive evaluations stimulate approval of UK membership, whereas pessimistic evaluations have the opposite effect. Immigration is especially potent and has a much stronger effect than judgements about the NHS. The analysis suggests that judgements about immigration exert stronger effects than do reactions to economic conditions, a finding that is important given the eventual outcome of the 2016 referendum and the factors that motivated the vote for a Brexit (see Chapter 7). Perceptions that the EU controls what happens to the British economy also have a strong influence on attitudes towards EU membership – those who think that Britain has lost control are more likely to be Eurosceptics. This is true as well for those who think that neither Britain nor the EU controls the economy.

In terms of people's individual characteristics, we find that high-status, well-educated individuals are indeed more likely to approve of EU membership than low-status, poorly educated people. Also, men are more supportive than women, and young people are more supportive than the middle-aged or elderly. Finally, respondents living in Wales and Scotland are more likely to favour membership than those living in England, with the difference being particularly marked for Scottish residents.

Turning to the multilevel model in the third column of Table 4.6, we see that the coefficients in the individual-level part of this model are not affected by the inclusion of aggregate-level predictors. The results reinforce the conclusion regarding reactions to economic conditions, since, controlling for everything else, increases in inflation and unemployment reduce support for EU membership. In addition, each of the three general elections that took place during this period had the effect of temporarily reducing support for UK membership, although elections to the European Parliament were not influential. Finally, the coefficient for the Coalition Government dummy variable indicates that anti-EU sentiments among the electorate grew after the Conservative–Liberal Democrat Government was formed in the wake of the 2010 general election.

Conclusion: Valence Politics and EU Membership

This chapter has documented that there are powerful relationships between British public attitudes towards EU membership and key factors that lie at the heart of the 'valence theory' of electoral choice. People's assessments about how established politicians performed on the key valence issues, their images of party leaders and psychological attachments to parties have all influenced how they think about their country's EU membership. Importantly, we have shown how these effects were operating for more than a decade before the 2016 referendum. Why does this matter? Our findings strongly suggest that while the actual referendum campaign during the first half of 2016 may well have changed some people's minds, the fundamentals of public opinion had been in place a long time ago.

Crucially, the all-important valence issues of the economy and immigration exerted powerful effects on public support for EU membership. Also, and as past studies suggested, people's judgements about how their domestic government had performed on key issues were particularly important, as were a perceived loss of economic control to Brussels and entrenched fears about immigration and its effects.

In later chapters we develop these points by examining the rise of anti-EU sentiment in elections that led up to the 2016 referendum (Chapter 6) and then investigate the referendum vote itself (Chapter 7). But another key for understanding the referendum outcome concerns the role of UKIP, the only party in England that called unequivocally for a Brexit. This is the focus of the next chapter.

5 | *The People's Army*

Let's take back control of our country. Let's control our borders and have a proper immigration policy. Let's stop giving away £55 million a day to a club that we don't need to be a part of. Let's re-embrace the big world, the twenty-first century global world. Let's strike trade deals with India, New Zealand, all of those emerging parts of the world. Let's free ourselves up and in doing so give an example to the rest of Europe. I know the people are behind this. I would urge people, come and join the People's Army. Let's topple the establishment who've led us to this mess.

Nigel Farage, in debate with Nick Clegg, April 2014

Nigel Farage and UKIP play a central role in the story of how Britain came to leave the EU. The party's rise has been one of the most striking developments in modern British politics. Particularly after 2010, UKIP and Farage captivated the national political debate and raised difficult questions not only for the established parties but also for those who, in the 2016 referendum, campaigned to keep Britain in the EU. There are two particularly important questions. The first, which we examine in this chapter, focuses on the issue of who responded to Farage's call to join his self-proclaimed 'People's Army'. What are the backgrounds, political histories and beliefs of the ordinary men and women who pushed this Eurosceptic party forward? The second question, which we examine in Chapter 6, is what were the electoral effects of UKIP's revolt on the right in the run up to the 2016 vote?

UKIP has attracted widespread attention, but a number of fundamental questions remain unanswered. As well as examining the backgrounds and attitudes of the party's members and activists, it is important to know how politically engaged they are and, above all, how they compare to the rest of population. Answering these questions will assist in understanding UKIP and how and why Britain voted for Brexit. In this chapter we draw on unprecedented amounts of survey data to put individual UKIP members under the microscope – to describe the ordinary men and women who decided to join the party and campaign at the grassroots for Brexit.

The Rise of UKIP: 1993–2016

Since its formation in 1993, UKIP has been guided by the goal of withdrawing Britain from the European Union. During its early years the party struggled to attract support and at the 1997 general election was overshadowed by the Referendum Party, a new and much better-resourced movement that had been formed by the billionaire Sir Jimmy Goldsmith to push for a referendum on EU membership. It was not until after the Goldsmith's death and the collapse of his party that UKIP began to occupy a more prominent role in British politics.

UKIP's rise began under Tony Blair's first New Labour Government and while William Hague was the leader of the Conservative Party. In 1999, this small Eurosceptic party won its first three seats in the European Parliament, including one for a young activist named Nigel Farage. While the new party struggled to make an impression in domestic general elections under the first-past-the-post electoral system, winning just 1.5 per cent of the vote in 2001, UKIP continued to poll strongly in the European Parliament contests that use proportional representation to allocate seats. In the 2004 European Parliament elections, UKIP forced its way into the headlines after securing 16.1 per cent of the vote and 12 seats. Then, in 2009, amid a Westminster parliamentary expenses scandal that caused an uproar in the media and tarnished the reputations of all three of Britain's mainstream parties, UKIP finished second with 16.6 per cent of the vote and 13 seats. The party was on its way.

It was not until after the 2010 general election, which produced a Coalition Government between David Cameron's Conservative Party and Nick Clegg's Liberal Democrats, that UKIP experienced a far more significant increase in support. Although Farage and his activists won only 3.1 per cent of the vote in the 2010 general election, over the next three years they replaced the Liberal Democrats as the third most popular party in the national opinion polls. UKIP's increasing popularity was reflected in its performance in local elections. In 2009, the party had contested only 25 per cent of the vacancies that were up for election, attracting just 4.6 per cent of the vote and securing eight local government seats (see Figure 5.1). But, by 2013 the party was

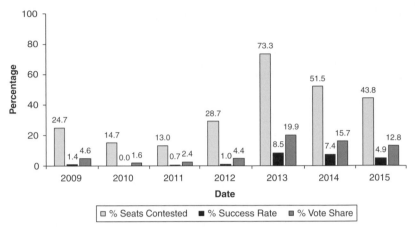

Figure 5.1 UKIP's Local Election Performance, 2009–2015.
Source: Rallings and Thrasher 2009–15.

emerging as a more serious force. In that year local elections were held across England's southern shires, which tended to be dominated by the Conservative Party – places like Buckinghamshire, Dorset, Hampshire, Somerset and Surrey. UKIP contested 73 per cent of the available vacancies, attracted almost 20 per cent of the vote and elected 147 councillors. 'We are not going away', said Farage in the aftermath. 'We are a political party that says we have been failed by the establishment, they've given away our country, they've led us to near bankruptcy and we want a different kind of politics.'[1]

By this time UKIP was consolidating its presence by devoting more energy to contesting parliamentary by-elections. Between 2011 and 2014 the party finished second in six of these contests, five of which had been held in seats controlled by Labour. In areas like Barnsley, Middlesbrough, Rotherham and South Shields, UKIP was demonstrating its ability to connect with more industrial, working-class and economically 'left-behind' sections of the country. The party's change of fortunes coincided with a change of strategy. Since his election as party leader for the second time in 2010, Farage had modified UKIP's message, fusing its traditional call for a Brexit with strident opposition to mass immigration and the free movement of EU nationals. This dual strategy of communicating both anti-EU and anti-immigration messages was accompanied by populist attacks against the established parties. Speaking to his followers ahead of the 2014 European

Parliament elections, Farage had underscored his party's new emphasis on immigration: 'It's the biggest single issue facing this country. It
affects the economy, the NHS, schools, public services, the deficit. But
the establishment has been closing down the immigration debate for
20 years. UKIP has opened it up.'[2] Immigration would remain at forefront of the party's offer to voters.

By the time of the 2014 European Parliament elections the geography of UKIP's support was also beginning to crystallize. The party
had notable strongholds throughout the eastern half of England, from
Lincolnshire down to Cambridgeshire, Norfolk, Essex, Kent, Suffolk,
Sussex and Hampshire. In 2014, against the backdrop of a strident
national debate about the numbers of EU workers from such Central
and Eastern European states as Bulgaria and Romania, UKIP finished
first at the European Parliament elections. Farage had benefited from
a wave of publicity that followed two high-profile debates with the
leader of the Liberal Democrats, Nick Clegg, but he had also doubled
down on his controversial strategy of targeting immigration. UKIP
had put up a series of billboards that focused on the negative effects
of a flood of workers from other EU member states and delivered
a simple message: 'Take Back Control'. As Farage explained in one
interview: 'The goal was to get into people's heads that immigration
and Europe are the same thing and that we are impotent.'[3]

The message resonated with the public. UKIP received over 27 per
cent of the vote and 24 seats in the European Parliament. The result
was especially embarrassing for Labour, the main opposition party,
and its leader Ed Miliband, who were pushed into second place. This
was the first time since 1984 that the main opposition party had failed
to finish first at a European Parliament election. There were other
warning signs for Labour as well. Its share of the vote was 20 points
lower than what it had polled in 1994, the last time that the centre-left
had fought a European Parliament election in opposition.

UKIP's transition from the margins to the mainstream was underscored by a decision taken by the regulatory Ofcom authority to
award it 'major party status'. Shortly afterwards, UKIP remained in
the headlines after attracting two defecting Conservative Members
of Parliament – Douglas Carswell, MP for Clacton in Essex, and
Mark Reckless, MP for Rochester and Strood in Kent. Their defections triggered parliamentary by-elections that UKIP subsequently
won, bringing the party its first seats in the House of Commons since

the party's formation.[4] UKIP almost gained a thir seat at a parliamentary by-election in Labour's northern constituency of Heywood
and Middleton that had been called following the sudden death of
the local MP. By finishing within 700 votes of Labour, UKIP demonstrated once more that all was not well in the Labour camp.

At the 2015 general election UKIP was confronted with the for-
midable obstacle of the single-member plurality electoral system.
Although Farage announced that his party would run a very targeted
campaign, focusing its resources on no more than 30 constituencies,
a major breakthrough remained elusive. UKIP emerged with just one
seat, the constituency of Clacton, where Douglas Carswell was re-
elected, albeit with a reduced majority. The party lost its only other
seat, Rochester and Strood, which returned to the Conservatives, and it
failed to capture any new seats. Although UKIP finished second in 120
constituencies, 44 of which were held by Labour, they had once again
been taught a harsh lesson about the barrier to entry for insurgent
parties that is imposed by the first-past-the-post system (see Goodwin
and Milazzo 2015). Farage had encountered the barrier at first hand.
In the Conservative constituency of South Thanet in Kent he failed to
win election to the House of Commons and finished second with 32
per cent of the vote, six points behind the Conservative candidate, who
was himself a former high-ranking UKIP official. It was the seventh
time that Farage had failed to win election to Westminster.

The result of the 2015 general election – a majority Conservative
Government – surprised many observers. Prior to the contest there
had been a broad consensus among academic forecasters, media pundits and pollsters that a hung parliament was in the offing (Clarke
et al. 2016a: ch. 4). Aside from handing the Conservative Party its first
majority government for 23 years, the election outcome had made a
referendum on Britain's continued membership in the EU a priority
item on the political agenda.

Meanwhile, UKIP was embroiled in infighting. On the day after the
2015 election, Friday 8 May, Farage resigned as leader, claiming that
he was fulfilling a pledge that he had made during the campaign to
stand down should he fail to win a seat at Westminster. But, by the
end of the weekend, he had seemingly changed his mind. On the following Monday, he announced that his resignation had been rejected
by UKIP's ruling committee and that he would resume as leader. In
the aftermath UKIP was almost torn apart by internecine conflicts

among its leading activists, some of whom wanted Farage to leave and disagreed with how the entire episode had been managed. One senior activist, UKIP's former Director of Communications Patrick O'Flynn, who had been recruited by Farage, publicly criticized Farage's leadership style, describing him as 'snarling, thin-skinned and aggressive' and suggesting that the events left UKIP looking 'like an absolutist monarchy or a personality cult'.[5]

While the infighting would continue and never truly be resolved, with the EU referendum on the horizon, Farage was back in control and bracing his 'People's Army' for the political battle of their lives. By the end of 2015 he was leading a party that had forced its way into the mainstream and, according to opinion polls, become the third most popular party in the country. But who, exactly, responded to Farage's call to join this 'People's Army', a grassroots revolt that was about to play a significant role in the campaign to leave the EU?

UKIP Members: Who Are They?

We can answer this question by reporting the findings of a large survey of grassroots UKIP members we undertook between November 2014 and January 2015, when UKIP was at its peak. The survey of 29,500 UKIP members was made possible by the prior approval of the party's national executive. Respondents were drawn from UKIP's membership list that was made available to the authors. The survey was conducted using an online survey platform[6] and was supplemented with a mail survey sent to 3,000 members chosen at random from the list of members who did not supply valid email addresses. More than 14,000 members responded to the online survey, representing a healthy response rate of 48 per cent, while 1,000 answered the offline mail survey, a slightly lower response rate of 33 per cent. Members were asked a wide range of questions about their backgrounds, beliefs, attitudes and behaviours. Taken together, these data provide unprecedented insight into the men and women who joined and campaigned for the populist right in British politics.

Who joined UKIP? Figure 5.2 shows that the typical UKIP recruit is white (99 per cent), male (83 per cent) and over 55 years of age (72 per cent). Almost one in two are retired, underscoring how UKIP quickly became a political home for an older generation of Britons, many of whom had first voted during the early 1970s or before. Many were old

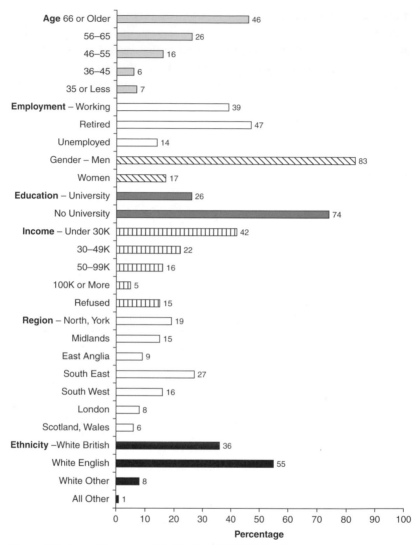

Figure 5.2 Socio-Demographic Profile of UKIP Members.
Source: UKIP Activists Survey.

enough to have voted in the country's first referendum on Europe, in 1975, to have witnessed the rise and dominance of Margaret Thatcher and the strident debates about immigration, race and Europe that took place during that era. Members also are more likely to identify themselves as English (55 per cent) rather than British (36 per cent), underscoring the importance of feelings of 'Englishness' for under-standing UKIP's attraction. Contrary to the popular portrayal of UKIP members as affluent Tories who live on wealthy country estates, most of them are not rich – 42 per cent said that their annual household income was less than £30,000, while fewer than one in four said that it was £50,000 or greater.

Where are they based? UKIP has enjoyed relatively strong support in eastern England and this is where we find a large cluster of mem-bers. Overall, 27 per cent of members were based in southeast England and a further 9 per cent in East Anglia. There are also notable clusters of members in the North and Yorkshire, the Southwest and Midlands. Fewer than 1 in 10 reside in London and only around 1 in 20 live in Scotland or Wales. These numbers provide further evidence that UKIP's revolt is primarily an English phenomenon.

What are their political backgrounds? We asked the members who they had voted for in the previous (2010) general election. While 51 per cent said they had voted for UKIP, 39 per cent had cast a Conservative ballot, revealing how disillusioned Conservatives were the main source of membership recruitment for the insurgent party. In sharp contrast, only 4 per cent had voted for the Liberal Democrats and 3 per cent had supported Labour.

Our survey allows us to paint a detailed picture of how members joined UKIP, when they joined and how their involvement with the party evolved over time. Interestingly, the vast majority of members said they had joined on their own initiative through UKIP's website; a total of 73 per cent joined in this way, whereas only 10 per cent joined after attending a UKIP event, 7 per cent had been introduced to the party by family or friends and 10 per cent had joined in some other way. These numbers reveal how most UKIP recruits were 'self-starters' who relied more on their own initiative than social networks that surround the party and its events. This is perhaps a reflection of the fact that UKIP is a young party that does not have a highly devel-oped infrastructure on the ground that can reach out and recruit new members via traditional inter-personal networks.

When did people decide to join UKIP? The party did not enjoy its main breakthrough until after the 2010 general election and only 10 per cent joined the party before 2005 and an additional 12 per cent joined between 2005 and 2010. Thus, fewer than one in four mem-bers had enrolled before 2010. Most members (58 per cent) did not

enrol until UKIP's 'take-off' period between the 2010 general election and the 2014 European elections, when support for the party
was growing quickly, Farage was frequently in the press and rumours
of Conservative defections were swirling around the nation's media.
A further 20 per cent said that they joined after the 2014 European
Parliament elections, meaning that fully 78 per cent of all members
had signed up since 2010.

This sheds light on a potential challenge for the party. Between 2010
and the 2016 referendum, the party experienced strong growth in electoral support, raising its visibility and pushing itself to the forefront of
British politics. During the same period UKIP attracted a large influx
of recruits who had no long-term loyalty to the party. This raises an
important question: how many of these people will stay with the party
if its wider support among the public falls away? Indeed, it is worth
noting that six months after the 2015 general election there were
reports that UKIP had lost around one quarter of its membership, as
well as influential donors who had been disappointed by its failure to
take its revolt into the heart of Westminster.[7]

How do new members who joined in 2013 or later compare to
older members who had joined UKIP before 2013, when the party
experienced its first notable breakthrough in the local elections? In
most respects, the two groups have very similar demographic profiles. Over four in five are men and only one in four have attended
university. Also, most members in both groups tend to have modest
incomes – two-fifths have annual incomes of £30,000 or less and only
1 in 20 are earning more than £100,000. They also tend to reside in
the same areas; despite UKIP's growing strength in the Midlands and
the North from 2013 onwards, approximately a third of both groups
reside in one of those regions, and over half live in East Anglia, the
Southeast or Southwest. Fewer than 1 in 10 in either group live in
the London area. Age and employment status differentiate the groups
most strongly. Both groups have large numbers of older individuals,
but newer entrants tend to be younger, with 35 per cent of those joining in 2013 or later reporting that they are over 65 as compared to 54
per cent of those who joined earlier. In keeping with these age differences, 40 per cent of the newer entrants and 54 per cent of the earlier
joiners are retirees.

The survey data point to another problem for UKIP. While the party
has recruited a large cadre of older members, it also has attracted a

lot of people who are not very active. Members were asked a series of questions about their levels of activism – such as how many meetings they attend, how many hours they devote to party activity, what kinds of activities they undertake and generally how active they would consider themselves to be. Given that our survey was conducted when UKIP was enjoying regular breakthroughs, one might expect to find a membership that is highly energized and committed to working for the party at the grassroots. Yet this is not the case. UKIP's advance in British politics appears all the more remarkable considering the rather low rates of activity among many of its members.

When asked how many meetings they had attended during the past year, only one fifth had attended five meetings or more, while slightly more than half had not attended a single one (see Figure 5.3). A similar picture emerges when we consider other measures of activity. When asked how many hours they spend working for the party when there is no election going on, over three-fifth of the members said 'none' and only 1 in 20 said nine hours or more (see Figure 5.4). During election campaigns, this distribution is largely unchanged, with 59 per cent saying they do no party work at all and 12 per cent saying they work 9 hours or more. Similarly, when asked to describe their level of activism, a large majority said they were either 'not at all active' or 'not very active'. A comparison of levels of activism by the year that members joined underlines the problem the party faces. While those members who had joined UKIP in earlier years, typically before 2004, were more likely to say that they were 'very active', more recent recruits who enrolled during the 'take-off' period were notably less likely to report high levels of activity. This suggests that the party was failing to motivate its membership to be active on its behalf.

Figure 5.4 reports the kinds of activities that UKIP-ers reported doing 'occasionally' or 'frequently'. The most popular are 'support' activities that require relatively little time to accomplish – fully 73 per cent said they had donated money to the party, 60 per cent say they had signed a petition in support of it and 47 per cent had displayed a poster. In contrast, 'engagement' activities that are more time-consuming are less popular, with 43 per cent attending party meetings, 37 per cent delivering leaflets and 31 per cent canvassing. Not surprisingly, 'office-seeking' activities that consume large amounts of time and effort are the preserve of small minorities. As Figure 5.5 shows, 13 per cent report that they had stood as a UKIP candidate at a local

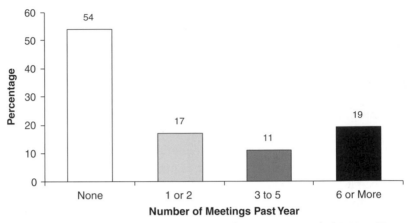

Figure 5.3 Number of Meetings UKIP Members Have Attended in Past Year.
Source: UKIP Activists Survey.

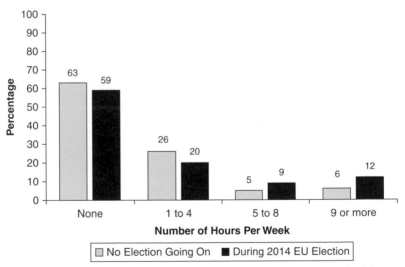

Figure 5.4 Number of Hours Per Week UKIP Members Have Worked for Party during Past Year.
Source: UKIP Activists Survey.

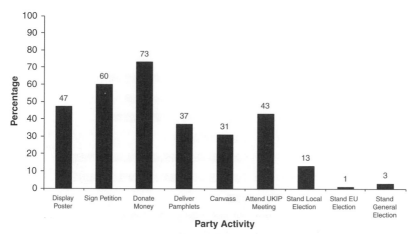

Figure 5.5 Percentages of UKIP Members Doing Various Party Activities 'Occasionally' or 'Frequently' and Percentages Who Have Run for Public Office.
Source: UKIP Activists Survey.

election, and only 3 per cent and 1 per cent, respectively, had run as a candidate in a general or European Parliament election. Overall, UKIP-ers appear similar to members of other parties in Britain and elsewhere.[8] Many support the party financially or in other ways, but high levels of personal engagement are the exception, not the rule. Candidacy for public office is rare.

Why Join the 'People's Army'?

Our surveys allow us to explore why UKIP members decided to become involved in politics. Their answers indicate that many got involved in response to what researchers call 'purposive' incentives (e.g. Kornberg et al. 1979; Seyd and Whiteley 1992). As Figure 5.6 shows, fully 81 per cent said that they decided to become politically active because they believed that UKIP can change Britain, 61 per cent thought that members could help to make the party more successful, 57 per cent agreed that citizens can make democracy work and 54 per cent said that people who are dissatisfied have a duty to become politically active. The idea that many UKIP-ers believed that they had an obligation to get involved is also reflected in the finding that more than three-quarters of them said that they would be seriously neglecting their civic duty if

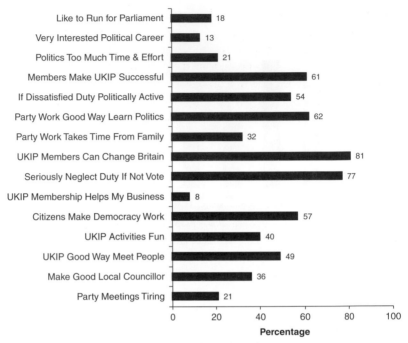

Figure 5.6 UKIP Members' Motives for Political Activity.
Source: UKIP Activists Survey.

they failed to vote, with over three-fifths saying that party work was a good way to learn about politics.

Other motives are evident as well, such as using the party as a vehicle for social networking. Nearly half of those surveyed indicated that joining UKIP was a good way to meet people and two-fifths said that UKIP activities were fun. However, fewer than 1 in 10 thought that membership was useful for promoting their business and relatively few saw party activities as a way to become a professional politician. Although slightly over one third thought that they would make a good local councillor, fewer than one in five stated that they would like to run for Parliament and just over 1 in 10 claimed to be 'very interested' in having a political career. These numbers suggest that most UKIP members are more interested in contributing to the 'greater good' than in pursuing politics for individual gain or a career in Westminster.

Finally, although many UKIP-ers were not particularly active, most did not think that party activity was burdensome. Specifically, only one third said that party work takes time away from their family, one fifth reported that party meetings were tiring and one fifth thought that politics takes too much time and effort. The finding that relatively few members were concerned about the costs of party membership is sensible – after all, joining the party is purely voluntary and members can pick and choose how active they wish to be and what kinds of activities they prefer. If they find that membership is a burden, they can simply exit.

What Do They Think?

Since its inception, UKIP has been portrayed as a home for people who hold extremist views, a right-wing populist party that is out of step with mainstream opinion. Is this stereotype true? To answer this question, we asked UKIP members a series of questions identical to those that appear in our monthly Essex Continuous Monitoring Surveys (ECMS). This enables us to see just how far, if at all, UKIP members deviate from the electorate as a whole. We start by examining where the members locate themselves on the 'left–right' ideological scale and then explore their attitudes towards issues like immigration and Europe, comparing UKIP members with a representative sample of the British electorate.

Figure 5.7 displays the distributions of UKIP members and the electorate as a whole on a summary 11-point ideological scale where 0 means 'left' and 10 means 'right'. Consistent with the party's small 'c' conservative reputation, the vast majority of UKIP-ers place themselves to the right of centre (5) on the ideology scale, with fully 84 per cent giving themselves scores of 6 or greater. Only 4 per cent, or fewer than 1 in 20, place themselves on the left side of the scale with scores of 0 to 4. In sharp contrast, the general public is more evenly balanced, with 40 per cent on the left of centre and 39 on the right of centre. UKIP members' greater ideological conservatism is underscored by the fact that their mean score is fully 7.2 as compared to 4.9 for the public.

Again, it does not surprise that UKIP members are more negatively disposed towards immigration and the EU than is the average person. As Figure 5.8 illustrates, there is virtual unanimity among UKIP members that immigration should be decreased (99 per cent) and that the Government has handled it badly (98 per cent). And fully 75 per cent think the problem is getting worse. However, it bears emphasizing

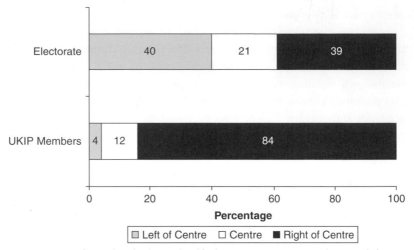

Figure 5.7 Left–Right Ideological Self-Placement, UKIP Members and the British Electorate.
Source: UKIP Activists Survey and ECMS Election Survey, 2015.

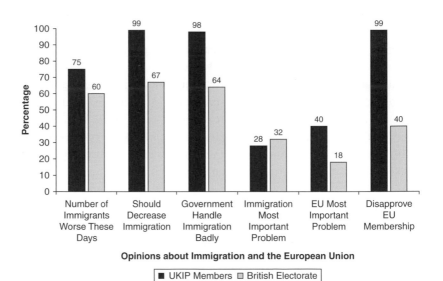

Figure 5.8 Opinions about Immigration and the EU, UKIP Members and the British Electorate.
Source: UKIP Activists Survey and ECMS Survey, January 2015.

that many people in the country as a whole are quite negative towards immigration, with 67 per cent believing that immigration should be reduced and 64 per cent judging that the Government has handled the problem badly. Moreover, three in five in the electorate think immigration is getting worse. Twenty-eight per cent of UKIP members and 32 per cent of people designated immigration as the most important issue facing the country.

Regarding their attitudes towards EU membership, not surprisingly UKIP members are almost unanimous (99 per cent) in favour of leaving the EU as compared to 40 per cent of the population (interviewed in January 2015). Similarly, two-fifths of the former group but slightly less than one fifth of the latter rank the 'European Union' or 'Europe' as the most important problem facing the country. Overall, it is evident that large majorities of UKIP members and ordinary people are exercised about immigration but, when our surveys were carried out, far fewer in the general public were preoccupied with the issue of EU membership.

UKIP has been widely characterized as a political home for people who distrust and dislike governing elites and the 'establishment' that dominates Britain's economy, polity and society. The survey data displayed in Figure 5.9 confirm this portrayal, with large majorities (ranging from 62 per cent to 79 per cent) of UKIP members agreeing that excessive profits by banks, corporate greed, economic inequality and social injustice are major problems. It is striking that similarly large majorities in the electorate as a whole share these sentiments; 79 per cent believe that corporate greed is a major problem and 77 per cent judge that banks are making excessive profits. Solid majorities of people at large also think that economic inequality and social injustice are major problems. Overall, the average difference between UKIP-ers and the wider electorate in responses to these four questions is less than 4 per cent.

Majorities of both groups also feel dissatisfied with their treatment by Government and the way that democracy is functioning in Britain. In both cases, UKIP-ers are more likely to be dissatisfied – fully 81 per cent are unhappy with the way that British democracy is working as compared to a bare majority (53 per cent) of the electorate as a whole. Viewed generally, however, it is the similarities, not the differences, between UKIP-ers and people in general that stand out. Discontent with the operation of Britain's economic, social and political systems is

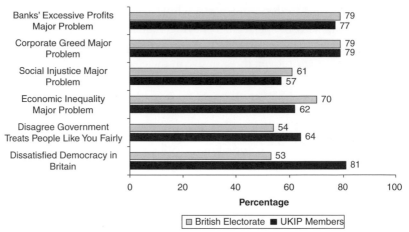

Figure 5.9 Populism: UKIP Members and the British Electorate.
Source: UKIP Activists Survey and ECMS Survey, January 2015.

widespread in both groups. A large majority of UKIP members express populist sentiments, but so too does much of the British electorate.

During the 2016 US presidential election campaign, Hillary Clinton, the Democratic Party's candidate, famously stated that one half of those people who were supporting her opponent, the Republican candidate Donald Trump, belonged in a 'basket of deplorables' who were 'racist, sexist, homophobic, xenophobic, Islamophobic – you name it' (*Time*, 10 September 2016). In Britain, UKIP has similarly been repeatedly criticized in the media for being a refuge for people who hold reprehensible views and was once described by David Cameron as being filled with 'fruitcakes, loonies and closet racists'. With this in mind, we asked UKIP members and people in general about their feelings towards different minority groups including Whites, Asians, Eastern Europeans, Blacks and Muslims. Survey respondents were asked to give these groups a rating on a scale from 0 ('strongly dislike') to 10 ('strongly like'). Figure 5.10 displays the average scores for UKIP members and the general public.

As Figure 5.10 illustrates, UKIP members and the public exhibit very similar feelings about various minorities. The average score for Asians among UKIP-ers on the 0–10 scale was 4.4 and among the public was 4.2. Again, UKIP members gave Eastern Europeans an average score of 4.0 and the public gave them an average of 3.8.

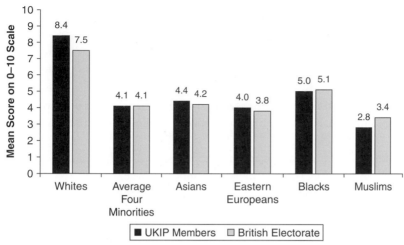

Figure 5.10 Attitudes towards Minority Groups, UKIP Members and the British Electorate.
Source: UKIP Activists Survey and ECMS Survey, January 2015.

For Blacks, the average scores given by UKIP-ers and the public were even closer at 5.0 and 5.1, respectively. Both groups liked Muslims the least, with UKIP members giving them a score of only 2.8, while the public gave them a score of 3.4. If we average scores for all four minority groups, UKIP-ers and the general public both accorded these groups identical scores of 4.1. In contrast, both UKIP members and the public at large felt much more positively about Whites; UKIP-ers gave this group an average score of 8.4 on the 0–10 scale and the general public gave them a slightly lower, but still very positive average of 7.5.

These data testify that UKIP members are much more favourably disposed towards the white majority than they are towards ethnic and racial minorities. Also, their feelings about minorities are not uniform across the board; they are especially negative towards Muslims. However, UKIP-ers' attitudes towards various minorities are not atypical – a sizeable segment of Britain's electorate holds very similar feelings, revealing how electoral potential for parties that adopt negative positions towards minorities is both entrenched and fairly widespread. This is an important point to remember when we turn to consider why, at the 2016 referendum, the Leave campaign's anti-immigration message resonated so strongly.

Why Do They Become Active?

We have already seen how UKIP members vary sharply in their levels of activity. But what accounts for these differences? To answer this question, we begin by using a statistical technique (exploratory factor analysis) to study how various activities cluster together. The results of this analysis show that there are three distinct dimensions of party activism, which we label 'organizational engagement', 'party support' and 'office-seeking'.

Engagement activities include things such as delivering pamphlets and canvassing, the number of hours per week a member works, the number of party meetings attended and reports of how active the member is in the local UKIP organization. Support activities are more passive, with an emphasis on donating money to the party and displaying UKIP posters. As observed earlier, office-seeking activities are quite rare, and they include running for local council offices, running as a UKIP candidate for the European Parliament or for a seat in the House of Commons. The analysis produces individual-level 'factor scores' which are overall summaries of these various kinds of activities.

Previous research has suggested a number of hypotheses for why some members are more active than others (see, e.g., Kornberg et al. 1979; Whiteley and Seyd 2002; Clarke et al. 2004, 2009a). Some explanations emphasize the material and intellectual resources that facilitate high rates of activity, such as having higher levels of education and higher incomes. Other explanations focus on people's psychological involvement with politics and their views of themselves as effective political actors. Individuals who are interested in politics and believe that they can 'make a difference' are more likely to be active than are those who lack interest and do not feel that they can make a difference.

Another perspective emphasizes the perceived benefits and costs of participation; individuals who believe that the success of their party will produce beneficial policy outcomes for society as a whole or for groups that they care about will be more likely to participate, as will those who think that the costs of participation are minimal. Still others participate because they perceive there are personal rewards to be gained or, in contrast, because they believe they have a civic duty to get involved regardless of possible payoffs.

Yet another perspective focuses on perceived grievances and argues that individuals who experience feelings of economic deprivation or think they have been 'left behind' or mistreated by political and economic elites are more likely to adopt extreme ideological positions and become politically active, particularly in right-wing populist movements. As we discuss in Chapter 6, this is a recurrent theme in studies of the rise of UKIP and populist right-wing parties in continental Europe.

To help specify a model of factors that might transform members into activists, we can begin by exploring their expressed motives for political activism, as shown Figure 5.6. An exploratory factor analysis indicates that the several motives can be subsumed by four factors: political change and civic duty, personal political ambition, social networking and costs of involvement.[9] The first of these motivational factors brings together the desire to effect political change with the sense that it is a citizen's duty to achieve it, while the second involves using party activity to satisfy personal career goals. The third factor summarizes motives that involve opportunities for making social and business contacts. The fourth factor – costs – focuses on the downside of party activity in terms of the time and effort that it requires.

We employ these four motivational factors as predictors in our models of the three party activity factors (organizational participation, party support and office-seeking). Following past research, we also include measures of political interest and a sense of political efficacy, as well as variables capturing negative attitudes towards immigration, disapproval of EU membership and placement on the left–right scale. Still other predictors focus on economic evaluations, populist sentiments (excessive profit-taking by banks, corporate greed, income inequality, feelings of social injustice), and general dissatisfaction with the performance of democracy in Britain. Four socio-demographic variables (age, education, gender and income) also are included. And, in keeping with the earlier discussion, we include a variable that identifies whether a UKIP member joined before the party's surge in popularity in 2013.[10]

The results are displayed in Table 5.1. It is immediately evident that a great many of the predictor variables have statistically significant effects on the three party activity factors. Specifically, there are 19 (of 20) significant predictors in the analysis of the organizational engagement factor, and 13 and 12 significant predictors, respectively, in the

Table 5.1 *Predictors of Extent of Involvement in UKIP*

Predictor	Organizational Engagement	Party Support	Office-Seeking
	ß	ß	ß
Political Change and Civic Duty	.101***	.167***	.013
Personal Ambition	.323***	.015†	.119***
Social Networking	.182***	.080***	−.003
Costs of Involvement	−.157***	−.009	.071***
Attention to Politics	.014**	.031***	.018***
Political Efficacy	.072***	.031***	.044***
Economic Evaluations	−.034***	−.053***	−.015
Left Behind Economically	−.024***	.003	−.020***
Left–Right Ideology	.098***	.008†	−.011***
Left–Right Ideology Squared	−.010***	–	–
Disapprove EU Membership	.061***	.141***	.025
Negative Attitudes Immigration	−.018†	.075***	−.006
Populist Attitudes	.055***	−.017	.033***
Dissatisfaction Democracy	.004	.003	.012†
Join UKIP before 2013	.304***	.563***	.096***
Age	−.067***	.033***	−.027***
University Education	.075***	−.119***	.043*
Gender	−.067***	.051*	.052*
Income	−.037***	.004	−.006
Constant	−1.524***	−2.169***	−.382***
R^2 =	.28	.16	.05
N = 12,059			

Note: * = $p \leq .05$; ** = $p \leq .01$; *** = $p \leq .001$; † = $p \leq .10$, one-tailed test.
– = variable not included in model.
Parameters are estimated using OLS regression analysis.

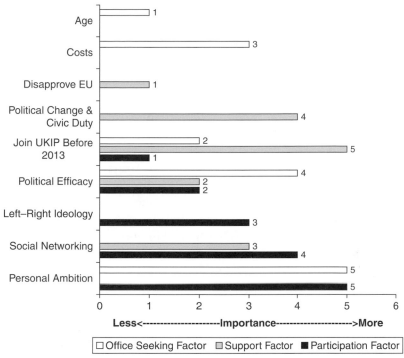

Figure 5.11 Five Most Important Predictors of Three Party Activity Factors (5 = Most Important, 1 = Least Important).

Note: strength of predictor variables measured using standardized regression coefficients from OLS regression analyses reported in Table 4.1.

analyses of the party support and office-seeking factors. These findings indicate that a great many factors influence how active UKIP members are in their party. Rather than discussing all of these effects in detail, we focus on the five predictor variables that have the largest impacts on each of the three activity factors.

Considering organizational engagement, Figure 5.11 shows that personal political ambition has the strongest effect. Although relatively few UKIP-ers say they are interested in party or public office, those who do tend to be *very* active. The second and third strongest predictors of organizational activity are social networking opportunities and position on a left–right ideological scale. UKIP's reputation for attracting persons holding extreme right-wing positions notwithstanding, those with somewhat more moderate views (by UKIP standards) tend to be most organizationally active. Other relatively powerful significant predictors of organizational participation include having a relatively strong sense of political efficacy and the time when a member joined the party. Consonant with the earlier discussion, people who joined UKIP before 2013 tend to be most active in the party organization.

Considering the party support factor, recall that this factor is dominated by activities such as donating money to UKIP, signing petitions and displaying signs. Figure 5.11 shows that the time of joining the party has the strongest effect and, again, those who joined before 2013 are the most active. Desire for political change and a perceived duty to bring it about and social networking are the second and third most powerful motivators. In fourth and fifth places are sense of political efficacy and disapproval of EU membership. As expected, those who feel efficacious and are highly negative about the EU are more likely to engage in party support activities.

Unsurprisingly, the third type of activity, office-seeking, is most strongly explained by personal political ambition and feelings of efficacy. Once more, members who joined UKIP before 2013 are more likely to be office-seekers. Other relatively strong predictors of office-seeking are feelings of being left behind economically, and being (relatively) younger. Finally, we note that people who recognize the costs of party activity are more likely to want to use UKIP to satisfy their goal to hold public office. Although this might seem counter-intuitive, it is consistent with the idea that people who might wish to use the party to advance their political careers but come to recognize that achieving this goal will entail significant costs, abandon the goal and, perhaps, UKIP. Those who remain acknowledge the costs and are willing to bear them.

At a broad level, then, the results present a mixed picture. UKIP's image as a strongly ideologically motivated party notwithstanding, it is incorrect to assume that UKIP-ers are driven to high levels of activity strictly by policy and ideological considerations. To be sure, sharply curtailing immigration and leaving the EU are key factors that have motivated public support for UKIP and are consensual goals among members. However, helping to achieve these goals is not the only thing that has driven higher rates of activism among UKIP's more committed followers. Political ambitions, a feeling that one can make a difference and social networking opportunities have helped to turn members into activists. And, all else aside, UKIP-ers who joined the party before 2013 – when it was still more movement and less party – are significantly more active than are those who joined more recently, suggesting that the party may have a difficult future unless it is able to encourage its more recent recruits to become more active.

Conclusion: A People's Army

Over the years, UKIP and its followers have often been portrayed in the press as a reprehensible group of right-wing extremists, whose views are highly unrepresentative of ordinary, 'decent' people. Indeed, by some accounts UKIP-ers are an unruly gang of racist, street-fighting yobs, keen to pour out of their local pub and give a good kicking to any hapless immigrant who has the misfortune to be walking by. Data presented in this chapter suggest that this characterization is very wide of the mark. True enough, UKIP members are overwhelming male, but they also are overwhelmingly quite elderly and many are pensioners. Many joined UKIP only recently. But within the party there is also a significant cadre of 'old hands', an earlier generation of activists who have stayed loyal to UKIP for a decade or more. Although many UKIP-ers content themselves with passive, but not unimportant activities such as donating some money to the cause, active minorities are engaged in various organizational activities during and between elections and, as in other more well-established parties, a small cadre aspires to use the party as a vehicle for advancing a career in politics.

Members of UKIP are united in their strong desire for Britain to leave the EU and the vast majority are very keen to reduce immigration into Britain from the EU and elsewhere. Yet while the 2016 referendum revealed how their desire to leave the EU is not shared by 48 per cent of the electorate, their hostility towards large-scale immigration is shared by a large number of people in the electorate as a whole. As we have seen in this chapter, UKIP members' relatively negative attitudes towards ethnic and racial minorities are closely mirrored in the wider public. Media rhetoric notwithstanding, our survey data clearly show that UKIP-ers' feelings towards various minorities are virtually identical to those expressed by a representative national sample of the general public. This suggests that regardless of the result of the 2016 referendum there is likely to remain a significant reservoir of potential support for movements like UKIP that seek to channel anxiety about immigration into electoral politics.

The similarities do not end there. In ideological terms UKIP members certainly place themselves further to the right than the average voter. But, when it comes to their populist views these two groups are also remarkably similar. Across much of the Western world, from Donald Trump to Marine Le Pen, populists are actively seeking to tap into feelings of anger among voters over unregulated markets, the behaviour of financial elites and increasingly massive disparities in income distribution. In the UK we have shown how these feelings are by no means unique to people who have already turned to the populist right. On the contrary, large majorities of UKIP members and the general public feel deeply concerned about rapacious banks, corporate greed, economic inequality and social injustice. Substantial numbers in both groups are worried that they have been 'left behind' by the rapid economic changes that have accompanied globalization. Also, many in both groups believe that Government is not treating them fairly and are dissatisfied with how democracy is working. These findings point strongly to the conclusion that irrespective of UKIP's future there is ample 'issue space' for populist politics in the contemporary United Kingdom.

Since 2010, Nigel Farage and UKIP have been in the vanguard of a populist uprising that has disrupted 'politics as usual'. The analyses presented above reveal how discontent with political and economic elites is by no means confined to a small minority. On the contrary, many of the views about the direction of the country and the performance of British democracy expressed by UKIP members are shared widely in the electorate as a whole. UKIP members may look more like a 'Dad's Army' than a 'People's Army', but their willingness to actively support a party that champions the concerns of many voters has helped to make their party a disruptive and unexpectedly potent political force. In the next chapter, we investigate factors responsible for UKIP's electoral success, particularly after 2010, with the aim of explaining the build-up to the referendum vote of 2016.

6 | *The Rise of UKIP*

The rise of UKIP helped to pave the way for the historic Brexit vote. Through two national elections – the 2014 European Parliament elections and the general election in 2015 – the populist right imposed itself on UK politics. Together, these contests set the stage for the victory for UKIP and the Eurosceptics in the 2016 referendum. As we will see, many of the dynamics that were in play during this period also were evident in the vote to leave the EU. It is inaccurate to view the rise of UKIP in isolation from the vote for Brexit.

In this chapter we examine why this remarkable change of fortune took place. We start by looking at some theories in past research about why radical right parties like UKIP attract support. We explore the aggregate dynamics of support for the party since 2004 and then develop an individual-level model to explain what motivated people to vote for UKIP at the 2014 and 2015 elections, the two major contests that preceded the 2016 referendum. The results of these analyses provide clear and important signposts for what would then happen at the 2016 referendum.

Why Support the Radical Right?

There are two general theories that have been offered for understanding the growth in support for radical right parties like UKIP.[1] One focuses on a syndrome of individual grievances based on economic marginalization and perceived threats from immigration and minorities. An alternative approach puts more emphasis on growing disillusionment among voters with the performance of mainstream parties and, more generally, declining trust in politicians and the institutions of democracy (Whiteley et al. 2015)

The grievances identified in the first perspective are animated by changes in society and economy brought about by globalization and reinforced by the growth in decision-making powers at the EU level.

The decline in political trust associated with the second perspective is driven largely by perceptions that political parties and institutions of the state such as Parliament and the Executive no longer work effectively to deliver what people want. Explanatory variables in these two perspectives operate to stimulate public discontent with the established political class, thereby creating space for the radical right that seeks to give voice to public discontent.

In the United States, the Tea Party, a loosely organized group exercising substantial influence in the Republican Party, and then populist Donald Trump have been the principal expressions of right-wing protest. Their counterpart on the left was Bernie Sanders's insurgent bid to become the Democratic Party's nominee in the 2016 presidential election. In Europe, some right-wing populist parties, such as Golden Dawn in Greece and Jobbik in Hungary, have been labelled anti-system or even neo-Nazi parties, whereas others such as Geert Wilders's Party for Freedom in the Netherlands, Morten Messerschmidt's Danish People's Party and Marine Le Pen's National Front in France operate within the existing framework of democratic politics but well to the right of the political spectrum. Many of these parties have performed well in EU and domestic elections and some of them, such as the Freedom Party of Austria or the National Alliance in Italy, have been coalition partners in recent national Governments.

As for UKIP, since its founding in 1993 the party has portrayed itself as a 'common-sense' alternative that vigorously champions the interests of ordinary people – interests that it claims are being progressively subverted by a cartel of unresponsive cultural, economic and political elites. According to UKIP's populist narrative, self-serving elites dominate Britain's mainstream parties and have willingly ceded national sovereignty to the EU. UKIP has emphasized the irreversible nature of this 'sovereignty ratchet', arguing that as long as Britain remains a member of the EU it faces an insurmountable 'democratic deficit' and loss of control. The result has been that ordinary people are burdened by an ever expanding supply of vexatious regulations promulgated by unelected and unaccountable Brussels bureaucrats.

These arguments are not without substance. The Treaty of Lisbon that came into force in 2009 gave the EU exclusive competence over a wide range of policy areas including a customs union, competition rules, monetary policy for members of the eurozone, a common fisheries policy, commercial policy and the negotiation of international agreements (Piris 2010). Further shared competences were introduced in which member states are unable to make changes once the rules have been agreed with the EU. These restrictions apply to a broad range of policies including the internal market, agriculture, the environment, transport, energy, security and justice. The issue that has had the most immediate resonance in Britain has been the free movement of labour, one of the four key pillars of EU trade policy along with free movement of capital, goods and services. Allowing any citizen of the other twenty-seven EU member states unlimited rights to work in Britain made immigration a potent issue.

Free movement of labour represents both an economic and cultural challenge. On the one hand, economic theory and a considerable body of evidence suggest that labour mobility brings about economic growth and boosts employment (Acemoglu 2009). But, in Britain there is evidence that large-scale labour mobility has undermined domestic wage levels, particularly for semi- and unskilled workers. A study by Dustmann and colleagues (2013) showed that the biggest impacts on wages of immigration into Britain occurred among low-wage workers. Their analyses suggested that a 1 per cent increase in the share of migrants in the UK-born working age population produced a 0.6 per cent decline in the wages of the 5 per cent lowest-paid workers. They also found that immigration was associated with an increase in the wages of higher-paid workers, so it has distributional effects that widen inequalities in the labour market. In part, this may explain why different occupational groups had different views about EU membership in the June 2016 referendum.

Regarding effects on employment, the Migration Advisory Committee studied the impact of immigration on the employment of UK-born people using data from the Labour Force Survey (Migration Advisory Committee 2012). Their research suggested that while EU migrants appeared to have no impact on UK-born employment, non-EU immigration was associated with a reduction in the employment of UK-born workers. In addition, the analysis showed that the likelihood of a negative impact of immigration on the employment rates of UK-born workers was greatest during economic downturns. The implication is that negative effects on employment were made worse by the Great Recession and eurozone crisis.

The cultural challenge has come from the arrival of large numbers of immigrants with different languages, values and religious practices that are radically at odds with those of the local population. Rapid immigration can transform a neighbourhood in a relatively short period of time in ways that can be quite disturbing for longstanding residents. This can produce what sociologists call 'culture shock', which affects local residents, particularly if there is little attempt by immigrants to integrate into society (Ward et al. 2001). The cultural impact of immigration depends on the numbers involved and rates of arrival, since indigenous communities have greater difficulty adjusting to change in the face of large numbers arriving over short periods of time. Past research in the UK has underlined the importance of these cultural anxieties to public hostility to immigration (McLaren 2003).

Another aspect of UKIP's appeal concerns the claim that successive governments have experienced a loss of control over policy-making in an increasingly globalized world. UKIP applies this argument to the EU but it applies well beyond Europe. Research in the 1980s, while acknowledging the growing importance of globalization, suggested that it did not fundamentally erode the autonomy of states to pursue independent policies (see Rose 1980; Castles 1982; Schmidt 1996; Keman 2002). As Garrett (1998: 2) stated in his book on politics and globalization: 'the impact of electoral politics has not been dwarfed by market dynamics'. However, later research has tended to contradict this conclusion. One example is the contention that an independent monetary policy is no longer possible in a globalized world (Boix 1998). More generally, it is argued that the autonomy of the state is now quite limited in many aspects of policy-making, particularly in relation to the economy (Caul and Gray 2000; Huber and Stevens 2001; Hellwig 2014).

This tendency for the autonomy of the nation state to be eroded by globalization has been reinforced in Europe by the growing importance of policy-making at the level of the European Union (Featherstone and Radelli 2003; Hix 2004). This has fed perceptions that national Governments face an increasing 'democratic deficit' that alienates voters from what they perceive to be unresponsive EU institutions (see Norris 2011). National parliaments are seen to have ceded major powers to the EU, whose elected element, the European Parliament, is viewed as remote and subservient to a powerful bureaucracy in Brussels. These perceptions of inefficacy may help to explain the decline in turnout in European Parliament elections over time. Average turnout in the first EU elections was 62 per cent in 1979, but by the eighth round of elections in 2014 it had decreased to only 43 per cent.[2] The implication is that voters are gradually abandoning European elections because they believe that elected representatives to the EU Parliament are basically powerless.

The sense of alienation from democratic institutions was given a significant boost by the financial crash that started in 2008 and subsequently evolved into the 'Great Recession', which lasted for the best part of six years (Reinhart and Rogoff 2009; Krugman 2012). This massive setback to prosperity had a serious effect on the economies of many EU member states. In the case of Ireland and southern European countries such as Italy, Greece, Spain and Portugal, the impact was extremely damaging. The recession significantly reduced living standards and increased unemployment, although the effects were far from uniform, since the impact on northern European countries was significantly less than that on southern Europe.

As we have already discussed in this book, the performance of the British Government in managing the economy and immigration and a feeling that the country has 'lost control' of its ability to make independent policy choices are all aspects of the valence model of electoral choice (e.g. Clarke et al. 2009a, 2016a, 2016b; Whiteley et al. 2013). A poor performance by incumbent parties, either as a consequence of mistaken policies or because they have limited ability to influence outcomes, creates opportunities for an insurgent party like UKIP to attract adherents. In one study of the UKIP vote by Matthew Goodwin and Robert Ford (2014) the authors summarize the factors that drove support for UKIP. These included Euroscepticism, hostility to immigration, dissatisfaction with the performance of the established parties and a pessimistic outlook on life. These factors are all related to developments discussed earlier. They have their origins in economic deprivation and growing inequality, cultural disruptions precipitated by mass immigration and a feeling of alienation from mainstream politics among marginalized groups in society.

One important theory that is used to explain political protests focuses on people's sense of 'relative deprivation' (Runciman 1966; Muller 1979; Walker and Smith 2002). The idea is that people make comparisons between what they expect out of life and what they actually experience. These expectations are formed, in part, by people comparing themselves with others who are similar to themselves. Blue-collar workers, for example, may compare themselves with other workers rather than middle-class professionals or wealthy entrepreneurs who are more remote from their immediate circumstances.

If this comparison with others produces a large gap between expectations and actual experiences, it can lead to frustration and aggression that can trigger political action in the form of protests and demonstrations (Walker et al. 2002). Relative deprivation can operate in people's personal lives arising from their social status and standards of living, but it can also be applied to the political system in general. If the system is seen as being unresponsive to the concerns of ordinary people and fails to deliver equitable and fair outcomes, the result is to trigger a sense of relative deprivation. This produces a situation in which the larger the gap between people's expectations of how their Government should be performing and their assessments of how it is actually performing, the greater is the sense of relative deprivation.

Relative deprivation can operate at the level of specific issues such as perceptions that the economy does not work for ordinary people, or a feeling that immigrants and minorities are receiving special treatment when they come to Britain. Alternatively, it can work at the political level, when people feel that politicians have become remote and isolated and are not listening to their constituents' views. It is important to observe that objective measures of deprivation such as low income or unemployment do not necessarily automatically translate into political action. This is because poverty and deprivation can produce apathy and cynicism about the value of participating in elections or politics generally. So there is no simple relationship between low income, lower socio-economic status and poverty on the one hand and support for a party like UKIP on the other. It is only when these indicators of objective deprivation trigger a sense of injustice and psychological deprivation, and a party succeeds in providing these concerns with a voice, that there is a translation into political action. The role of parties and leaders in articulating this sense of deprivation is crucial for creating a narrative that makes sense to people and mobilizes them to enter the political arena.

This dynamic means that insurgent parties need the 'oxygen of publicity' to be heard. In the event, after 2010 UKIP's success in local elections, European Parliament elections and by-elections, as well as heavy media coverage of the party's surge in the polls, generated a flood of publicity. The party's leaders, particularly Nigel Farage, magnified this by reacting adroitly to political events and the mistakes of his opponents. After 2010, the party enjoyed a virtuous circle of electoral success followed by escalating media coverage in a context where Euroscepticism was rapidly increasing, as the analyses in Chapter 4 showed. In turn, this generated further success because it encouraged previously inattentive voters to consider what UKIP was saying. Some of these people liked what they heard, and this increased the likelihood that they too would support the party.

Identity politics is another idea that is useful to consider when exploring the increase in UKIP's support. This was discussed extensively in Chapter 4. It is clear that national identities play a role in explaining the vote in the referendum on UK membership, since a majority of the English and Welsh voted to leave the EU, whereas the Scots and Northern Irish voted to stay. The role of national identities in the referendum is discussed fully in Chapter 7 but, insofar as voting for UKIP in the 2015 general election is concerned, the party took 14.1 per cent of the vote in England and 13.6 per cent in Wales. In sharp contrast, in Scotland UKIP received only 1.6 per cent. Since UKIP was far more popular in England and Wales than it was in Scotland, it appears that identity politics played a role in explaining support for the party. The fact that English identity is on the rise in England and Scottish identity is increasing north of the border, while British identity is declining more or less everywhere, is clearly an influential factor in the UK (Kenny 2016). That said, identity politics is unlikely to dominate explanations of the rapid rise in support for UKIP after 2010 because national identities change rather slowly. The role of national identity will be examined in the individual-level analyses of UKIP voting presented below.

In the next section we analyse a dynamic model of UKIP support based on monthly aggregate ECMS data from April 2004 to April 2015, just prior to the general election. The focus is on understanding the *dynamics* of support for UKIP over 11 years.

The Aggregate Dynamics of UKIP Support

Our aggregate model of UKIP support builds on the analysis in Chapter 4, which analysed factors affecting public attitudes towards EU membership. Figure 6.1 shows trends in voting intentions in our monthly ECMS surveys for the four major parties in British politics since 2004. What is readily apparent is that UKIP's support remained

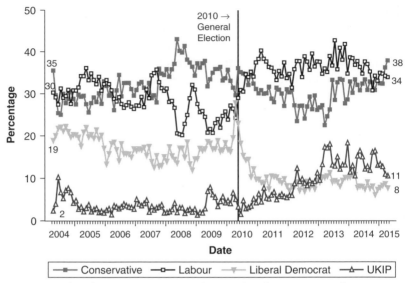

Figure 6.1 Trends in Conservative, Labour, Liberal Democrat and UKIP Vote Intentions, April 2004–April 2015.
Source: ECMS Surveys, April 2004–April 2015.

fairly static at around 4 per cent, subject to some fluctuations, until 2010. After the 2010 general election UKIP voting intentions started to trend upwards and reached 15 per cent just prior to the 2014 European Parliament elections, nearly three times larger than the party's average vote intention share before 2010. Support for the party then continued at this new high level until the 2015 general election.

Another interesting feature of UKIP vote intentions is that they are characterized by periodic bursts of volatility. The ECMS surveys began just before the 2004 European Parliament elections. UKIP's support rose and fell rather rapidly before the 2005 general election before settling down to a more sedate pace in later years. Another period of turbulence occurred in 2009, at the time of the European Parliament elections, and continued until the 2010 general election. A third period of increasing volatility then occurred in 2014 and 2015, again coinciding with the European Parliament elections and 2015 general election. A dynamic model of UKIP support needs to take account of this volatility.

To this end, we specify a model of the aggregate dynamics of UKIP vote intentions in the form of a 'Generalised Autoregressive

Conditional Hetereoscedasticity' or 'GARCH' model (Enders 2014; Clarke et al. 2016b). A GARCH model takes into account the volatility of a time series variable like monthly UKIP support when modelling relationships. In the past, volatility of this kind was seen as a nuisance that could inhibit inferences about which explanatory variables were exerting significant effects but, in financial econometrics where the GARCH model originated, volatility is a standard measure of market uncertainty and attendant risk. For example, there will probably be an upsurge in share trading in stock markets in response to an unexpected 'shock event' like Brexit, and this gives rise to an increase in the volatility of stock prices. Increased volatility thus reflects uncertainty about the effects of such an event. Interpreting enhanced volatility as a signal of increased risk, traders attempt to avoid possible losses (Shiller 2000). As a result, volatility in asset prices feeds back to affect price levels. This is what econometricians call a GARCHM (Garch in Mean) effect (e.g. Enders 2014: ch. 3).

Here, volatility in UKIP support means that some voters are looking at the party and considering its message, and some of them are deciding to support it. This occurs because at various times the party is likely to receive the extra 'oxygen of publicity' of the type referred to earlier. This can occur because of rapidly increasing polling numbers, a strong election result or favourable publicity following speeches by the leader. Indeed, for a party with low levels of support, it is plausible that even negative publicity can help to boost support by helping to raise its profile and exposing its message to a larger group of voters, some of whom will find it attractive. For a small insurgent party trying to get on voters' 'radar screens' as a credible option, virtually any news can be good news.

In our model the dynamics of UKIP's support are explained by five factors. First and foremost are attitudes towards Britain's continued EU membership. Given that opposition to the EU long has been at the core of UKIP's programme, we hypothesize that attitudes towards the EU will track UKIP support in dynamic equilibrium over time. Such a cointegrating relationship between EU attitudes and UKIP support implies that changes in attitudes to EU membership influence changes in UKIP support in the short run. In addition, there is a long-run relationship between these two variables such that they tend to 'travel together' through time. This cointegrating relationship is the fundamental force driving the dynamics of UKIP support but it can be disturbed by other factors, including reactions to salient issues and political events.

The second component of our dynamic model involves three valence issues – voters' judgements about how the Government of the day is handling the economy, immigration and the National Health Service, with the latter being an indicator of how satisfied voters are with the delivery of public services more generally.[3] The indicators are coded so that optimism about the economy and the health service is associated with positive scores on the factors, and negative attitudes towards immigration produce positive scores on its factor. The implication is that negative judgements about the economy and the NHS encourage people to vote for an opposition party like UKIP, as do negative attitudes towards immigration.

The relationship between two of the variables that make up the economic evaluations scale used to study UKIP support is shown in Figure 6.2. One of these variables focuses on evaluations of the state of the national economy and the other on evaluations of personal finances. It can be seen that people were increasingly pessimistic about both the national economy and their personal finances in the period after the 2010 general election. This period coincided with rising

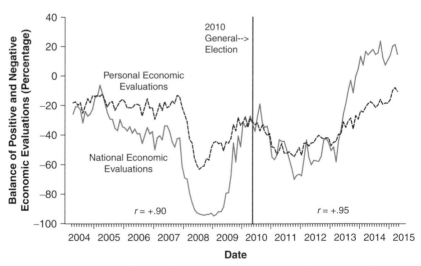

Figure 6.2 Trends in Balance of Positive and Negative Evaluations of the National Economy and Personal Finances, April 2004–April 2015.
Source: ECMS Surveys, April 2004–April 2015.

support for UKIP. However, in 2013 optimism about the economy began to return fairly rapidly. Optimism about personal finances also started to revive, but did so much more slowly. During this later period UKIP's vote intention share tended to level off at about 13 per cent, but did not subsequently decline to levels seen before the 2010 general election. Many of the voters who had switched to UKIP when the economy was in decline did not return to their previous parties after economic conditions began to recover.

It is important to understand the background to the pessimistic evaluations of the economy that voters expressed after the 2010 general election. To a substantial extent, the pessimism was prompted by reactions to the austerity policies that were pursued by the then-new Coalition Government (see Clarke et al. 2016a). Prime Minister Cameron and Chancellor of the Exchequer George Osborne focused on reducing the budget deficit, which they argued was the main barrier to economic recovery, and proceeded to do this with vigour. The emergency budget that was introduced soon after the election included spending cuts of £32 billion per year by 2014/15, an £11 billion reduction in welfare spending and a two-year freeze in public sector pay. These harsh measures were accompanied by an increase in VAT from 17.5 to 20 per cent, which cut disposable incomes by £8 billion. The Government also introduced further taxation measures affecting National Insurance as well as a bank levy and increased capital gains tax. The emergency budget report in 2010 summarized the measures as follows: 'A total consolidation of the £113 billion per year by 2014–15 and £128 billion per year by 2015–16, of which £99 billion per year comes from spending reductions and £29 billion per year from net tax increases' (HM Treasury 2010).

This was an enormous fiscal squeeze at a time when the economy was struggling to recover from the Great Recession. The consequence was to prolong the recession, and in the words of financial journalist William Keegan (2014: 149) the result was: '[t]he slowest recovery from recession on record – slower even than the recovery from the Great Depression of 1929–31, which took two years fewer than 2008–14'. Unemployment had risen rapidly after the start of the recession in 2008, but stabilized at about 8 per cent by the time of the 2010 election. The austerity policies produced further increases in unemployment and it peaked at 8.6 per cent by the start of 2012. The relationship between the unemployment rate and the economic optimism scale was hugely negative ($r = -.93$) in the period after the 2010 general election. Rising joblessness translated fairly rapidly into economic pessimism in the minds of the voters (Clarke et al. 2016a: 61).

These problems were reinforced by the emergence of the eurozone crisis, which erupted towards the end of 2009. The crisis involved Cyprus, Ireland, Greece, Portugal and Spain announcing that they were unable to pay or refinance their financial obligations, producing a sovereign debt crisis that caught markets unprepared. This was thought to be virtually impossible when the eurozone was originally created. The crisis largely arose from attempts by these governments to bail out their banks following the financial crash (Daianu et al. 2014). The fact that the eurozone shares a common currency but does not have common taxes or fiscal policies exacerbated the situation, since it prevented transfer payments between countries to alleviate these imbalances. Equally, the European Central Bank, which had the main responsibility for dealing with the crisis, was very slow to respond and waited until September 2012 before announcing that it would provide unlimited support for the economies of all eurozone countries. These events had an effect in Britain as we observed in Chapter 4, since public disapproval of the UK's EU membership soared after the crisis began. Again, these developments boosted public support for UKIP.

One important reason for the recovery in economic evaluations that can be seen in Figure 6.2 was that in 2012 the Government changed its policy by easing the fiscal squeeze and effectively abandoning the goal articulated in the post-election budget of reducing the deficit to zero by the time of the 2015 general election (Clarke et al. 2016a). This change was not publicly announced but it came about, in part, because of the politically damaging 2012 'Omnishambles' budget that was widely criticized by the press and voters alike. More generally, the austerity policies were failing to produce the anticipated recovery and it became increasingly apparent to Cameron and his colleagues that if the recession continued it would jeopardize the Conservatives' electoral chances in 2015. Backing off on the fiscal squeeze combined with a very interventionist policy of low interest rates and quantitative easing by the Bank of England helped to stimulate recovery and unemployment started falling in early 2013. In turn, this had the effect of reviving economic optimism among voters.

Immigration is the second major issue important for understanding the rise in UKIP. Figure 6.3 shows the relationship between UKIP's

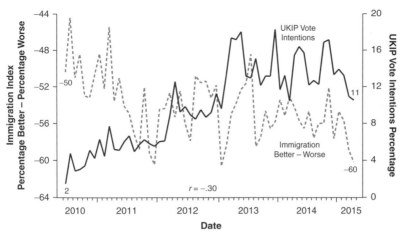

Figure 6.3 Trends in UKIP Vote Intentions and Attitudes towards Immigration, June 2010–April 2015.
Source: ECMS Surveys, June 2010–April 2015.

support in monthly ECMS surveys and attitudes towards immigration in the years after the 2010 election. The latter is measured by the percentage of respondents who thought that immigration had got better (decreased) during the previous year minus the percentage who thought that it had got worse (increased). This variable is one of the components of the attitudes towards immigration scale used in the UKIP model. Pessimism about immigration massively exceeded optimism and this produced negative scores on this variable throughout the entire 2004–15 period. In addition, net optimism gradually declined over time. These trends helped UKIP to gain additional support as the electorate became more pessimistic about immigration and its effects.

The background to increasing public negativity about immigration was the doubling of annual net migration rates into Britain between 1997 – the year of Tony Blair and New Labour's landslide victory – and the 2005 general election. This was largely the result of the Blair Government's decision to allow the free movement of labour into Britain from states in Central and Eastern Europe as soon as these countries joined the EU in 2004. As a result of this decision, net immigration increased to an average of just over 200,000 a year between 2005 and 2010 (Clarke et al. 2016a). Following the eurozone crisis, net immigration rose to 260,000 by 2014 and continued to increase

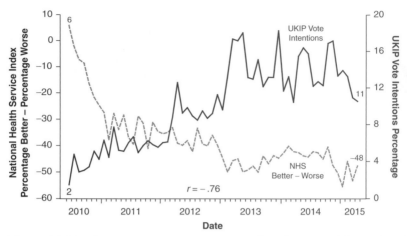

Figure 6.4 Trends in UKIP Voting Intentions and Evaluations of the National Health Service, June 2010–April 2015.
Source: ECMS Surveys, June 2010–April 2015.

after that. The UK immigrant population was growing by almost 1 million people every three years during the latter part of the decade. These developments fuelled public concern about the issue and increased receptivity to UKIP's argument that Britain had lost control of its borders.

Regarding public services, Figure 6.4 shows the relationship between UKIP support and judgements that the National Health Service was deteriorating. The correlation between the two is very strong ($r = -.76$). After the 2010 election, evaluations of the performance of the health service had become increasingly pessimistic and this strong correlation suggests that the growing negativity about the NHS also helped UKIP. The pessimism was rooted in growing pressures on the healthcare system that were coming from an ageing population, the mounting costs of technology and new drugs. The situation had been exacerbated by the failure of a massive reorganization of the NHS that had been introduced in the Health and Social Care Act 2012, sponsored by Andrew Lansley, then Minister of Health in the Coalition Government.

Lansley's reform proposals were the most comprehensive plans introduced for changing the NHS since it had been founded in 1948. They covered commissioning of health services, regulation of care quality, governance of the system and the relationship between the NHS and private-sector health provision. The scale of the changes was so large

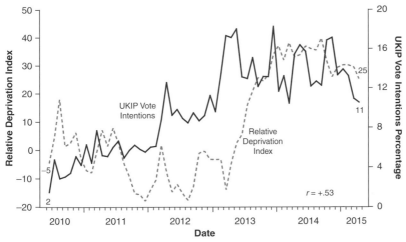

Figure 6.5 Relative Deprivation Index and UKIP Support, April
2004–April 2015.
Source: ECMS Surveys, June 2010–April 2015.

that the Chief Executive of the NHS at the time, David Nicholson,
quipped that the reforms were 'so big you can see them from space'
(Ham et al. 2015: 10). They severely disrupted the provision of healthcare at a time when resources being put into the NHS were declining.
Health spending as a percentage of gross domestic product peaked
at 9.4 per cent in 2009, falling to 8.8 per cent by 2013 (Clarke et al.
2016a: 48). In retrospect, it is evident that the plans were a failure and
the negative public mood reflected the declining quality of healthcare.

As discussed above, a gap between people's expectations and their
actual experiences can give rise to relative deprivation. This is a third
contributor to the rise in UKIP support, in addition to negative attitudes towards EU membership and the valence issues (the economy,
immigration, healthcare). UKIP was able to give voice to the sense
of relative deprivation, winning additional support among disaffected
voters. As Figure 6.5 shows, after a period of economic pessimism following the 2010 election, optimism returned in 2013, but a growing
gap emerged between people's evaluations of the national economy
and their own financial position. If people were optimistic both about
the economy and their own finances, feeling that they were doing as
well as or better than their peers, then this would not generate a sense
of relative deprivation. In contrast, if they were pessimistic about their

own finances while also believing that the economy was doing much
better than they were, this is likely to create a sense of relative deprivation. For this reason, we use the difference between personal and
national economic optimism to index feelings of relative deprivation
in our analysis of the dynamics of UKIP support.

Voters' images of political leaders are also major explanatory variables in the valence model and, like partisanship, leader images provide a simple mechanism that voters can employ to help them decide
who to support. Judgements about the likeability of a leader are a
'fast and frugal' heuristic (Gigerenzer 2008), which people can use
to decide whether that leader is likely to deliver the policies they care
about. It turns out that affective reactions to various leaders are good
proxy measures of perceptions of their honesty, competence, strength
and other desirable traits (Clarke et al. 2009a). Accordingly, likeability
is an ideal summary measure of leader images.

The best variable to use in the aggregate model of UKIP support
would be an indicator of the likeability of the party's leader, Nigel
Farage. Unfortunately, a question that asked people how they felt
about Farage was included in the surveys only from the start of 2014.
However, another measure is provided by people's images of David
Cameron, Ed Miliband and Nick Clegg combined. Eleven-point 'likeability' scales for the Conservative, Labour and Liberal Democrat
leaders were included in every survey since 2004 and can be summed
to give an overall image scale for major party leaders.[4]

A high score on this combined leader likeability scale means that a
survey respondent liked one or more of Farage's main rivals, and so
positive scores should be negatively related to support for UKIP. In
contrast, a low score on the scale means that the respondent disliked
all of the leaders of the major parties, which could increase the likelihood that they would be favourably inclined towards UKIP. Figure 6.6
displays the relationship between UKIP support and the leader image
scale. As expected, there is a strong negative relationship between the
two measures ($r = -.57$), indicating that disliking the major party leaders is strongly associated with UKIP support.

The fifth and final component of our UKIP voting model is a series of
political events that might be expected to influence the party's support.
These include the occurrence of five elections – the 2004, 2009 and
2014 European Parliament elections and the general elections in 2005
and 2010. In addition, there were other events that might have been

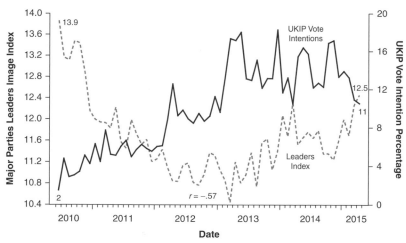

Figure 6.6 Trends in UKIP Vote Shares and Major Party Leaders Image Index, June 2010–April 2015.
Source: ECMS Surveys, June 2010–April 2015.

expected to influence the party's support. In March 2012, Chancellor of the Exchequer, George Osborne, introduced the 'Omnishambles' budget referred to earlier. This poorly received budget introduced taxation on pasties (a type of meat pie) and caravans (camping trailers), both thought to be associated with working-class lifestyles. The result was a blizzard of negative media coverage.

Another important event was Cameron's widely publicized 'Bloomberg speech' in January 2013. Cameron promised that if the Conservatives won a parliamentary majority in the next general (2015) election, he would hold a referendum on EU membership after renegotiating the terms of this relationship. The speech was welcomed by Eurosceptics, particularly within the Conservative Party. But many saw it as a thinly veiled ploy to curb the political fall-out from growing anti-EU sentiment among Conservative identifiers and the wider electorate. UKIP claimed that it had forced Cameron into conceding its longstanding goal of holding a referendum and this boosted support for the party.

Yet another newsworthy event took place in January 2014 when UKIP was obliged to suspend one its local councillors for voicing racist and homophobic remarks. This produced a wave of publicity that showed the party in a bad light and had the potential to reduce support among uncommitted voters. Finally, Douglas Carswell and Mark Reckless, two Eurosceptic Conservative MPs, defected to UKIP in August and September 2014 respectively. Carswell and Reckless resigned their seats in the House of Commons and stood in by-elections in their respective constituencies. In both cases they won, giving an instant boost to UKIP, which could now claim to have two Members of Parliament as well as a sizeable cadre of MEPS.

Finally, the GARCH process in the model captures the 'oxygen of publicity' effects associated with the volatility in UKIP's support.[5] Elections were the most obvious catalyst in this process (see Figure 6.1), but the other events already discussed had the potential to play important roles as well. In particular, the cointegrating relationship between opinions about EU membership and UKIP support suggests that declining support for the EU affected the volatility in UKIP's support. Substantial decreases in EU support translated into both upward movements and increased volatility in UKIP's support in the polls. In turn, this volatility and the publicity associated with it raised UKIP's profile and generated additional support.

Table 6.1 contains results for the analyses of the aggregate UKIP vote intention models using monthly observations between 2004 and 2015. The first column contains the estimates of the cointegrating relationship between UKIP vote intentions and attitudes to UK membership of the EU. This is a baseline model where changes in UKIP voting intentions are driven by levels of these voting intentions measured in the previous month, together with changes and lagged levels of approval ratings of the UK's EU membership. Model estimates indicate that a decrease in the level of support for EU membership translates into growing support for UKIP in the month in which support for the EU falls. In addition to this short-term effect, the analysis documents the expected long-run cointegrating relationship between attitudes towards the EU and UKIP support. The results indicate that a shock to UKIP support from whatever source would be eroded at a rate of 8 per cent in each subsequent month. This shows that while public attitudes towards EU membership were fundamental for understanding the long-run dynamics of UKIP support, there was considerable 'play' in the system, and that other factors had considerable potential to affect how people felt about the party.

The second model in Table 6.1 incorporates the additional explanatory variables including the measure of volatility to capture feedback

Table 6.1 *Models of the Dynamics of UKIP Vote Intentions, April 2004–April 2015*

Predictors	Δ UKIP Vote 2004–15	Δ UKIP Vote 2004–15
UKIP Vote Intentions (*t*–1)	–.08**	–.13***
Δ Net Approval of EU Membership	–.16***	–.07***
Net Approval of EU Membership (*t*–1)	–.04**	–.01***
Δ Leadership Evaluations (*t*–1)	–	–.39***
Δ Evaluations of the Economy (*t*–1)	–	–.04**
Δ Evaluations of Immigration (*t*–2)	–	.31***
Δ Evaluations of the NHS (*t*–1)	–	–.31***
Δ Relative Deprivation and the Economy	–	–.02***
European Parliament Election 2004	–	2.43***
European Parliament Election 2009	–	.71
European Parliament Election 2014	–	3.31***
General Election 2005	–	1.10**
General Election 2010	–	.14
'Omnishambles' Budget 2012	–	1.03***
David Cameron Announces Referendum, 2013	–	3.51***
UKIP Wins a Parliamentary By-Election	–	4.25***
UKIP Councillor Suspended	–	–2.38***
Moving Average Residual Model	–	–.67***
Log(GARCHM Feedback Effect)	–	.44***
Constant	.54**	–1.34***
Error Variance (*t*–1)	–	1.73***
Δ Net Approval of EU Membership (*t*)	–	–.04*
Adjusted R²	.19	.48
AIC	3.97	3.26
BIC	4.06	3.48

Note: *** = $p < .01$; ** = $p < .05$; * = $p < .10$; N = 141.

effects discussed above. The long-run relationship between UKIP voting and attitudes to EU membership remains statistically significant but it is clear that other factors also influenced support for the party. Pessimism about the economy, immigration and the NHS all increased support for UKIP, whereas optimism about these issues had the opposite effect. In addition, if people thought that there was a gap between national and personal economic well-being and they felt left behind, they were more likely to support UKIP. Similarly, if people felt positively about the major party leaders, they were less likely to support UKIP.

Events mattered too. Support for UKIP was boosted by European Parliament elections of 2004 and 2014 and the 2005 general election, though not in 2010. The 'Omnishambles' budget of 2012, which triggered the changes in economic policy discussed earlier, gave UKIP a short-term boost, as did Cameron's announcement of a referendum in his 2013 Bloomberg speech.

Finally, we see that rising approval of EU membership had a negative impact on the volatility of UKIP support, suggesting that voters were less likely to consider the party when there was growing approval of EU membership. Rising disapproval, in contrast, prompted greater volatility in UKIP support. Interpreted as helping to provide the 'oxygen of publicity' needed to attract public attention, volatility in UKIP's support had a positive effect on its support, net of all other considerations. When UKIP's vote intention share in public opinion polls surged, it made news that worked to produce further increases in the party's support.

Overall, while attitudes regarding EU membership clearly played a significant role in explaining the dynamics of UKIP support, other factors associated with the valence model of electoral choice were important as well. In the next section we examine an individual-level model that enables us to study voters' feelings about the party in greater detail.

Who Supported UKIP? An Individual-Level Analysis

To gain a stronger insight into UKIP voting we can pool the survey data from 2004 to 2015 to estimate a model of the party's support at the individual level. This involves expanding the valence model of electoral choice by incorporating the leadership effects for Nigel Farage after 2013, when survey data on his public image were first collected, and adding additional variables relevant for understanding why UKIP supporters are discontented about the way the British political system works.

The first important addition to the dynamic model discussed in the previous section is party identification. Partisan attachments predispose people to support particular parties and reflect a type of 'brand loyalty' that people acquire when they believe that the party is performing well. Clearly, UKIP partisans are more likely to vote for the party than are voters in general, but the interesting question is how they compare with Conservative, Labour and Liberal Democrat partisans. On the face of it, someone who identifies with one of the other three parties should be less likely to vote for UKIP, since their partisanship should act as a barrier to them switching support to another party. But some of these voters may be sympathetic enough to UKIP to consider voting for the party, so it is not certain that loyalties to rival parties automatically preclude UKIP voting.

In addition, it is important to investigate the willingness of individuals who claim to have no partisan attachments at all to vote for UKIP. Between 2004 and 2015 an average of slightly under 14 per cent of our ECMS respondents claimed to have no attachment to any party, so non-partisans comprise a significant segment of the electorate. If people are not psychologically attached to any party, it should be easier for them to switch to UKIP. Many of these non-partisans can be described as 'protest' voters who will readily switch between parties in response to current concerns about the performance of the main parties. In this regard, it is noteworthy that the Liberal Democrats, traditional recipients of protest voting, were a partner with the Conservatives in the 2010–15 Coalition Government. This meant that voters who wished to protest against the Coalition's policies or performance in office could no longer turn to the Liberal Democrats. UKIP was an available alternative.

With regard to leadership, variables measuring feelings about the three major party leaders were combined into a single scale in the aggregate analysis, but it is interesting to treat these variables separately in the individual-level analyses. This makes it possible to determine whether positive feelings about all of the major leaders provided barriers to voting for UKIP. We know from earlier research that favourable evaluations of Farage provided a big boost to voting for UKIP at the 2015 general election (Goodwin and Milazzo 2015; Clarke et al. 2016a: 116). The effects of feelings about Farage and his major party rivals can be investigated using the ECMS survey data from January 2014.

As for issues, the analyses include economic evaluations and judgements about immigration and the state of the NHS. The valence politics model suggests that individuals who evaluate the performance of the economy negatively, are concerned about levels of immigration and worried about the state of the health service are all more likely to support UKIP. Equally, attitudes towards EU membership are clearly important and should stimulate support for the party among those who disapprove of membership.

The model includes three additional issue indicators. First, ECMS respondents were asked, using an open-ended question, to name issues facing the country that were most important to them. Answers to this question covered a wide variety of concerns, although they tended to be dominated by the economy, immigration and public services. This 'most important issue' question was followed by a question that asked respondents to indicate which party they thought was best at handling the issue that they had chosen as most important.[6] When asked to choose the 'best party', respondents were able to say that none of the parties was best suited to address their issue of primary concern. This is an additional measure of dissatisfaction with the performance of parties.[7]

A third issue indicator is based on responses to a question asking which of the major parties is best at managing the economy. Once again, respondents could say that none of the parties was competent on this issue. This enables us to examine whether voters who were disillusioned with all of the parties on the economy might consider UKIP.

Finally, the analysis included a broader measure of valence judgements based on a question that asked respondents to indicate their level of (dis)satisfaction with the state of democracy in Britain. This variable can be regarded as a valence assessment of the political system as a whole, not just in relation to specific issues such as the economy or immigration. Over the entire 2004–15 period about half of the ECMS respondents indicated that they were either 'a little' or 'very' dissatisfied with British democracy, indicating the presence of a reservoir of generalized political discontent that UKIP might be able to tap.

We discussed the possible impact of relative deprivation on UKIP support earlier and, as in the aggregate analysis presented above, we measure this sense of deprivation as the discrepancy between evaluations of personal financial conditions and judgements about the state of the economy. We supplement this with two additional measures that also are designed to capture a sense of deprivation. Respondents were asked to if they felt that the Government treats people like them fairly. This is a very direct measure of feelings of deprivation, and over the entire 11-year period between 2004 and 2015 nearly 60 per cent said that the government did not treat them fairly. There is clearly widespread dissatisfaction with the way that the government treats its citizens. Once again, the expectation is that people who think that they are being treated unfairly are more likely to support an 'outsider' party like UKIP.

Another measure of deprivation concerns an important issue in the referendum debate, namely that Britain is losing control of its ability to manage its own affairs to Brussels. This is the issue of sovereignty and it was a key theme in the Leave campaign. Here, we investigate the ability of perceptions that the country has lost sovereignty to boost support for UKIP by using responses to a survey question that asked respondents whether they thought the British Government or the EU controls the UK economy. A 0–1 dummy variable identified those respondents who thought that the EU controls the UK economy. This sense of a loss of control to the EU is an additional source of a sense of deprivation.

The individual-level model allows us to probe how individual characteristics, such as age, gender, formal education and occupational status, are related to UKIP support. Education is measured by university graduate status, occupation distinguishes between people who are in professional or higher managerial jobs and those in blue-collar or working-class jobs. Given the earlier discussion we expect that graduates and professionals will be less likely to vote for UKIP, whereas less well-educated people and those engaged in manual occupations will be more likely to do so. It is also anticipated that men and older people are more likely to support the party than are women and younger individuals.

Table 6.2 presents the results of analysing UKIP's vote in three different periods.[8] The first model pools all of the survey data from 2004 to 2015. The second focuses on the period after 2010, when UKIP's support began to expand, and the third looks at the 2014–15 period, when it was possible to include feelings about the party's leader, Nigel Farage.

The first model fits the data quite well as judged by the McFadden R^2 statistic (.55) and, with one exception, all coefficients accord with expectations. Focusing first on the effects of issues, not surprisingly if voters disapproved of EU membership they were more likely to say

Table 6.2 *Multilevel Logistic Regression Models of UKIP Vote Intentions*

Predictors: Individual Level	2004–15	2010–15	2014–15
UKIP Best on Respondent's Most Important Issue	2.42***	2.25***	1.17***
No Party Best on Most Important issue	.72***	.50***	.22*
Conservative Partisanship	.54***	.94***	.12
Labour Partisanship	−.23***	−.26***	−.82***
Liberal Democrat Partisanship	−.37***	.26*	−.21
UKIP Partisanship	3.28***	3.65***	2.85***
No Partisanship	1.19***	1.46***	1.26***
Evaluations of Labour Leaders	−.06***	−.10***	−.16***
Evaluations of Conservative Leaders	−.20***	−.14***	−.18***
Evaluations of Liberal Democrat Leaders	−.05***	−.03***	.01
Evaluations of UKIP Leader	–	–	.40***
Economic Evaluations	.12***	−.05*	−.30***
Evaluations of Immigration	−.37***	−.41***	−.40***
Evaluations of the NHS	−.07***	−.11***	−.10**
Relative Deprivation on the Economy	−.13***	−.04*	.01
Satisfaction with Democracy	−.04***	−.10***	−.09***
Perceptions that Government is Fair	−.27***	−.17***	−.48***
Perceptions that EU Controls UK Economy	.18***	.09*	.32***
Perception that No Party is Best on the Economy	.77***	1.05***	.77***
Approval of UK Membership of the EU	−.51***	−.47***	−.26***
Graduate	−.02	−.04	−.17*
Professional Occupation	−.04	−.13**	.18*
Working-Class Occupation	−.09**	−.13**	.08
Male	.35***	.39***	.34***
Age	.01***	.01***	.01***
Respondent Lives in England	.10	.29***	.14
Respondent Lives in Scotland	−.65***	−.54***	−1.19***
Constant	−2.57***	−2.83***	−3.79***
McFadden R²	.54	.58	.64
AIC	29,620.2	15,372.2	4,683.5
BIC	29,885.2	15,613.8	4,899.4

Note: *** = p <.01; ** = p < .05; * = p < .10; max. N = 135,167.

they would vote for UKIP. Equally, people who chose UKIP as the party that could best manage their most important issue were very likely to support it. But this also was true for those who thought that no party was capable of handling important issues. When people judged that none of the major parties was able to deliver on the issues that they considered important, this benefited UKIP. Also, the key issues of the economy, immigration and the NHS all had significant effects on UKIP support. In the case of immigration and the NHS, people who felt that these had been badly managed were more likely to vote for Farage and his party.

What about the effects of feelings about parties? As expected, we find that people who expressed a sense of psychological attachment with UKIP were more likely to support the party, while those who aligned with Labour or the Liberal Democrats were less so. Interestingly, across the entire 11-year period people who identified with the Conservatives were more likely to support UKIP. However, Conservative loyalty is not significant in the third model, which includes evaluations of Farage. This suggests that some Conservative partisans were attracted to UKIP by Farage, and when his popularity is taken into account, Conservative partisanship does not directly affect UKIP voting. Finally, people lacking partisan attachments were more likely to opt for UKIP, implying that the party was able to pick up support from individuals who did not identify with any party.

Leadership images have consistent effects. If voters liked the Labour, Conservative or Liberal Democrat leader they were less likely to support UKIP. Feelings about David Cameron had particularly strong effects in inhibiting a move to UKIP. It is noteworthy that feelings about Cameron continue to have a negative impact on UKIP support in the model containing feelings about Farage. At the same time, positive feelings about Labour Leader, Ed Miliband, continued to negatively impact UKIP voting in the period after 2014. So the popularity of two major party leaders acted as a barrier to UKIP support. In contrast, feelings about Liberal Democrat Leader Nick Clegg were irrelevant.

The relative deprivation variables also behave as expected. People who perceived a gap between their own economic situation and that of the country as a whole were more likely to support UKIP, although the effect weakened after 2010. Similarly, individuals who felt that the Government was not treating them fairly were more supportive of UKIP. The broader measures of valence politics relating to satisfaction with democracy in Britain and perceptions that the EU controls the British economy also perform as anticipated. People who were dissatisfied with the state of democracy and believed that the EU runs the British economy were more likely to say that they would cast a UKIP ballot.

Socio-demographic characteristics had only weak effects. That said, university graduates appear less likely to support UKIP, although the effect is only statistically significant in the third model in Table 6.2. Also as anticipated, older individuals and men are consistently more likely to support the party than are younger voters and women. The relationship between occupational status and UKIP support is particularly interesting. Those in working-class occupations were less likely to vote for the party over the whole period, indicating that while many working-class people voted to leave the EU in the referendum this does not necessarily translate into support for UKIP in an election setting. Being working class per se matters less than having attitudes supportive of UKIP. This point is reinforced by the fact that the relationship between professional status and UKIP voting appeared to be negligible in the model for the entire period, although there were inconsistent effects in the later period. Finally, if someone lived in England, that had a positive impact on voting for UKIP after 2010, and if they lived in Scotland this reduced support for the party.

Thus far, we have examined an aggregate time series model of UKIP voting and a more fully specified individual-level model. We can bring these two approaches together by modelling effects at the individual and aggregate levels of analysis simultaneously by using a multilevel modelling approach (Hox 2002; Raudenbush and Bryk 2002). One interesting line is to examine how the effects of the different variables in the individual-level model changed over time, if at all. Some coefficients may have strengthened, implying that a variable became more important over time, while others may have weakened or stayed the same.

This question can be examined by incorporating an aggregate time trend into the analysis and then examining how this interacts with the coefficients in the individual-level models. In this multilevel analysis, the first level repeats the individual-level model in Table 6.2 and the second level uses a linear time trend to see if the coefficients in the individual level model grow stronger or weaker over time. In effect, the second level is modelling variations in the strength of the coefficients in the first level.

Table 6.3 *Cross-Level Interactions in Multilevel Models of UKIP Vote Intentions*

Predictor Variables	Cross-Level Interaction Coefficient	Effect of Interaction on Variable
No Party Best on Respondent's Most Important Issue	−.004***	Weakens
UKIP Partisanship	.010***	Strengthens
Conservative Partisanship	.010***	Weakens
Liberal Democrat Partisanship	.017***	Weakens
No Partisanship	.008***	Strengthens
Evaluations of Labour Leaders	−.001***	Weakens
Evaluations of Conservative Leaders	.001***	Weakens
Satisfaction with Democracy	−.001*	Strengthens
No Party Best on the Economy	.014***	Weakens
Male	.003***	Strengthens

Note: *** = p < .01; ** p = < .05; * = p < .10; max. N = 135,167.

The results of this analysis appear in Table 6.3, where non-significant effects have been excluded. Taken as a whole, the analysis suggests that UKIP support has become consolidated as the coefficient of UKIP partisanship became stronger over time and the coefficients for the other parties weakened or remained unchanged. This is also true for the effects of Labour and Conservative leader images, which both weakened over time.[9] In addition, it is apparent that the effects of non-partisanship strengthened as UKIP became more successful at appealing to voters who did not identify with any party. Many of these people may have felt dissatisfied with the performance of the main parties and the political system more generally.

It is also interesting to note that several issues are not represented in Table 6.3. This is because although the economy, immigration and the NHS had strong effects in Table 6.2, these effects did not change over time. The two issue indicators that did change were perceptions that no party could manage the most important issue, and perceptions that no party was best at managing the economy. Both of these effects weakened over time, although they remained significant in the individual-level model. Finally, the one demographic variable that changed was gender, with support by men relative to women strengthening over time. In the next section we apply the individual-level model to the task of explaining UKIP voting in the 2014 European Parliament elections and the 2015 general election.

Bringing It Together: The 2014 and 2015 Elections

The 2014 European elections were the key breakthrough for UKIP since it won more votes and seats than any other party. Up to this point our analysis of UKIP support has concentrated on modelling the party's support using data from monthly surveys that were carried out between 2004 and 2015. But from May to August 2014 the ECMS surveys also included a question that asked respondent to recall which party they voted for in the recent European Parliament elections. This provides a more focused measure of actual voting as distinct from intentions to vote for the party in a hypothetical election. In addition, a pre–post internet panel survey was conducted during the 2015 general election and respondents were asked in the post-election wave of this survey how they had voted. Responses to these questions enable us to study factors prompting UKIP voting in these two important elections.

Table 6.4 uses the model presented in Table 6.2 to investigate what motivated support for UKIP at the 2014 European Parliament elections, together with the 2015 general election. The goodness of fit statistic for the European elections model has a McFadden R^2 of .49, which is only slightly smaller than the R^2s for the vote intention models. The estimated coefficients suggest that six variables stand out as being important for explaining UKIP voting in the European elections. These are attitudes towards EU membership, concerns about immigration, leader images, partisanship, perceptions of loss of sovereignty to the EU and feelings of relative deprivation.

As expected, attitudes towards EU membership played a very important role. However, of the three valence variables discussed earlier, only immigration stood out as being important in the voting model. Individuals who were exercised about immigration clearly picked up

Table 6.4 *Individual-Level Logistic Regression Models of Voting for UKIP in the 2014 European Parliament Elections and 2015 General Election*

Predictors	2014	2015	2015
UKIP Best on Respondent's Most Important Issue	.57***	1.21***	1.22***
No Party Best on Most Important Issue	.06	.77***	.81***
Conservative Partisanship	.26	−.71*	−.72*
Labour Partisanship	.61**	−.33	−.35
Liberal Democrat Partisanship	.38	−.00	−.06
UKIP Partisanship	1.22***	.08	.08
No Partisanship	.44	.28	.31
Evaluations of Labour Leaders	−.05*	−.05	−.05
Evaluations of Conservative Leaders	−.03	−.08**	−.08**
Evaluations of Liberal Democrat Leaders	−.07**	.00	.00
Evaluations of UKIP Leader	.42***	.42***	.43***
Economic Evaluations	.15*	.05	.06
Evaluations of Immigration	−.49***	−.23	−.22
Evaluations of the NHS	−.02	.02	.01
Relative Deprivation on the Economy	−.17***	−.16*	−.16
Satisfaction with Democracy	.01	.01	.01
Perceptions that Government is Fair	−.21	−.16*	−.15
Perception that the EU Controls the UK Economy	.27**	.06	.05
Perception that No Party is Best on the Economy	.31*	.19	.14
Approval of UK Membership of the EU	−.56***	−.37***	−.37***
Graduate	.01	.11	.09
Professional Occupation	.28*	−.11	−.14
Working-Class Occupation	.02	−.07	−.07
Male	.30***	−.02	−.03
Age	.03***	.01**	.01**
Respondent Lives in England	.47*	−.14	−.08
Respondent Lives in Scotland	−.17	−2.04	−1.98**
UKIP Campaigning	−	−	.54**
Conservative Campaigning	−	−	−.44*
Labour Campaigning	−	−	−.00
Liberal Democrat Campaigning	−	−	−.03
Other Party Campaigning	−	−	.23

Table 6.4 (*cont.*)

Predictors	2014	2015	2015
McFadden R^2	.49	.45	.45
AIC	2,049.2	936.8	941.1
BIC	2,225.8	1,103.5	1,137.4
N	4,061	2,838	2,838

Note: *** = p < .01; ** = p < .05; * = p < .10.

the UKIP message that the UK had lost control of its borders and so were more likely to vote for the party. Judging that UKIP was the best party at handling the issue deemed most important was also a highly significant predictor. There was some overlap between this measure and evaluations of the economy, immigration and EU membership, since a number of survey respondents cited these as being the most important issue as far as they were concerned. But this did not negate the impact of immigration and EU membership on the propensity to vote for UKIP.

Leader images continued to be influential as well. Comparing Farage with his rivals shows how he took centre stage in influencing the UKIP vote. In contrast, favourable evaluations for Ed Miliband and Nick Clegg weakened the likelihood of casting a UKIP ballot. However, the same point could not be made about David Cameron, who had a negligible influence on voting for UKIP. We saw earlier that over the entire period from 2004 onwards positive feelings about successive Conservative leaders limited the growth of support for UKIP (see Table 6.2). But in the 2014 European Parliament elections this was not true. By the time of this contest Cameron's pledge to hold an 'in or out' referendum had been in place for more than a year, a move that had been designed to fend off UKIP and critics in his own party. Either way, the tactic clearly failed, because neither feelings of loyalty to the Conservative Party nor feelings about Cameron influenced support for UKIP in the 2014 EU Parliament elections.

Regarding partisanship, as expected, identifying with UKIP had a large positive effect on voting for the party in the European elections. Although Conservative and Liberal Democrat partisanship did not influence the UKIP vote, Labour partisanship actually boosted support for UKIP. This did not occur in any of the models in Table 6.2 and it suggests that for the first time UKIP was able to broaden its appeal to include Labour identifiers. People who thought of themselves as Labour partisans but were Eurosceptics were willing to lend their vote to UKIP in these elections, focused as they were on the EU. Finally, those who had no partisan attachments were more likely to vote UKIP, although the effect was not statistically significant at conventional levels.[10]

Regaining sovereignty – taking back control – was a major theme in the 2016 referendum. The potential of this theme to influence voting in the referendum is suggested by the fact that people's belief that the UK had lost control of its economy to the EU had a significant effect on UKIP support in the 2014 European elections. Equally, people who felt that they had been 'left behind' in the economic recovery were also more likely to support UKIP in those elections. In addition, another measure of relative deprivation – perceptions that the Government does not treat people like them fairly – was close to being a significant predictor.[11] These effects speak to wider concerns about democratic accountability and indicate the presence of discontent about how the Government was handling the economy and other key valence issues.

The second model in Table 6.4 relates to the 2015 general election, and it has a marginally weaker fit than the European elections model. This is partly because of the fact that the context in which the two elections were held was different. The European elections focused on the relationship between the EU and Britain and, since this is UKIP's flagship issue, it gave the party greater visibility. In contrast, in the 2015 general election the issue of EU membership was well down the list of priorities (see Clarke et al. 2016a). The fact that turnout in the European elections was under 36 per cent while it reached 66 per cent at the general election reveals how voters who cared about the EU were more likely to vote in the former election compared with the latter. This is confirmed by the fact that some 22 per cent of our survey respondents who voted in the European Parliament ranked Europe as the most important issue compared with only 14 per cent in the general election.

There are major similarities but also differences between factors affecting voting in the two elections and they relate principally to the effects of leader images and issues. Farage had a big impact on the UKIP vote, both in the European elections and the general election. But there was a clear difference between the effects of other leaders on the vote in 2015 compared with the European elections. Unlike 2014, positive feelings about David Cameron acted as a barrier to UKIP in the 2015 general election, and the popularity of Ed Miliband and Nick Clegg had no effect, even though it had been significant the previous year. Similarly, Conservative loyalty had a weak negative impact on UKIP voting in 2015 compared with a negligible impact in 2014. This suggests that in the general election, where Cameron had spent considerable energy framing the Labour Party as the principal electoral threat, there was a 'rally around the flag' effect in the Conservative camp. Conservative supporters who voted for UKIP in the European elections were less willing to do so at a general election when there seemed to be a possibility that Labour might win. Similarly, Labour loyalty had no impact on UKIP voting in the general election, whereas it did have a positive impact in the European elections, again suggesting that Labour identifiers reverted to their traditional loyalties in 2015.

Perceptions that UKIP was the best party at managing voters' most important issues were very important in 2014 and 2015, but perceptions that no party could handle this issue were important in the general election though less so in the European elections. This suggests that UKIP continued to pick up support from voters who did not believe that the political system delivered for them in 2015, but it worked through the issue most important to them. In addition, feelings of relative deprivation influenced UKIP balloting in the general election. Perceptions of a gap between one's personal circumstances and the economy as a whole and a feeling that the Government did not treat people like themselves fairly helped to drive people to vote UKIP in 2015. The third model in Table 6.4 adds indicators of campaigning to the set of predictors in the UKIP model, and it shows clearly that UKIP was helped by its own campaign but harmed by Conservative campaigning. The campaigns run by the other parties appeared to have had no effect on UKIP's support.

UKIP's Coalition: Conservatives and Others

The impact of an insurgent party like UKIP depends in part on which elements of the electorate it can attract. In this regard, a study of UKIP voting in the 2009 EU elections reported that the party was more likely to appeal to disaffected Conservatives than adherents of other parties

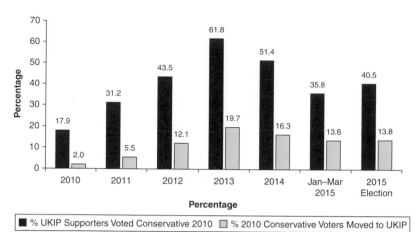

Figure 6.7 UKIP Supporters Who Were Former Conservatives, 2010–2015.
Source: ECMS Surveys, January 2010–May 2015.

(Whitaker and Lynch 2011). This finding is consistent with the idea that UKIP's anti-EU platform has acted as a magnet for Eurosceptics, many of whom are former Conservatives. The findings presented above reinforce the point that up to and including the 2015 general election, party competition between the Conservatives and UKIP was fiercer than between Labour, the Liberal Democrats and UKIP. The sizeable negative correlation ($r = -.67$) between trends in Conservative and UKIP support in the monthly surveys conducted between June 2010 and April 2015 is consistent with this observation.[12]

Our individual-level analysis reinforces the conclusion that many, but certainly not all, of UKIP's voters were erstwhile Conservatives. Specifically, the surveys conducted after the 2010 election show that large numbers of those who intended to vote for UKIP were ex-Tories, with the number reaching a maximum of nearly 62 per cent in 2013 (see Figure 6.7), although that clearly still leaves a large number of UKIP voters who were not former Conservatives. After that, UKIP's coalition broadened, with only 36 per cent of those participating in one of the surveys in early 2015 saying that they had voted Conservative in 2010. Similarly our 2015 ECMS election survey shows that 41 per cent of UKIP voters had cast a Conservative ballot in 2010. This represented slightly fewer than one in seven of those voting Conservative in that year. The ability of UKIP to attract sizeable numbers of former Conservatives had interesting implications for the 2016 referendum.

If UKIP could attract disaffected Tories, if it could join forces with Conservatives in a common albeit awkward alliance to take Britain out of the EU, this would be a powerful stimulus to the Leave campaign. This is of course exactly what happened and is investigated further in the next chapter.

Conclusion: UKIP on the Move

The rise of UKIP is one of the most important developments in British party politics in the past quarter century. The findings presented in this chapter reveal how the rise of the controversial party was propelled first and foremost by negative public attitudes towards the country's EU membership. Over the years, these attitudes have been quite volatile and, as expected, UKIP's support has ebbed and flowed with them.

However, we have also shown how UKIP's support has been driven by several other factors. People's negative judgements about how the Government of the day performed on key issues such as the economy, immigration and healthcare, all worked to UKIP's advantage. In this regard, the Liberal Democrats' decision to join a governing coalition with the Conservatives after the 2010 general election provided a valuable opportunity for UKIP to attract voters who were unhappy with the Government's performance on these valence issues.

Support for UKIP was also clearly enhanced by the fact that Labour's image for managerial competence had been badly damaged by the Great Recession and a record surge in immigration that occurred during its lengthy term in office. Party leader images were relevant too. Positive feelings about Farage raised the probability that voters would cast their ballots for UKIP, and so, while divisive, he is a very important part of the story about why the party was able to force its way to the very forefront of UK politics. Meanwhile, positive feelings about the leaders of other parties made it less likely that people would jump on the UKIP bandwagon.

These valence politics considerations aside, UKIP was affected by other factors as well. Voters who experienced a sense of relative deprivation – feeling that their financial circumstances had not kept pace with the economy as a whole – were more likely than others to be drawn to the party. This underlines the importance of the so-called 'left behind' in UK society (Ford and Goodwin 2014). Finally, the success of an insurgent minor party depends heavily on its ability to attract public attention to its message and UKIP benefited from an 'oxygen of publicity' effect that helped to drive its support upwards in a self-reinforcing spiral of media attention and favourable poll numbers. UKIP became a focal point of media attention, which, in turn, gave the party the broad audience it needed to move centre stage. By the time of the 2015 general election, UKIP had become a significant force and its anti-EU message had a broad and sympathetic audience. In the next chapter, we will study forces that translated that message into a vote for Brexit at the 2016 referendum.

7 | Voting to Leave

On 23 June 2016 the United Kingdom made a historic decision to leave the European Union. The 2016 referendum was the second such event in the country's history. The first referendum, in 1975, had asked voters whether they wanted to stay in the Common Market, as it was then called, and they had endorsed continued membership by a strong two to one margin (Butler and Kitzinger 1996). But the 2016 result was very different. When all votes were counted 51.9 per cent of those casting ballots had opted to leave the EU, with the margin between Remainers and Leavers approaching 7 per cent in England.[1]

What motivated this vote for a Brexit? Was the decision to leave the EU motivated mainly by instrumental considerations concerning the perceived costs and benefits of the country's EU membership? Were judgements about the perceived adverse economic effects of EU membership concentrated among people who felt they had been 'left behind' as the UK's economy had revived after the Great Recession? Or was the Leave vote driven more strongly by feelings of national identity and anxiety over perceived threats to the native in-group, from immigration and the free movement of EU nationals, worries that the two Leave campaigns had sought to amplify during the campaign? How influential were risk perceptions? What were the roles of cues from prominent politicians, such as David Cameron, Boris Johnson and Nigel Farage, in motivating people to vote to remain or leave?

In this chapter we address these questions using data gathered in a national panel survey of the electorate conducted just before and immediately after the referendum. Using these data, we will show how the vote for Brexit was not caused by 'one' factor alone. Rather, the narrow Brexit decision reflected a complex and cross-cutting mix of calculations, emotions and cues. While some of the factors, such as people's attitudes towards immigration and their feelings of national identity, were 'baked in' long before the referendum campaign began, others, such as how people felt about the different political leaders, produced strong effects nearer to the vote itself. There were many drivers, not merely one, behind the Brexit vote.

How to Explain Voting in the EU Referendum

Our expectations about what influenced the 2016 referendum are based on past research on what shapes attitudes towards the EU. This research was discussed in Chapter 4. Taken together, these studies emphasize the importance of cost–benefit *calculations*, feelings of attachment to a wider *community* and *cues* from political leaders in shaping the outcome of referendums, like that held in 2016 (Hooghe and Marks 2005; Hobolt and de Vries 2016; see also LeDuc 2003). Overall, the fundamental issue was: is the EU delivering the policies and performance that people want?

Considering calculations first, seen from this perspective the 2016 referendum was a 'soft' rational choice exercise in which voters evaluated the benefits of EU membership, such as in relation to the national economy and their own financial position, and then weighed these benefits against perceived costs. We explore this hypothesis using a battery of survey questions that were designed to capture how these perceived costs and benefits affected voting. Linked to this idea is the claim that 'left-behind' groups in Britain were especially likely to conclude that the costs of EU membership outweighed any benefits. We examine this idea by looking at the impact of perceived discrepancies between people's judgements about the national economy and their own economic well-being.

As the referendum campaign and its aftermath revealed, public attitudes towards EU membership also have a powerful emotional component. Although some people have a strong affinity with the notion of being a member of a wider community, others strongly resist this idea. Recent research on affective reasoning suggests that emotional aspects of decision-making have substantial effects on the political choices that people make (see, e.g., Marcus et al. 2000; Neuman et al. 2007; Garry 2013) For this reason, our survey included a question designed to capture the emotions people feel when they think about the EU. The expectation is that positive emotional reactions promoted voting for Remain and while negative emotions prompted voting for Leave.

Another important consideration involves the effects of people's perceptions of risk. As discussed earlier, in his review of research on referendums LeDuc (2003) identified a 'status quo bias' in voters' decision making. When faced with a complex and difficult choice of the type posed by major 'polity-shaping' events like the referendums on Scottish independence or EU membership, voters who are risk-averse typically prefer to opt for 'the devil they know'. Prior to the beginning of a referendum campaign sizeable numbers of people typically tell pollsters that they support the change being proposed. But as the campaign progresses and decision day nears, some have misgivings, reconsider and, after a period of indecision, end up voting to keep things as they are. This pattern – 'LeDuc's law' – is consistent with research in experimental economics and cognitive psychology that emphasizes the importance of risk orientations when individuals are making choices in the context of high stakes and abundant uncertainty (Gigerenzer 2008; Kahneman 2011). This is why it is important that we explore how the perceived risk of leaving the EU affected voting decisions in the 2016 referendum.

Turning to community, which taps people's feelings of identity, we investigate how the vote was influenced by people's identities as British, English, Scottish, Welsh, European or something else. As observed above, scholars have argued the case for the effects of such identities on attitudes towards the EU. However, our expectations about the impact of identities on choices made in the 2016 referendum are tempered by recent research on voting in the 2014 Scottish independence referendum and the SNP in elections to the Holyrood Parliament, which discounts the importance of identity (Johns et al. 2013). More generally, identities tend to be stable over extended periods of time. So, if identity considerations are important then their effect will likely be found well back in the chain of factors that influenced the 2016 vote, rather than having an immediate effect on the decision to remain or leave.

Past research on how cues affect referendum voting emphasizes the roles of political parties and party leaders. In the case of the EU referendum the minor parties and their leaders, such as UKIP and Nigel Farage, the SNP and Nicola Sturgeon and the Liberal Democrats and Tim Farron, adopted clear and well-publicized positions. In contrast, both the Labour and Conservative parties were divided – the latter much more so than the former. During the referendum campaign, Prime Minister David Cameron campaigned vigorously for Remain while former London mayor Boris Johnson – himself a very prominent

Conservative politician – campaigned to leave. Johnson, who aligned himself to the official Vote Leave campaign, quickly became the unofficial leader of the Leave campaign and was followed closely by the media throughout the campaign. This put Johnson in an important position, giving him ample opportunity to 'cue' the public about how to vote. Reflecting the divisions among the Conservatives, he was accompanied by several other Eurosceptic cabinet ministers, such as Michael Gove, Chris Grayling and Priti Patel, and more than a hundred Conservative MPs who, to varying degrees, made the case for Leave. Because the Conservatives were divided and articulated contradictory messages about the EU, this probably muted the impact of a more general Conservative Party cue.

Labour was more united on the country's EU membership, although a handful of MPs, among them Gisela Stuart, Frank Field, Kate Hoey and John Mann, advocated a Brexit. However, internal party discord over the unpopular leadership of Jeremy Corbyn, who provided only a lukewarm endorsement of continued EU membership, meant that Labour had also sent mixed messages to the electorate. Corbyn's refusal to make a clear and compelling case for the Remain side was traced by many journalists to his well-documented Eurosceptic sentiments in earlier years. This does not surprise, given his view that the EU was basically a bureaucratic device to service the interests of uber-capitalism (Shipman 2016). In the event, Corbyn's half-hearted campaign efforts, together with the Conservative divisions, eroded the strength of the cues given by the major parties.

The Ballots Counted

When the first results were announced on the evening of 23 June, it was clear that Leave was performing better than many observers had anticipated. Sunderland, famous for its early reporting of election results, put Leave on 61 per cent and Remain on only 39 per cent, handing the Brexiteers a resounding 22-point victory margin. This startling tally proved to be a harbinger; as the night wore on it was clear that Leave had performed stronger than many had expected.

Although London delivered a predictably large harvest of Remain votes, other major urban areas with large minority populations such as Sheffield and Birmingham provided Leave majorities. The latter was late to report but, when it did, the game was up. In the end, it is estimated that nearly three-quarters of constituencies held by the Conservative Party voted for a Brexit.[2] The three highest votes for Brexit were recorded in the Conservative-held seats of Boston and Skegness (75 per cent), South Basildon and East Thurrock (73.1 per cent) and Castle Point (72.7 per cent), although over half of the 100 most pro-Brexit seats also had Conservative MPs.

The result also revealed how Brexit and the closely linked issue of immigration had cut directly across the political geography of the Labour Party. While nearly three-quarters of Conservative seats had voted for Brexit, so too had nearly two-thirds (64 per cent) of Labour-held seats. But Labour MPs also represented solid Remain territory, too, which added to the party's new dilemma. Of the 100 seats that provided the strongest votes for a Brexit, slightly over half (53) had Conservative MPs and a sizeable 46 were held by Labour. But of the 100 seats that gave the strongest votes to Remain only 20 were held by the Conservatives, while 41 were held by Labour. In the shadow of the referendum Labour thus found itself torn between seats where more than 7 in 10 voters had turned out to endorse Leave – like Kingston-upon-Hull East, Stoke-on-Trent North, Doncaster North, Walsall North, Mansfield, Stoke-on-Trent South and Normanton, Pontefract and Castleford – and seats where similarly large majorities had turned out to endorse Remain – seats like Hornsey and Wood Green, Streatham, Bristol West, Hackney North and Stoke Newington, and Edinburgh South.

When all of the ballots were counted, 72.2 per cent of the eligible electorate had cast a ballot and Leave had a 51.9 per cent share across the UK as a whole (see Figure 7.1). England and Wales both had Leave majorities, at 53.4 per cent and 52.5 per cent, respectively. These totals could not be offset by strong Remain performances in Scotland and Northern Ireland. In Scotland, only 38.0 per cent voted to leave and in Northern Ireland, 44.2 per cent did so. To the surprise and consternation of many commentators at home and abroad, the UK electorate had chosen Brexit.

Although the overall margin between Leave and Remain was a modest 3.8 per cent and Scotland voted decisively for Remain, anti-EU sentiment was widespread throughout much of the rest of Britain. This point can be illustrated by aggregating the vote totals that were reported by local authorities to the constituency level. Although the fits between local authority jurisdictions and constituency boundaries

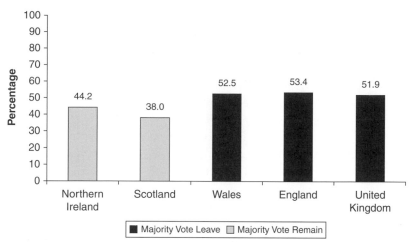

Figure 7.1 Percentages Voting Leave in 23 June 2016 UK Referendum on Continued EU Membership.
Source: Electoral Commission.

are typically imperfect, it is helpful to estimate how the vote played out across individual constituencies. As Figure 7.2 illustrates, across 632 British constituencies, 401 (63.4 per cent) are estimated to have had Leave majorities. In England, outside of greater London, the percentage of constituencies with Leave majorities varies from a low of 69.0 per cent in the Southeast and East Anglia to a high of fully 87.6 per cent in the Midlands. Similarly, 72.5 per cent of constituencies in Wales had Leave majorities. In sharp contrast, the London figure is only 21.9 per cent and Scotland's is a miniscule 1.7 per cent (one constituency). These latter numbers aside, it is clear that, if they were listening, a large majority of British MPs would have heard their constituents supporting Brexit.

When combined with census data and information from the 2015 general election, the constituency-level referendum vote estimates enable us to see which kinds of constituencies were most likely to favour Brexit. Opinion polls conducted before the referendum portrayed Leave voters as older, less well-educated and white people who identified themselves as being English and were often working in manual occupations. Also, although not active politically, many of them were well integrated into their communities in the sense of being long-time residents and home owners. A multivariate statistical analysis (OLS

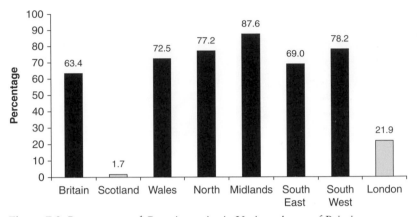

Figure 7.2 Percentages of Constituencies in Various Areas of Britain Estimated to Have Voted Leave.
Source: Chris Hanretty's Website (https://medium.com/@chrishanretty).

regression) of the constituency-level data testifies that this portrait of Leave voters has considerable credibility.

As Table 7.1 shows, voting for Leave was highest in English constituencies that had relatively large proportions of home owners, manual workers and older people. In contrast, Leave voting tended to be lower in constituencies with high percentages of young people, university graduates and larger proportions of ethnic minorities. Also, as indexed by turnout in the 2015 general election, Leave voting tended to be higher in areas where political activity and civic engagement were relatively low.

Finally, it is noteworthy that Leave voting tended to be more prevalent in areas where UKIP had performed well in the 2015 general election. The existence of a positive relationship between UKIP support and anti-EU sentiment is unsurprising, but its strength is nevertheless impressive – the constituency-level correlation (r) between the percentage of people that voted for UKIP in 2015 and the percentage that voted Leave in the 2016 EU referendum is fully +.85. This once again underlines the important role that the party played in cultivating public support for leaving the EU in the build-up to the 2016 referendum.

The picture sketched by these constituency-level findings fits well with the results of earlier research (e.g. Ford and Goodwin 2014) showing that support for UKIP and anti-Europe attitudes tended to be

Table 7.1 *OLS Regression Analysis of Factors Affecting Constituency-Level Leave Voting in Great Britain*

Predictors	ß	s.e.
Percentage University Degree	−.791***	.042
Percentage Manual Workers	.236*	.102
Percentage Home Owners	.246***	.029
Minority/White Ethnicity Ratio	−1.033*	.530
Age		
Percentage 18–29	−.288***	.054
Percentage 65 and Older	.131*	.066
Percentage Turnout 2015 Election	−.334**	.056
Country		
Scotland	−14.812***	.650
Wales	−5.033***	.650
Constant	81.266***	.102
R^2 = .89		
N = 632		

Note: *** = p < .001; ** = p < .01; * = p < .05, one-tailed test.

concentrated among groups in society that went on to vote strongly for Leave in the 2016 EU referendum. However, while these findings are interesting they do not tell us about what actually motivated people to vote for Leave at the referendum. We investigate this topic in the next section.

Referendum Voting: Why They Did It

The survey data used to study how people voted in the EU referendum were derived from a national panel survey that we conducted before and after the vote.[3] The first wave of our survey was in the field from 18 to 20 June and the second wave was conducted shortly after the referendum, between 27 and 29 June. The sample sizes for the pre- and post-referendum waves were N = 2,218 and N = 1,993, respectively. The panel design is well suited for studying how various factors affected voting at the referendum. Voting behaviour was measured in the post-referendum wave, while, with the exception of campaign contacts, all of the predictor variables were measured in the pre-referendum wave. Modelling the data in this way helps to alleviate threats to inference that can bedevil analyses that rely on cross-sectional survey data measured at one point of time (Whiteley et al. 2016).

In the pre-referendum wave of the referendum panel survey, 46.4 per cent of respondents intending to vote reported that they would vote Remain and 47.9 per cent indicated they would vote Leave, with the remaining 5.8 per cent saying they 'didn't know'. If, as discussed earlier, many in the latter group ultimately would decide to stick with the status quo, these numbers suggest that Remain might have been able to secure a narrow victory. Of course, that did not happen. Vote totals in the post-referendum wave of our survey closely mirrored the result, with 50.7 per cent stating they had voted Leave and 49.3 per cent saying that they had voted Remain.[4]

We begin by investigating relationships between the referendum vote and the social and demographic characteristics of voters.[5] The results fit well with the constituency-level findings reported above. As shown in Figure 7.3, there is a sharp and virtually steady age gradient in referendum preferences, with the percentage of Leave voters increasing from a low of 25 per cent among 18–25-year-olds to 66 per cent among those over 65 years old. There also are strong ethnic differences: 53 per cent of those identifying themselves as 'White British' voted to leave as compared to only 23 per cent of those in an ethnic minority group. Educational and social class differences are readily apparent as well: among university graduates, 37 per cent voted Leave as compared to 60 per cent of those with no university education. Similarly, the percentage of Leave voters increases steadily from 35 per cent among people in the upper and upper-middle class (A/B) group to fully 64 per cent among those in the working or lower classes (D/E). Finally, we see that Leave voting did not vary by gender. Among both men and women, 51 per cent reported that they voted to leave.

We now consider how people's attitudes have affected their voting behaviour. If past research on major referendums is a reliable guide, benefit–cost considerations were likely to be very important. We begin by examining voters' evaluations of the costs and benefits of EU membership. For this purpose, we use survey items that tap survey respondents' perceptions of being either better off or worse off from leaving the EU with regard to a large number of issues, including their personal finances, immigration, terrorism, foreign affairs, sovereignty and

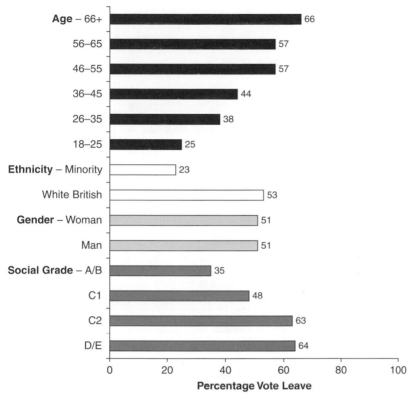

Figure 7.3 Leave Voting by Socio-Demographic Characteristics.
Source: ECMS Pre-Referendum Survey, June 2016.

the economy. As Figure 7.4 illustrates, respondents were inclined to think that if Britain left the EU then the economy would be worse off (39 per cent v. 24 per cent), as would their own financial circumstances (30 per cent v. 12 per cent). However, judgements about immigration were very different – fully 51 per cent thought that there would be less immigration and only 3 per cent thought that there would be more in the event the UK left the EU. At the same time, a plurality (41 per cent) agreed with the proposition that immigration provided workers for jobs that Britons are unwilling to do.

During the referendum campaign the Remain side claimed that the EU was a force for peace as well as prosperity. A plurality of the survey respondents agreed: 37 per cent believed that membership of the EU helped to keep the peace in Europe while 29 per cent thought

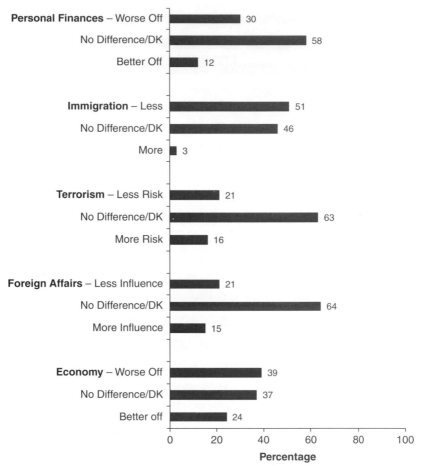

Figure 7.4 Perceived Benefits and Costs of Leaving the EU.
Source: ECMS Pre-Referendum Survey, June 2016.

the opposite (Figure 7.5). Regarding international affairs, 21 per cent believed the UK would have less influence in world affairs if it left the EU, while 15 per cent thought it would have more influence. At the same time, a majority (51 per cent) indicated that they thought EU membership eroded British sovereignty. Finally, there was a tendency to believe that continued EU membership enhanced the risk of terrorism. Specifically, 21 per cent stated that the risk would be greater if the country stayed in the EU and 16 per cent said the risk would be smaller. When asked a second question, the difference was larger – 47

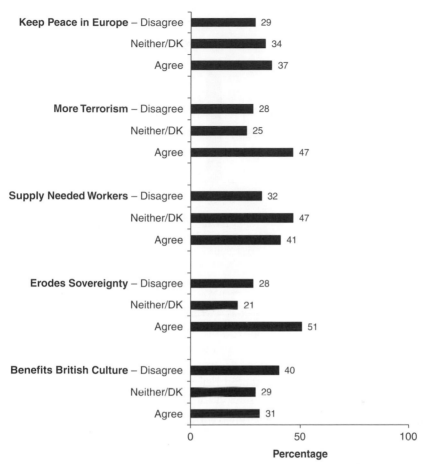

Figure 7.5 Perceived Benefits and Costs of Continued EU Membership.
Source: ECMS Pre-Referendum Survey, June 2016.

per cent agreed that there would be more terrorism if the UK remained in the EU and 28 per cent disagreed. Overall, then, most people tended to feel that a Brexit would be bad for the national economy and their own finances, but would also help the country to reduce immigration and reclaim national sovereignty, although many were unsure of the consequences or thought it would make no difference.

A statistical technique (confirmatory factor analysis; see Acock 2013) allows us to summarize the perceived benefits and costs of leaving the EU and suggests that two factors provide a useful representation of

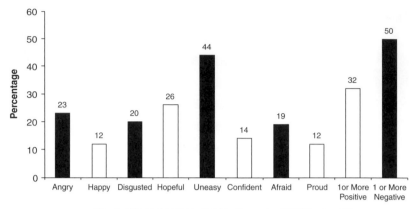

Words Selected to Describe Feelings about EU Membership

Figure 7.6 Emotional Reactions to UK Membership of the EU.
Source: ECMS Pre-Referendum Survey, June 2016.

the data. The results show that variables focusing on the economy and Britain's influence in the world load heavily on factor one, while items focusing on immigration and security issues load heavily on factor two. Factor scores derived from this analysis are employed in the multivariate modelling presented below.

What about the role of emotion in the referendum vote? Figure 7.6 contains frequency distributions for various emotional reactions to EU membership. These data are derived from a question asking respondents to describe their feelings about the country's EU membership by selecting up to four words from a list of eight descriptors. Four of the words described positive emotional reactions and four described negative reactions. The figure illustrates that feelings of unease dominated, with 44 per cent selecting this word. Although 26 per cent described their feelings as 'hopeful', and this was the second most popular choice, no other positive word was selected by more than 14 per cent. Overall, as the two bars on the far right of Figure 7.6 indicate, 32 per cent chose one or more positive words, while fully 50 per cent chose one or more negative words. Thus, on the eve of the referendum, negative emotions clearly outweighed positive ones when people thought about EU membership. To the extent that emotional considerations would drive referendum voting, this clearly was a problem for the Remain camp.

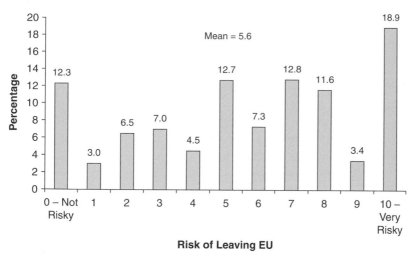

Figure 7.7 Perceived Risks of Leaving the EU.
Source: ECMS Pre-Referendum Survey, June 2016.

Figure 7.7 displays responses to a question that asked people to use an 11-point scale to indicate how risky leaving the European Union would be for Britain. On the scale, 0 indicates 'no risk' and 10 signifies 'very risky'. As the figure illustrates, risk perceptions were widely dispersed. Also, although the mean score (5.6) was very close to the scale's mid-point (5), opinion was tilted towards the 'risky' end, with a majority (54 per cent) assigning scores of six or greater. In contrast, only one third (33 per cent) gave scores below the mid-point, thereby indicating that they did not think the risks would be as severe. If risk assessments influenced referendum voting, the expectation is that the more risk people perceived the less likely they were to prefer Brexit. This was good news for Remain, because a large proportion of the electorate believed that exiting the EU entailed substantial risk.

The community aspect of attitudes to membership was measured by a survey question that asked respondents if they felt 'British', 'English', 'Scottish', 'Welsh', 'European' or some other nationality. In the event, 48 per cent described themselves as 'British', 33 per cent as 'English', 6 per cent as Scottish and 3 per cent as 'Welsh'. Only 3.5 per cent described themselves as 'European', with a further 6 per cent choosing another national identity or saying they 'didn't know'. As discussed above, the expectation is that national identities influenced the vote. Compared with those identifying themselves as British, we expect those thinking of themselves as English or Welsh will be less favourable towards EU membership, whereas those who see themselves as European or Scottish will be more favourable. This is because the former identities are narrower than a more inclusive identity of being 'British'. However, in the case of Scotland the recent upsurge of nationalism flips this relationship, since many Scottish identifiers see EU membership as an attractive alternative to remaining in the UK.

The potential role of party leaders providing cues to voters was measured by asking respondents to rate several prominent politicians using 11-point (0–10) 'likeability' scales, where 0 means 'strongly dislike' and 10 means 'strongly like'. These scales have proved very useful in summarizing important leader image traits such as competence, honesty, responsiveness and trustworthiness (Clarke et al. 2009a; Whiteley et al. 2013). The hypothesis is that respondents will be more responsive to cues provided by leaders they like rather than those they dislike. Given the positions taken by key leaders in the referendum, we would expect that positive feelings about David Cameron or, to a lesser extent, Jeremy Corbyn would encourage individuals to vote to remain in the EU, whereas positive impressions of Boris Johnson or Nigel Farage would encourage them to vote to leave.

Other possible cues in the referendum campaign came from the political parties and the Remain and Leave campaigns. The divisions in the Labour and Conservative parties over Brexit suggest that cues from these parties might be largely ineffective in influencing the vote because they were sending mixed or weak messages. In contrast, cues from the SNP, the Liberal Democrats and UKIP were much clearer and so attachments to these parties might well have influenced the vote. These possibilities are explored by including measures of whether people felt a sense of psychological attachment to one of the parties.

In addition, we investigate the influence of three other predictors. Two of these measure the amount of contact that people had with the Leave and Remain campaigns. The expectation is that people exposed to a campaign would be more likely to vote for that option. A third predictor is the perceived importance of 'Europe' as an issue. Over the years, 'Europe' has become a codeword for Euroscepticism and, accordingly, designating Europe as an important issue can be taken as a useful proxy for the strength of Eurosceptic sentiments that could have prompted Leave voting.

Finally, we consider the possible effects of four socio-demographic variables. During the campaign, numerous polls showed large differences in support for/opposition to EU membership across different age groups, with older people being more likely to express their desire for a Brexit than the young. Similarly, echoing previous research on attitudes towards the EU (Ford and Goodwin 2014), opinion polls revealed that less well-educated people and those in lower social classes were more likely to be Leave supporters. In contrast, polls showed only small gender differences in attitudes towards the EU.

We begin by estimating the direct effects of the several predictor variables discussed above on referendum voting. Since the dependent variable is a dichotomy (vote Leave = 1, vote Remain = 0), model parameters are estimated using binomial logit procedures (Long and Freeze 2014).[6] Table 7.2 presents the results of this analysis.

So what really influenced the choices voters made in the 2016 referendum? Our analysis reveals that both of the benefit–cost factors – economic–influence and immigration–terrorism – played very significant roles in explaining the vote to leave. Table 7.2 shows that respondents who were optimistic about the economy and Britain's role in the world if the country were to exit the EU were much more likely to vote Leave. Similarly, those who believed that Britain would be better able to control immigration and counter-terrorist threats if it were not part of the EU were more likely to vote Leave. As also expected, and unsurprisingly, perceptions of risks associated with leaving the EU have a highly significant impact on referendum voting. People who saw Brexit as risky were much less likely to vote to leave than those who minimized the risks. Emotional reactions to the EU were significant as well: positive reactions to the EU stimulated a vote to remain, whereas negative emotions promoted a leave vote. In addition, and again as expected, those who designated the EU as an important issue were more likely to vote to leave.

The national identity measures are not statistically significant, with the sole exception of Scottish identifiers, who were less likely to vote to leave than were those who identified themselves as British (see Table 7.2). Equally, socio-demographic characteristics had no effects apart from a very modest tendency for individuals in higher socio-economic grades to vote for remain. The cues variables indicated that party cues were largely irrelevant with the exception of a negative effect associated with Conservative partisanship, indicating

Table 7.2 *Binomial Logit Analysis of Factors Affecting Voting to Leave the EU*

Predictor	ß	s.e.
Benefits–Costs of Leaving EU		
Economy–Influence	2.500***	.578
Immigration–Terrorism	1.030**	.367
Risk Assessments of Leaving EU	−.371***	.062
Emotional Reactions to EU	−.304***	.096
Importance of Europe as Issue	.599*	.270
Left Behind in Economy	−.039	.147
Party Leader Images		
Cameron	−.029	.056
Corbyn	−.054	.053
Farage	.194***	.055
Johnson	.196***	.056
Partisanship		
Conservative	−.539*	.322
Labour	−.060	.321
Liberal Democrat	−.347	.443
UKIP	−.338	.563
SNP	1.416	.741
National Identity		
English	.185	.243
Scottish	−1.592**	.552
Welsh	−.323	.594
European	−.841	1.305
Other	−.287	.463
Campaign Contact		
Remain Campaign	−.083	.194
Leave Campaign	.270	.278
Socio-Demographics:		
Age	−.006	.007
University Education	.093	.236
Gender	.026	.221
Social Class	−.148†	.101
Constant	1.289	.753

McKelvey R^2 = .89
Percentage Voters Correctly Classified = 93.2
Percentage Reduction in Classification Error (Lambda) = 86.2 per cent
N = 1,780

Note: *** = $p \leq .001$; ** = $p \leq .01$; * = $p \leq .05$; † = $p \leq .10$, one-tailed test.
Dependent variable is scored: vote Leave = 1, vote Remain = 0.

that Conservative identifiers were more likely to vote to remain, other things being equal. Leader images were another story. Although feelings about Cameron and Corbyn were not influential, feelings about Boris Johnson and Nigel Farage had important effects. Controlling for the influence of other predictors, positive images of the leaders of the Leave campaign significantly enhanced the likelihood of voting to exit the EU.

Finally, we see that the variable measuring judgements of being left behind economically does not have a significant direct effect on how people voted. This is largely because the other measures capture this sense of being left behind, which is at root an indicator of the costs and benefits of continued EU membership. Overall, our statistical model fits the data very well – the estimated (McKelvey) R^2 equals .90 and 93 per cent of voters are correctly classified by the analysis, an 86 per cent reduction in prediction error. These summary statistics testify that the model provides an excellent statistical explanation of why respondents voted as they did.

Which predictor variables had the strongest effects on referendum voting? Since the binomial logit model of the referendum vote has a nonlinear functional form, interpretation of the effects of predictor variables is not straightforward (Long and Freese 2014). Accordingly, to illustrate the explanatory power of various predictor variables, we assess the impact of a change in a predictor variable from its minimum to its maximum value on the probability of casting a Leave vote while holding all other predictors at their mean values. Figure 7.8 shows that the economics–international influence and immigration–terrorism benefit–cost variables had the strongest effects on referendum voting. As the former moved from negative (very high costs, very low benefits of leaving) to positive (very low costs, very high benefits of leaving), the probability of voting Leave increased by fully .88 points (on a 0–1 scale). The latter also was very powerful – as benefit–cost calculations regarding immigration and terrorism moved from negative to positive, the likelihood of voting Leave increased by .75 points. People who judged that regaining control of immigration was a benefit of leaving the EU were very likely to vote to leave.

Risk perceptions worked as expected as well. Changing perceptions of risks associated with leaving the EU from their minimum to their maximum value reduced the probability of voting for Brexit by .71. This suggests that people's risk orientations were very influential in the

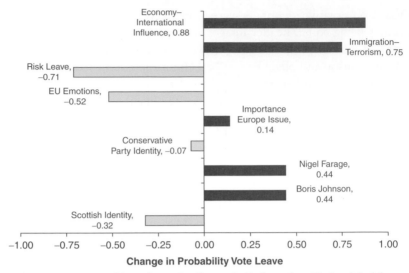

Figure 7.8 Impact of Significant Predictors in Referendum Voting Model on Probability of Voting Leave.

referendum, and thus it could be argued that Remain was correct in its assiduous efforts to amplify voters' apprehensions about the dangers of leaving the EU. Unfortunately for the Remain side, however, the effects of 'Project Fear' – powerful as they were – fell short of being able to change the overall result.

Emotional reactions to membership also exerted sizeable effects. Shifting from purely negative emotions about EU membership to purely positive ones reduced the probability of a Brexit ballot by .52 points. This suggests that the Remain camp might well have been wise to devote more attention to making the positive case for EU membership and trying to galvanize positive emotions about the country's EU membership rather than focusing so heavily on the negative consequences of a Brexit.

The cues provided by Nigel Farage and Boris Johnson were influential too – in both cases, as feelings about these two leading figures in the Leave campaign moved from negative to positive along the 0–10 'likeability' scale, the probability of voting Leave increased by .44 points. Viewed in this light, the UKIP leader was not a toxic asset for the Leave camp. On the contrary, by having both Johnson and Farage as leaders of two different Leave campaigns the Leavers

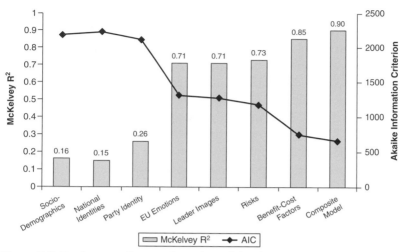

Figure 7.9 Explanatory Power of Rival Models of Voting in the EU Referendum.

were able to maximize their support among different groups of Eurosceptic voters.

Other effects were less powerful. Scottish identity reduced the likelihood of voting to leave by .32 points, while rating Europe as an important issue increased it by .14 points. The influence of Conservative partisanship was very weak, reducing the probability of a Leave vote by .07 points – a reflection of the extent to which the party was divided over the issue.

Figure 7.9 presents a comparison of the ability of different groups of explanatory variables to account for how people voted. The figure displays estimated R^2 and AIC values, measures of how well the models fit the data, for several models of the vote that use various combinations of predictors. When considering the numbers it is helpful to keep in mind that larger R^2 and smaller AIC values indicate that a model has greater explanatory power compared to its rivals.

As shown, the benefit–costs model dominates its competitors, with the largest R^2 (.85) and the smallest AIC (748.35). Other relatively powerful models include the risk assessment model (R^2 = .73), the emotional reactions to the EU model (R^2 = .71) and the leader cues model (R^2 = .71). The remaining models have much smaller R^2s and considerably larger AICs. Therefore, explanations that look only at the influence of party identification, national identities and people's background characteristics are weaker, with R^2 of .26, .15 and .16, respectively. Note also that the composite model that specifies all of the predictor variables (see Table 7.2 above) has better fit statistics (R^2 = .90, AIC = 658.02) than any of its sub-models. This finding testifies that the strongest explanation of referendum voting is provided by the composite model that incorporates all of the predictor variables. Several different factors worked together to drive referendum voting.

What influenced people's assessments of the benefits and costs? Table 7.3 steps back from the vote and examines the effects of various predictor variables on the benefit–cost scales, the two most important predictors in the vote model. In addition to predictors from the vote model, we also include a variable measuring negative attitudes towards immigration and a variable tapping perceptions that Britain has lost control of its economy to the EU.

Both models in Table 7.3 have strong explanatory power, with R^2 values of .69 and .75, respectively. The results show that although voters' impressions of Cameron and Corbyn did not directly influence the vote, the images of the two leaders exerted indirect effects by working to shape voters' benefit–cost evaluations of a Brexit decision. Feeling positively towards Cameron and Corbyn nudged people towards thinking that leaving the EU would bring fewer benefits and more costs, although the effects were significantly stronger for Cameron than Corbyn in the case of economic–international influence calculations. Predictably, if people felt positively about the two Leave leaders, Boris Johnson and Nigel Farage, this had the opposite effect – they were more likely to appreciate the benefits of a Brexit and less likely to think there were burdensome costs.

The partisanship measures show that Labour, Conservative and Liberal Democrat party identifications cued voters in expected ways, increasing perceptions of the benefits and reducing perceptions of the costs of remaining in the EU. Interestingly, the effects Conservative partisanship were weak, unlike those of Labour and the Liberal Democrat partisanship. This was probably because the Tories were so divided on the issue, and this served to weaken the ability of Conservative partisanship to cue voters about costs and benefits of membership. Finally, there is evidence that the Remain campaign affected voters' assessments of benefits and costs, whereas the Leave campaign appeared to have not to be influential in this regard. However, the Remain

Table 7.3 OLS Regression Analyses of Predictors of Perceived Benefits and Costs of Leaving the EU

Predictor	Benefits–Costs of Leaving EU			
	Economy and International Influence		Immigration– Terrorism	
	ß	s.e.	ß	s.e.
Negative Attitudes towards				
Immigration	.227***	.013	.474***	.020
EU Control of UK Economy	.140***	.023	.204***	.036
Left Behind in Economy	.007	.052	.012	.018
Party Leader Images				
Cameron	−.046***	.004	−.063***	.006
Corbyn	−.029***	.004	−.051***	.006
Farage	.039***	.005	.062***	.007
Johnson	.051***	.004	.082***	.007
Partisanship				
Conservative	−.044*	.028	−.093*	.042
Labour	−.090***	.026	−.133**	.040
Liberal Democrat	−.141***	.040	−.199**	.061
UKIP	−.050†	.038	−.092	.059
SNP	.020	.063	.006	.097
National Identity				
English	.042*	.021	.091**	.032
Scottish	−.098*	.047	−.085	.072
Welsh	.062	.052	.145*	.081
European	−.138*	.061	−.238**	.094
Other	−.067†	.046	.049	.071
Campaign Contact				
Remain Campaign	−.026*	.012	−.029†	.019
Leave Campaign	−.013	.018	.005	.027
Socio-Demographic:				
Age	.001	.001	.002*	.001
University Education	−.041*	.020	−.039†	.030
Gender	.006	.018	.018	.028
Social Class	−.024**	.009	−.023*	.013
Constant	−.020	.052	−.137†	.080
R² =	.69		.75	
N = 1,736				

Note: *** = p ≤ .001; ** = p ≤ .01; * = p ≤ .05; † = p ≤ .10, one-tailed test.
High scores on benefit–cost factors indicate pro-Leave perceptions.

campaign effect is very weak and so it is difficult to draw conclusions that one campaign had a bigger effect than the other when measured by campaign contact.

As noted above, with the exception of viewing oneself as Scottish, national identities did not directly influence the referendum vote. However, these identities did have a variety of modest but significant effects on benefit–cost evaluations. English identifiers were significantly more likely than those who viewed themselves as British to emphasize the benefits rather than the costs of exiting the EU. The opposite was true for those who saw themselves as Scottish or European. Welsh identifiers were an intermediate case; they were no different from British identifiers regarding the economic-influence and benefit–cost evaluations, but they were significantly more likely to have positive evaluations of immigration–terrorism if the UK left the EU.

Negative attitudes towards immigration had highly significant effects on both types of benefit–cost assessments. People who held negative attitudes about immigration were more likely than other people to extol the benefits of Brexit and to minimize the costs of leaving the EU. This effect was not only true for the immigration–terrorism factor but also for the economy–international influence factor. Perceptions that Britain's economic sovereignty had been lost to the EU mattered as well. Again, the effects are as hypothesized: those who believed the EU had seized control of the British economy were more likely than others to appreciate the benefits and minimize the costs of Brexit.

Finally, socio-demographic characteristics had noteworthy effects. As Table 7.3 shows, university graduates and those in higher social grades were significantly less likely to see the benefits of leaving the EU than were other people. In contrast, older voters were more likely to judge that Brexit would have benefits by helping to control immigration and reducing the threat of terrorism. Gender differences in benefit–cost assessments were small and insignificant.

What influenced people's perceptions of risk, the third most important predictor of how they voted at the referendum? Our statistical analyses show that the model fits the data very well, with the R^2 indicating that 69 per cent of the variance in risk assessments is explained (see Table 7.4). Two highly significant predictors in this model are negative attitudes towards immigration and perceptions that Britain no longer controls its own economy. Negative attitudes towards

Table 7.4 *OLS Regression Analysis of Predictors of Perceived Risks of Leaving the EU*

Predictor	ß	s.e.
Negative Attitudes towards		
Immigration	–.726***	.077
EU Control of UK Economy	–.722***	.139
Left Behind in Economy	–.213**	.071
Party Leader Images		
Cameron	.223***	.024
Corbyn	.143***	.024
Farage	–.200***	.027
Johnson	–.216***	.026
Partisanship		
Conservative	.412**	.163
Labour	.463**	.156
Liberal Democrat	.464*	.236
UKIP	–.115	.226
SNP	.089	.373
National Identity		
English	–.118	.123
Scottish	.356†	.278
Welsh	–.330	.312
European	.710*	.363
Other	–.139	.272
Campaign Contact		
Remain Campaign	.118†	.072
Leave Campaign	–.031	.106
Socio-Demographics		
Age	–.023***	.003
University Education	.046	.117
Gender	–.030	.108
Social Class	.068	.051
Constant	6.769***	.307

$R^2 = .56$
N = 1,780

Note: *** = $p \le .001$; ** = $p \le .01$; * = $p \le .05$; † = $p \le .10$, one-tailed test. Risk assessment scores vary from 0 to 10, with higher scores indicating greater perceived risks of leaving the EU.

immigration tended to dampen the perception that leaving the EU would be risky. This was also true of perceptions that Britain had lost control of its economy to the European Union.

Leader images were highly significant predictors of risk orientations as well. As anticipated, positive feelings about Cameron and Corbyn were associated with greater perceived risks of a Brexit. In contrast, if people felt positively towards Farage and Johnson, they were less likely to perceive Brexit as a risky proposition. Partisan identifications were at work too – Conservative, Labour and Liberal Democrat identifiers tended to think that the risks of leaving the EU were higher than did other party identifiers or non-identifiers.

Of the remaining predictors of risk assessments, feelings of being left behind economically have a statistically significant negative effect. This means that, as expected, people who judge themselves to be economically marginalized were more likely to minimize the risks associated with Brexit. It will be recalled that this variable did not influence the Brexit vote directly in Table 7.3, but this shows that it had an indirect influence by changing the way voters evaluated the risks of leaving the EU. As for national identities, the only significant identify was 'European': those who saw themselves as European rather than British were more likely to believe that exiting the EU would entail substantial risks. Among socio-demographics, age has a highly significant impact, with younger people being more likely to emphasize the risk of Brexit. Education, gender and social class are not influential. In the next section, we use the results of the multivariate analyses of referendum voting to consider a factor that might have been particularly important for pushing the country into a Brexit.

The 'Boris Effect'

The findings that we have presented so far reveal how a wide variety of factors worked to shape the decisions that voters made in the EU referendum. Some of these factors, such as people's attitudes towards immigration and their national identities, were established features of the psychology of the electorate well before the referendum campaign began. As such, their effects on the referendum vote were 'baked in' before the campaign began. However, this is not true for the cueing effects from political leaders. The way leader cues played depended, to a substantial extent, on how they were presented to voters during the campaign. As we have seen, leader images had a variety of strong effects in the models of forces that influenced referendum voting.

Of the country's political leaders, it is the effects associated with Boris Johnson, the high-profile, outspoken former mayor of London, that are particularly interesting. Unlike Nigel Farage, Johnson had supported the country's EU membership for many years and his conversion to the Brexit cause was a surprise to some of his colleagues, not least Cameron. Johnson announced his decision immediately after Cameron had announced the date of the referendum and he was quickly designated as an unofficial leader of the Leave forces. Johnson proceeded to campaign vigorously and the media gave him enormous publicity.

Our analysis above has already revealed Boris's potential impact on the referendum outcome; feelings about him had strong and statistically significant effects in the models of forces that affected the vote and this suggests that he was a major asset for the Leave camp. It is also noteworthy that Johnson was relatively popular, with an average likability rating of 4.5 on the 0–10 scale compared to 4.2 for Corbyn, 3.5 for Cameron and only 3.2 for Farage. During an interview with the authors, Johnson's influence was recognized by Andrew Cooper, chief pollster for the Remain campaign: '[d]uring the referendum campaign it was clear from all our tracking research that Boris was having a big impact. This came through clearly in the focus groups and in our (weekly, twice-weekly, then daily) polling, Boris invariably came top on the question of which politician has made the most persuasive impact (Cameron invariably came second).'

To learn more about the strength of the 'Boris effect', we can use the results our statistical analyses to calculate how the probability of voting Leave varied according to people's feelings about the affable Conservative politician. In addition to determining how feelings about Johnson influenced the vote directly, we also take indirect effects into account by calculating how these feelings affected people's calculations of the benefits and costs of a Brexit, as well as their assessments of the associated risks. We vary feelings about Johnson across the 0–10 likability scale holding predictors other than the benefit–cost and risk variables at their mean values. The results are shown in Figure 7.10.

Feelings about Johnson had very strong effects on the probability of casting a Leave ballot. For voters who really disliked him, the

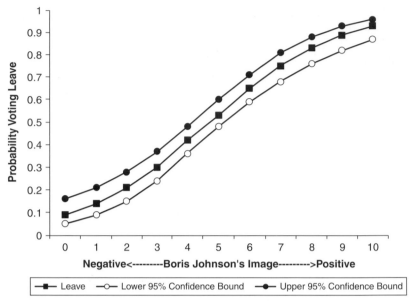

Figure 7.10 How Feelings about Boris Johnson Affected Probability of Voting Leave.

probability of voting Leave was only .09. However, it climbed sharply as people's feelings about Boris became increasingly positive. For those at top end of his likability scale, people who gave him a '10 out of 10', the probability of a Leave vote was fully .93. Even among people who gave Johnson a mid-point score of 5 on the 0–10 likability scale, the probability of voting Leave was .53. Since over half (50.5 per cent) of the voters accorded Johnson a score of 5 or more, this points to his ability to tip the outcome in Leave's favour and his important role in making the Brexit decision matter. These numbers indicate that over half the active electorate were at least lukewarm about the former mayor and, if they were otherwise average, they had a better than even probability of voting Leave. Although the close division of the vote on 23 June means that while it is not possible to conclude that 'it was Boris was wot won it' – as documented above, many factors influenced the vote – his boisterous and widely covered presence on the campaign trail was clearly very advantageous to the Leave side, whose only other salient leader was the much less popular Nigel Farage.[7]

Conclusion: The Brexit Choice

In this chapter we have investigated forces that shaped the choices that voters made in the historic 2016 referendum on UK membership of the EU. When the results are aggregated to the constituency level, we have seen how, outside of London, voters in a large majority of constituencies throughout England and Wales opted to leave the EU. Although Leave voting was greater among older, less well-educated 'white English' people in lower social grades, it would be an error to conclude that Brexit lacked broad-based support: public support for leaving the EU was relatively widespread. In the end only London, Northern Ireland, Scotland and the university towns were bastions of support for Remain. Elsewhere across the UK Brexit was the preferred option in most locales.

Our analyses of the vote have stressed the importance of people's calculations of the perceived benefits and costs of Brexit, their assessments of risks and their emotional reactions to EU membership. In addition, people's images of the individual political leaders on both the Remain and Leave sides had a variety of sizeable direct and indirect effects. Feelings about Boris Johnson were especially important. Although the multiplicity of forces at work means that it is not possible to conclude 'No Boris, No Brexit', it is clear that the widely unexpected presence of London's former mayor at the heart of the Leave campaign was a major asset for the Leave side.

The country's political parties played a significant role, too, although their effects were weaker and largely worked indirectly by shaping the evaluations of the benefits, costs and risks that people were thinking about. Other forces were working further back in the causal chain but nonetheless helping to shape the referendum vote; negative public attitudes towards immigration, as well as a feeling that Britain had lost sovereignty to the EU, and feelings of national identity, all influenced how people were assessing the benefits, costs and risks of the vote. Feelings of being economically marginalized or 'left behind' were also important, working indirectly to minimize the likelihood that people would see Brexit as a risk. People's age, education and social status also had effects, though not as strong as the factors already discussed.

As we saw in Chapter 3, during the referendum campaign itself Remainers focused almost exclusively on a narrative of economic risk. They deployed a veritable 'Davos A-list' of world leaders, politicians, civil servants, business moguls and celebrities to try to convince voters of the negative economic consequences that would ensue if they voted for a Brexit. 'Project Fear', as it came to be called, portrayed Brexit as an extremely risky, economically self-destructive and ill-advised course of action – a 'leap into the unknown'. Leavers, meanwhile, countered with dire warnings about how a vote to remain in the EU would mean uncontrolled immigration and vulnerable national borders, increase the threat of terrorism, threaten the country's sovereignty and further erode democratic accountability. What do our findings say about this campaign? Although the dark scenarios advanced by Prime Minister Cameron and his allies were insufficient to secure a victory for Remain, this does mean that their claims had no effect on voters. As our analyses have shown, both economic- and immigration-focused benefit–cost calculations had strong effects on the referendum choice. Combined with risk assessments, emotional reactions to the EU and leader image cues, these calculations were important immediate forces driving voting in the EU referendum. The narrow Brexit decision voters made on 23 June thus reflected a complex, cross-cutting mix of calculations, emotions and cues. In the next chapter we conduct analyses that help us to evaluate the pros and cons of this decision.

8 | *The Consequences of Brexit*

The previous chapters have told the story of the Brexit referendum, locating its origins in a variety of long-term political and economic developments in Britain and Europe. In the immediate aftermath of the referendum result, markets reacted quickly and the value of the pound plummeted along with the stock market. However, this reaction was not sustained for very long and the stock market recovered to its pre-referendum levels fairly quickly and the value of the pound started to rise again, although it did not achieve pre-referendum levels. As new economic data emerged in the immediate months after the referendum, it became apparent that consumer confidence was still buoyant and unemployment continued to fall. The dire warnings of an immediate economic crisis following a vote to leave had been proved wrong. Moreover, a few months after the vote the Bank of England's chief economist would publicly admit that his profession had both failed to foresee the 2008 financial crisis and misjudged the impact of the Brexit vote, with the latter being traced to a failure of economic models to cope with 'irrational behaviour'.[1] That said, concerns were expressed that Brexit would have serious long-term consequences for investment in Britain and could damage trade relationships in Europe in the long run.

After the vote it also became clear that the Government had made few preparations for a Leave vote, and so Whitehall had to start work on the mammoth task of separating Britain from the EU. Once installed as the new Prime Minister, Theresa May, who had advocated a Remain vote, created a new government department for 'Exiting the European Union' and put three prominent Eurosceptics in charge of preparing for the negotiations with the EU. Responsibility for managing the effort was divided between Boris Johnson in the Foreign Office, David Davis, who was put in charge of the new Ministry for Exiting the EU, and Liam Fox, the Secretary of State for International Trade.

Attention then switched to the long-term effects of the Brexit vote, although these still remain uncertain.

The aim of this chapter is to examine the longer-term economic and political consequences of Brexit. The process of leaving the European Union will take many years and the full consequences will not be known for a long time. Nonetheless, it is possible to examine plausible scenarios about what is likely to happen to the economy, to society and to British politics more generally. As discussed in Chapter 6, two key issues in the referendum were the economy and immigration, so we examine the likely consequences of Brexit for both of these issues. Subsequently, we consider the influence of the EU on democratic governance in Britain to assess the likely effects of Brexit on democracy and politics more generally. We begin by looking at the likely economic consequences of the UK leaving the European Union.

The Economic Consequences of Brexit

In April 2016 the UK Treasury produced a report on the long-term effects of UK membership and the consequences that might follow from leaving the EU (HM Treasury 2016). It examined three alternative scenarios for the likely consequences for the economy following Brexit. The report attracted considerable attention during the referendum campaign, when, amid many other warnings, George Osborne quoted a prediction of one of the scenarios that suggested the average family would lose £4,300 per year by 2030 if Britain left the EU.

The three scenarios were based, in part, on existing relationships between the EU and non-member states. The first, referred to as the 'Norwegian' option, was based on the assumption that Britain would join the European Economic Area (EEA) in much the same way as Norway. The latter is not an EU member state but has full access to the single market and has to pay for this privilege by contributing to the EU budget and accepting free movement of labour. The second scenario is based on the option of negotiating a bilateral agreement with the EU in a similar way to Switzerland and Canada. For example, the Comprehensive Trade Agreement between the EU and Canada lowers tariff barriers, co-ordinates trade regulations and promotes cooperation, but it does not involve free movement of labour. The third scenario is referred to as the 'WTO' option arising from trade agreements negotiated by the World Trade Organization over many years between a large number of countries that are designed to reduce tariffs and other barriers to trade.

The Treasury document provided an overall evaluation of these scenarios and concluded that:

The analysis in this document shows that under all 3 models, the UK's economic openness and interconnectedness would be reduced. Trade and investment flows would be lower. The UK would be permanently poorer if it left the EU and adopted any of these models. Productivity and GDP per person would be lower in all these alternative scenarios, as the costs substantially outweigh any potential benefit of leaving the EU. (HM Treasury 2016: 8)

Estimates of the costs of leaving derived from the three scenarios suggested that the annual loss of household incomes after 15 years would be £2,600 for the EEA option, £4,300 for the bilateral arrangement mentioned in the campaign and £5,200 for the WTO alternative. The report acknowledged that the estimates were subject to considerable uncertainty but reported them as being central tendency forecasts calculated from modelling of each of the alternatives. Thus, the overall story emerging from the report was one of significant long-run economic losses resulting from the Brexit decision.

To evaluate these forecasts, we have to look closely at the modelling upon which they are based. These forecasts were made using so-called gravity models of trade relationships between countries (Head and Mayer 2013). These models have been used in economic geography for many years and predict that trade flows between countries are dependent on their incomes, the size of their populations, their geographical proximity and their cultural similarities. The latter two considerations include measures of the physical distance between countries and variables identifying whether they share a common language and have a common border (HM Treasury 2016: 158). The basic idea is that countries with similar standards of living and close geographical and cultural ties are more likely to trade with each other.

The Treasury modelling proceeded by estimating the effects on trade of Brexit and then feeding the estimates from the gravity models into a more comprehensive econometric model called NiGEM to calculate the long-run impact on GDP. The NiGEM model was developed at the National Institute for Economic and Social Research and is used extensively by Governments and economic forecasting agencies.[2] The scenarios were forecast up to 15 years into the future on the grounds that the long-run consequences of Brexit should be known by then. This whole approach represents current practice in econometric modelling, but it can be criticized as suffering from three serious problems that cast considerable doubt on the validity of the forecasts.

The first problem is that the Treasury estimates of the gravity models provide a poor forecast of trade flows, an argument that has now been accepted by orthodox economists. In a comprehensive analysis of the Treasury's gravity model estimates, a report from the Centre for Business Research at the University of Cambridge concluded that:

Gravity model analysis by HM Treasury of the potential impact of various outcomes for trade outside the EU is examined and found wanting. The gravity model approach is replicated but with data only from the UK's main trade partners and not from a large number of emerging economies with which the UK does little trade. The results suggest that the approach is unstable but if anything the impact of EU membership on UK trade is much less than suggested by the Treasury. (Gudgin et al. 2017: 1)

The second problem is uncertainty, something that has been known about for a long time. It is really impossible to project economic growth forecasts some 15 years into the future with any chance of obtaining reliable results because there is so much uncertainty about how the economy will develop. All forecasts are based on projections of what has happened in the past and these become increasingly uncertain the further they look into the future. To illustrate this point, very few economists forecast the financial crash and the subsequent Great Recession that had such a major impact on the world economy from 2008 onwards. Any economic forecaster working in 2006 who made the prediction that interest rates in Britain would fall to near zero in real terms by 2008 and stay that way for many years would have been regarded as deluded. But this is exactly what happened.

The great economist John Maynard Keynes made the following observation about the problem of uncertainty in the 1930s:

If we speak frankly, we have to admit that our basis of knowledge for estimating the yield ten years hence of a railway, a copper mine, a textile factory, the goodwill of a patent medicine, an Atlantic liner, a building in the City of London, amounts to little and sometimes to nothing. (Keynes 1936: 149–50)

The third problem is more general and questions the validity of the theories that underpin the econometric modelling. The unorthodox economist Hyman Minsky (1982, 1986), writing well before the financial crisis, argued that the problems of instability and recessions in capitalist economies have not been solved by contemporary theory. As his biographer points out, Minsky deals harshly with current theories explaining their failure in the following terms:

The neoclassical approach that provides the foundation for mainstream macroeconomics is applicable only to an imaginary world, an economy focused on market exchange based on a barter paradigm. Money and finance are added to the model as an afterthought – they really do not matter. Because an invisible hand supposedly guides rational individuals who have perfect foresight towards an equilibrium in which all resources are efficiently allocated, there is little role for government to play. The current crisis has shown this approach to be irrelevant for the analysis of the economy in which we live. (Wray 2016: 60)

Minsky's argument is that economies are unstable because periods of prosperity create the conditions for subsequent recessions. The reasoning is that during an upswing in the business cycle, firms and banks become more and more optimistic and take on riskier financial commitments. They commit larger portions of their expected revenue to debt service and at the same time lenders accept smaller down payments and poorer-quality collateral for their loans. These developments increase financial fragility, and when inevitably income flows turn out to be lower than expected and interest rates rise, lenders react by curtailing their loans. At the same time debtors cut back on spending and in some cases are forced into a fire sale of assets in order to meet their debts This produces a financial crisis that then triggers a recession. In 2008 the problem was made much worse by years of deregulation and the creation of very risky financial instruments by banks and other financial institutions, many of them held offshore and so subject to no effective regulation. This meant that when the crash came financial institutions had little in the way of adequate reserves to stabilize the situation. Governments had to step in and save them from collapse to prevent the entire financial system from a catastrophic meltdown. 'Too big to fail' was the order of the day.

The dominant view in the economics profession is that the economy is fundamentally stable and self-correcting and so will be resistant to shocks of the kind that produced the Great Recession (Blaug 1962). This view is grounded in 'general equilibrium' theory that underpins the NiGEM model and pervades contemporary economic reasoning in the form of a belief in the 'invisible hand'. General Equilibrium theory originated in the nineteenth century and argues that a unique equilibrium can be found in the economy that maximizes the welfare of all participants (Arrow and Debreu 1954). However, subsequent theoretical work has shown that this result requires very stringent assumptions that cannot be met in any real-world economy (Debreu 1974). As Offer and Söderberg put it: 'The invisible hand is magical thinking ...' (2016: 15). Belief in a hidden stability in the economy is largely a matter of faith rather than science. Of course, debates about the stability of the macro-economy are highly contentious but, if Minsky is correct, then the basic assumptions underlying the Treasury forecasts are unreliable, making projections 15 years into the future highly problematic.

To get a handle on the likely long-run economic consequences of Brexit, it is incumbent on forecasters to be much more modest about what can be reliably asserted about the future. One approach would be to look at the UK's economic performance over a long period of time in the past, and then try to assess what this means for the future of the UK economy once it is outside of the EU. The United Kingdom joined what was then called the European Community in 1973, so we can get some idea of how membership changed things by looking at the performance of its economy up to the early 1970s and then examining what happened after accession. If there was a discernible acceleration in growth and prosperity following accession, then it is reasonable to infer that joining the EU brought significant additional benefits to the UK economy. If so, Brexit may have damaging economic consequences for the country even if it is difficult to precisely estimate the size of these effects.

A further point is that if Britain's membership had no discernible effects on long-run growth after 1973, that throws considerable doubt on the pessimistic scenarios set out in the Treasury analysis. This is a much more modest exercise than trying to forecast what will happen in the year 2030. It is nonetheless a difficult one because it is necessary to take into account many other factors that influence the growth of the UK economy in addition to trade relationships with the EU. We take up this task in the next section.

The Effects of EU Membership on the British Economy

To calculate the effects of UK membership of the European Union it is necessary to specify a model that takes into account a number of important variables that can influence long-run growth. Economic growth has been the subject of systematic study since at least the eighteenth century. In his famous book *The Wealth of Nations*, first published in 1776, Adam Smith wrote:

The annual produce of the land and labour of any nation can be increased in its value by no other means, but by increasing either the number of its productive labourers, or the productive powers of those labourers, who had before been employed. (Smith 1976: 343)

Adam Smith set the context of subsequent work on growth by focusing on labour and capital inputs into the process. In recent years there has been a veritable explosion of research into the topic and the influence of many factors have been investigated (Acemoglu 2009). Models using cross-national comparisons over time have been developed to estimate the effects of Government spending (Barro and Lee 1994), religious traditions and the existence of political rights (Barro 1999), economic openness and trade (Sachs and Warner 1995), the effectiveness of different types of capitalism (Hall and Jones 1999), legally enforced protections for property rights (Acemoglu et al. 2001), the role of political institutions (North 1990), the impact of social capital (Knack and Keefer 1997; Whiteley 2000), the extent of market freedoms (De Haan et al. 2004) and the role of ideas and culture (McCloskey 2015).

In an influential paper Levene and Renelt (1992) conducted a meta-analysis of the empirical literature on economic growth and argued that few of the variables tested in cross-national analyses were robust predictors. Thus, many effects failed to hold up in varying specifications of the models tested over different time periods and in different sets of countries. However, their analysis did show that there were some stable and robust predictors, including capital investment, levels of employment and investment in human capital in the form of education and training, trade openness and a variable called 'catch-up'. The latter refers to more rapid growth among countries with relatively low standards of living as they copy the technological and organizational innovations of their richer rivals. Trade openness is a strong predictor in these analyses and it suggests that if barriers to trade are created between Britain and the European Union this will reduce long-run prosperity.

Currently, there is no consensus model of economic growth and to some extent the sources of growth remain a mystery (see Helpman 2004). However, there is agreement that in addition to trade openness, education and training play important roles in raising productivity (Romer 1994). Furthermore, capital investment that increases productive capacity and raises the skills of the workforce has been recognized as an important driver of growth ever since Adam Smith (Barro and Sala-i-Martin 2004).

Based on these results we specify a relatively parsimonious model of economic growth in Britain using these robust predictors, and test it using data from the Penn World Tables. This database provides estimates of annual rates of real growth of GDP across a large number of countries over the post-war period (Heston et al. 2006). The time series data for Britain runs from 1950 to 2014 in the most recent version of the database (Feenstra et al. 2015). The use of annual observations that correct for inflation focuses attention on long-run growth rather than short-run fluctuations in economic activity, although it is important to take these into account as well as key shocks to the system during this period. Thus, the modelling examines growth in real GDP at constant national prices over this 64-year period.[3]

We hypothesize that growth is driven by capital investment, levels of employment, which refers specifically to capacity utilization of the economy, an index of the quality of human capital and two indicators of the openness of the economy. The latter are the value of exports and imports combined together, which provides an overall measure of how open the economy is, together with the pound–dollar exchange rate that measures the price of exports.[4] A rising pound relative to the dollar makes imports more expensive and exports cheaper, and a falling pound has the opposite effect. Since the 1920s it has been argued that a high value for the pound depresses economic activity, since a reduction in the demand for exports creates unemployment, which is not offset by the rising demand for imports since this generates employment abroad rather than in Britain (Keynes 1925; Dow 1998).

This relatively simple model is used to investigate both the short-term and long-term impact of the predictor variables on the change in real GDP. The model incorporates lagged versions of these variables

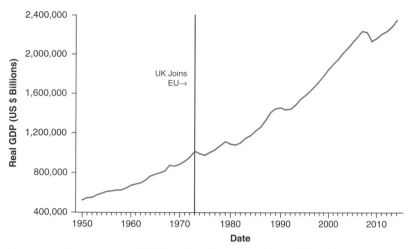

Figure 8.1 Trends in Real GDP in Britain, 1950–2014 ($US Billions).
Source: Penn World Tables.

in levels to capture long-run effects, together with changes in them to capture short-run effects. In addition, we include various dummy variables that measure the effects of major economic events that occurred over this period. Figure 8.1 charts trends in the gross domestic product in Britain in constant prices over the period 1950 to 2014 using data from the Penn World Tables. The figure shows that growth was quite steady over much of this period, averaging just less than 2.5 per cent per annum, subject to some fluctuations. This meant that standards of living in Britain were about five times higher at the end of the period compared with the beginning.

Figure 8.1 suggests that growth was influenced by the trebling of oil prices following the Arab–Israeli war of 1973, which stoked very high levels of inflation in Britain and disrupted the world economy. It also appears that growth was influenced by the 'monetarist experiment' which occurred after the election of Margaret Thatcher's Conservative Government in 1979. Her Government broke with traditional Keynesian methods of macro-economic management and embarked on an experiment designed to squeeze inflation out of the system by raising interest rates to very high levels. This followed monetarist doctrines that argued that inflation can be controlled entirely by restricting the supply of money (Friedman and Schwartz 1963). It meant imposing austerity on an economy that was already in recession and in the end it failed and was abandoned (Desai 1981). But, as Figure 7.1 suggests, the monetarist experiment had the effect of slowing growth in the early 1980s.

A third shock to the system occurred in 1992, when John Major's Government attempted to tie the value of the pound to the European Exchange Rate Mechanism (ERM), the predecessor of the euro single-currency zone. The aim was to lay the groundwork for Britain to join the eurozone at a later stage. Yet the Government was forced to abandon the ERM on 'Black Wednesday', 16 September 1992, after a spectacular run on the pound took place in the financial markets. The currency crisis had a large negative effect on support for the Conservative Government and it seriously eroded confidence in the ability of Mr Major and his colleagues to manage the economy effectively (Clarke et al. 2004). Yet another shock was the impact of the Great Recession of 2008–12, the effects of which are very apparent in Figure 8.1.

Table 8.1 summarizes three models of the effects of various predictors on growth. In these analyses growth is measured by the change in real GDP in billions of US dollars. The first model (Model A) focuses only on the five key drivers of growth discussed earlier. The first predictor in this model is lagged levels of real GDP, which has a negative impact on the change in GDP over time. This is the familiar reversion to the mean process that can be found in many economic relationships. It indicates that there is a tendency for a large increase in the level of GDP in a given year to be followed by a smaller increase in the following year, producing a negative relationship between the lagged level of GDP and the subsequent change in GDP. This means that growth does not continuously accelerate over time.[5]

The second predictor is the rate of employment, and it shows that an increase in the percentage of the workforce employed in the short run has a positive impact on growth. This is consistent with Okun's law, a well-established relationship between employment and growth in advanced industrial economies. In his original paper Arthur Okun (1962) suggested that a 1 per cent rise in employment in the USA would produce a 2 per cent rise in potential GDP, while acknowledging that this was likely to vary between countries and over time. The estimates in Table 8.1 suggest that an increase of 1 million in the numbers employed in Britain in a given year would increase the GDP by nearly $35.5 billion. Interestingly, the lagged level of employment

Table 8.1 *Determinants of Growth in Real GDP in Britain, 1950–2014*

Predictors	Model A ∆ Real GDP	Model B ∆ Real GDP	Model C ∆ Real GDP
Real GDP (t–1)	–.34***	–.38***	–.34***
∆ Employment Rate	35,479.3***	32,574.4***	38,797.8***
Employment Rate (t–1)	–1,812.78	–1,158.7	–
∆ Human Capital Index	–210,447***	–2,370,326***	–1,979,935***
Human Capital Index (t–1)	598,880.8***	564,409.5***	509,102***
∆ Capital Stock	.28***	.23**	.22***
Capital Stock (t–1)	–.01	.00	–
∆ Exchange Rate	–144,786.3**	–127,305.7**	–118,717.8**
Exchange Rate (t–1)	–126,598.8**	–177,928.5***	–139,607.4***
∆ Imports plus Exports (Openness)	–42,209.3	–184,751.8	–
Imports plus Exports (t–1)	71,463.8	–17,615.4	–
UK Joined the EU	–21,048.9	–7,334.5	–11,104.5
Oil Crisis 1974–5	–	–29,847.9**	–28,905.2**
Monetarist Experiment 1981–2	–	–21,884.8	–
Sterling Crisis 1993	–	11,089.8	–
Great Recession 2008–12	–	–1,069,343***	–997,642.9***
Adjusted R²	.64	.71	.72
Durbin Autocorrelation χ² Test	.11	.18	.15
Likelihood Ratio ARCH Test	.02	.00	.16
AIC	1,443.8	1,433.4	1,426.4
BIC	1,471.9	1,470.1	1,450.2

Note: *** = p ≤.001; ** = p ≤ .01; * = p ≤ .05, one-tailed test.

does not have a direct effect on economic growth once changes in employment are taken into account. It is the flow rather than the stock of employment that influences growth.

The human capital index in the Penn World Tables builds on the work of Barro (1991) and others who use average years of schooling as an indicator of education and training in developing countries (Barro and Lee 1994). This is a less useful measure in an advanced economy like the UK's, which has compulsory education up to the age of 16. Consequently, it has been suggested that enrolments in higher education are a better measure of human capital in advanced countries (Vandenbussche et al. 2006). However, the human capital index is the standard measure in the Penn World Tables data and so it is included in the modelling. There appears to be a short-run negative effect on growth of changes in the human capital index, but this is an unreliable finding since changes in the index are tiny because it grows very slowly over time.[6] The positive effect of human capital in levels is the key relationship and it shows that investment in education and training has a long-term positive impact on economic growth in Britain.

Changes in capital stock that measure capital investment also have a strong positive impact on economic growth. This is to be expected, although the levels of capital stock do not affect growth in the long run once the changes in investment are taken into account. Again, this is largely because both investment and growth are flows, and once these are taken into account stocks of capital goods need not necessarily influence the latter. This is particularly true if high stocks of physical capital are accompanied by low levels of investment, since in these circumstances capital will become obsolescent and therefore less productive over time.

As the earlier discussion indicated, the two indicators of openness in Model A are the pound/dollar exchange rate and the combined level of imports and exports. The latter capture trade flows and are the focus of attention in the Treasury model discussed earlier. It is noteworthy that the openness measure is not a statistically significant predictor of growth, either in the short or the long run. The UK economy became more open as time went by with greater imports and exports in real terms, but this did not stimulate growth. This casts some doubt on the dire predictions that increases in trade barriers between Britain and the EU after a Brexit will be disastrous for the UK economy.

In contrast to openness, it appears that a high value of the pound relative to the dollar reduces growth both in the short term and in the long term. As the earlier discussion indicated, it has long been recognized that a high value of the pound can reduce exports and increase imports, which, in turn, adversely affects the balance of payments and employment. In the decades before the 1970s Britain's currency was tied to the dollar at a fixed exchange rate, and so Governments regularly introduced austerity measures to try to deal with trade imbalances. They reduced pressure on the exchange rate caused by a balance of payments deficit by deflating the economy to reduce demand for imports with the aim of restoring the balance. Instead of exchange rates acting as an adjustment mechanism, consumer demand was targeted and this reduced growth.

This policy became known as 'Stop–Go' and it had the effect of slowing growth during the period up to the time that Britain abandoned fixed exchange rates in the 1970s (see Pollard 1982). The estimates in Table 8.1 imply that the decline in the value of the pound immediately following the referendum result actually helped to insulate the economy from any adverse short-term consequences of the Brexit vote. This illustrates the point that currency fluctuations appear to be more important than the total volume of trade when it comes to influencing growth.

Of particular interest in Model A is a dummy variable that scores one from 1973 onwards and zero otherwise. This is the year that Britain joined the Common Market, as it was then known. This variable is designed to identify whether there was a permanent increase in growth after Britain joined the EU. The coefficient shows that the effects of this variable were negative but not statistically significant. This suggests that in the long run the UK's membership of the EU made no difference to the rate of economic growth, controlling for the other factors.[7] Undoubtedly, EU membership has caused many changes to the UK's economy and to society more generally, but there is no evidence to suggest that it stimulated economic growth. Overall, Model A fits the data quite well with an adjusted R^2 of .64.

Model B in Table 8.1 includes the four additional economic shocks that were identified earlier. These estimates show that the oil-price crisis of the early 1970s that triggered high inflation and industrial unrest in Britain had a significant negative effect on growth. It is captured in the model with a dummy variable scoring one in 1974 and 1975 and zero otherwise. In contrast, the shocks associated with the monetarist experiment of the early 1980s and the 1992 sterling crisis were not significant, even though they had important political effects at the time. The Great Recession of 2008 to 2012 had a clear negative impact on growth, which is not surprising given that it was the worst economic crisis facing the country since the 1930s. Finally, it is noteworthy that the EU membership dummy variable remains nonsignificant in Model B.

The third model in Table 8.1 (Model C) is the most parsimonious version and includes only the statistically significant predictors from the earlier models. AIC and BIC model selection statistics show that that Model C is preferable to Model A,[8] so the two shocks played important roles in explaining long-run growth. It is important to stress that this is a relatively sparse model of growth aimed at estimating the effect of the UK joining the EU in 1973. The findings suggest that EU membership did not have a long-term influence on economic growth. An additional important finding is that trade openness was not important once the value of the currency is taken into account. In contrast, high values of the pound have historically reduced economic growth.

Taken together, these findings cast considerable doubt on the Treasury forecasts and, if the 64-year period examined has relevance for the future, they suggest that Brexit will not have a large and enduring deflationary effect on the British economy. Bearing in mind that the past may be a poor guide to the future, in so far as our models provide insights, they testify that the negative economic consequences of Brexit are probably exaggerated. We cannot confidently forecast 15 years ahead, as the arguments outlined earlier about the instability of contemporary advanced economies make clear, but if there is another recession waiting in the wings for the UK economy, it is unlikely that it will be caused by Brexit.

One possibility is that the United Kingdom is an exception to the rest of the EU when it comes to membership affecting growth. Recall that a key campaign theme in the 1975 referendum when a large majority voted to remain in the Common Market was that membership would bring increased prosperity because economic growth in the member states at that time was higher than it was in Britain (Butler and Ranney 1994). Figure 8.2 shows rates of growth in all 28 member states in the EU, separating out the pre-accession rates of growth from the post-accession rates. Different countries joined the EU at different points of time, with the original six countries joining in 1958, when the Common Market replaced the European Coal and Steel Community. Subsequently, there were significant enlargements in membership that took place in the early 1970s, the mid 1980s and the early 2000s.

Figure 8.2 shows that post-accession growth was lower than pre-accession growth in a total of 20 of these countries. This is true in

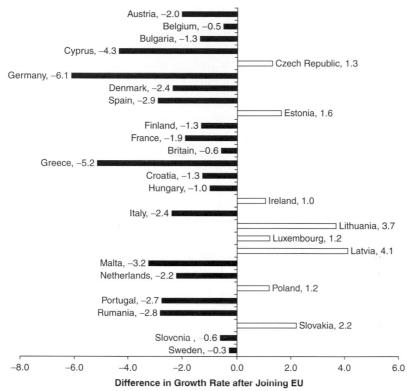

Figure 8.2 Differences in Growth Rate after Joining the European Union, 28 EU Countries.
Source: Penn World Tables.

Germany, a founding member; Denmark, which joined at the same time as the UK in 1973; Spain, which joined in 1986; Finland, which joined in 1995; and finally Romania, which joined in 2007. The eight countries that are exceptions to this pattern include Estonia, Lithuania, Latvia, Poland and Slovakia. These are all ex-communist countries that joined in 2004, more than a decade after the collapse of the Soviet Union and the introduction of democracy and market reforms. Increased growth in the 2000s in these countries could easily be explained by 'catch-up', which is the well-known phenomenon referred to earlier of countries catching up to their rivals by adopting technological and market innovations pioneered by their competitors. Membership of the EU may have facilitated this process but it is unlikely to have caused it.

Economic growth has many determinants and so it would be misleading to argue that EU membership had the effect of slowing growth in most EU member states after they became members. But the important inference that can be made from available evidence is that EU membership did not boost economic growth and prosperity in a way that many people thought might happen when their countries applied to join. The fact that the accession of different countries varied over time means that the slowing of growth was not the product of period effects, that is, events such as the oil-price crisis of the 1970s that might explain such a slowdown across many countries at the same time.

If it is hard to make the case that EU membership stimulated economic growth, it may be different for the other big issue that dominated the 2016 referendum, namely immigration. In Chapter 7 we saw that concerns about immigration had strong effects on the referendum vote, so it is important to assess the implications of Brexit for immigration to Britain in the future. We consider this topic next.

Brexit and Immigration

As we have seen, immigration was a key issue in the 2016 referendum campaign and was also central to explaining why the country eventually voted for Brexit. Claims and counter-claims surrounded this issue, with Leavers in particular arguing that Brexit would enable the UK to curb immigration levels that have been a source of anxiety among voters for many years. But how might Brexit influence immigration? If economic forecasting is difficult, it is even more difficult to forecast patterns of migration. In their recent review of the literature on migration forecasting, Disney and his colleagues conclude that:

[T]here are many social, economic and political drivers which can impact migration flows, making forecasting migration an extremely difficult task. In particular, migration is very susceptible to shock events which are, by their very nature, hard to predict, such as economic cycles, military conflict and policy changes. Changes in migration flows can be subject to extreme short-term fluctuations, thereby making migration forecasts prone to very high levels of error. (Disney et al. 2015: 3)

Migration forecasting has in the past utilized deterministic models that rely on both quantitative and qualitative evidence to make predictions about future trends in immigration and emigration. This approach has been adopted by the Office of National Statistics (ONS) in the UK when forecasting future population trends arising from net migration. In 2014 the ONS concluded that short-term net migration into Britain would be 165,000 per year over the next few years, a forecast that turned out to be quite wide of the mark (ONS 2014). A second approach to forecasting migration uses probabilistic models, which have the advantage of estimating measures of uncertainty associated with any predictions. A common method is to use Autoregressive Moving Average (ARIMA) models of the type pioneered by Box and Jenkins (1976), and sometimes these have been enhanced using Bayesian methods (Bijak 2010). A third approach is to use survey-based expert judgements to derive forecasts (Lutz et al. 2004). Overall, there appears to be no optimal approach to forecasting migration since all of these methods are subject to possibly sizeable errors (Disney et al. 2015).

Figure 8.3 shows long-term trends in immigration to and emigration from Britain involving all countries in the world over the 25 years from 1991 onwards. It can be seen that the two series were running at under 100,000 per year in the early nineties and they largely cancelled each other out. However, by 2015 immigration was running at more than 600,000 a year, over twice as large as emigration, and the gap between the two widened in each successive year. It is hardly surprising, therefore, that immigration became a major issue in the referendum campaign, especially as large numbers of migrants were coming to the UK from other EU member states.

As is well known, Britain is theoretically able to control immigration from outside the European Union but must accept free movement of labour from member countries as long as it remains a member of the EU. Figure 8.4 compares trends in immigration and emigration to and from the EU over the same 25-year period. Once again, in the early 1990s immigration and emigration to and from the EU were running at below 100,000 a year and were largely self-cancelling. Again, however, by 2015 immigration from within the EU was running at nearly 300,000 per year, nearly two and a half times greater than emigration, which was running around 125,000. The gap in net migration has grown rather dramatically since the 2010 general election and was clearly associated with Britain's emergence from the Great Recession.

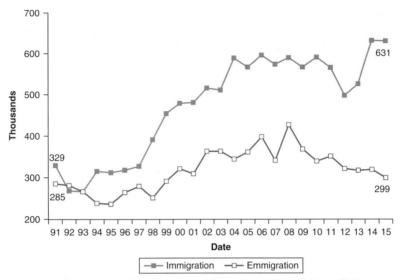

Figure 8.3 Trends in Migration to and from the UK Involving All Countries, 1991–2015.
Source: Office of National Statistics.

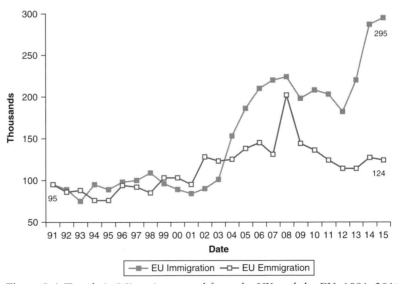

Figure 8.4 Trends in Migration to and from the UK and the EU, 1991–2015.
Source: Office of National Statistics.

It is instructive to observe that in 2015 the gap between immigration and emigration from outside the EU was 161,000 compared with a gap of 171,000 for net migration from the EU. Given that technically Britain can control immigration from outside the EU, we might expect net migration from outside the EU to be significantly lower than from inside the EU. But as Figures 8.3 and 8.4 indicate this is not what the data show. Instead, the two figures are quite similar and suggest that Britain has failed to control net migration when it has been in a position to do so. This carries the implication that leaving the EU may not have a big influence on net migration in the future.

Some insight into future trends in net immigration can be obtained by looking at the relationship between net migration and economic performance. Figures 8.3 and 8.4 suggest that economic recovery may have been responsible for the surge in net migration after 2010. We can test this idea utilizing ARIMA models of net migration from inside and outside the EU to estimate these effects. The 25 years of annual data provide only a rather limited sample, so we use quarterly data on net migration published by the ONS from 2006 to 2016 giving a total of 40 observations altogether.[9]

Table 8.2 displays estimates of net migration from inside and outside the European Union using first-order autoregressive models. These use lagged values of the series at time $t-1$ to forecast current values at time t. The series are clearly non-stationary since they trend upwards over time and so to avoid problems of spurious regression they are differenced in the analyses (Enders 2014). Model A in Table 8.2 shows that lagged net migration is a significant predictor of current net migration from the EU. This means that, not surprisingly, net migration into Britain from the EU is subject to considerable inertia.

The AIC and BIC model selection statistics enable us to compare Model A with Model B, which includes quarterly data on real growth in Britain as a predictor of net migration over the period 1991–2015. This revised model shows that economic growth was a statistically significant positive predictor of net migration from the EU. The model selection statistics are reduced in this revised model, suggesting that economic growth improves the overall fit. This analysis confirms the hypothesis that economic growth was a strong attractor of immigration to the UK from the European Union.

Models C and D in Table 8.2 analyse net migration from outside the EU and once again a first-order autoregressive model (Model C)

Table 8.2 *ARIMA Models of Net Migration to the UK from Inside and Outside the EU*

Predictors	Model A Net Migration from EU	Model B Net Migration from EU	Model C Net Migration from Outside EU	Model D Net Migration from Outside EU
Net Migration from Inside the EU $(t-1)$	.39**	.16	–	–
Net Migration from Outside the EU $(t-1)$	–	–	.43**	.42**
UK Economic Growth (t)	–	6.18**	–	.61
Ljung-Box Q	12.6	15.2	21.9	21.6
AIC	290.7	287.7	287.3	289.2
BIC	295.7	294.3	292.3	295.9

Note: *** = $p < .001$; ** = $p < .01$; * = $p < .05$, one-tailed test.

captures the relationship between current net migration and migration in the previous period. However, when economic growth is included in the specification (Model D), it fails to have a significant impact on net migration to Britain. This result indicates that the attraction of economic growth is significantly more important for EU migrants than it is for non-EU migrants. Arguably, this suggests that Home Office restrictions of various kinds on economic migrants from outside the EU are working. Net migration from outside the EU may be high, but it would be even higher without controls on economic migration.

These findings have important implications for the argument that Britain appears unable to control immigration from outside of the EU and so by implication Brexit will do little to control immigration from inside the EU. Table 8.2 suggests that this conclusion is wrong, since controls on economic migration from EU member states are likely to be effective in reducing immigration if the same rules are applied to the EU as to immigrants from the rest of the world. The question of free movement of labour is likely to be a very difficult issue in the negotiations over Brexit, since it is a central pillar of EU doctrine. However, if the UK Government accepts free movement of labour in the negotiations, economic migration into Britain will probably continue at high levels in the absence of a major shock that severely restricts future growth. Such an outcome would likely ensure that public concern over immigration will continue, providing an ongoing reservoir of support to parties like UKIP that campaign against the EU, the free movement of labour and large-scale immigration more generally.

Having reviewed the likely consequences of Brexit for the two issues that were at the forefront of debate in the EU referendum, in the final section of this chapter we broaden the discussion to investigate the effects of EU membership on the quality of democracy in the UK. Arguably, more than 40 years of membership of the European Union has fundamentally changed Britain's constitution and its politics, and so in this section we investigate the implications of Brexit for the future of democracy in the UK and in the EU more generally.

The European Union, Democracy and Governance

The growth of democracy across the world in the post-Second World War era has been a major topic of research in political science for many years (Dahl 1954, 1961; Lijphart 1977; Mansbridge 1983; Huntingdon 1991; Beetham 1994). The database developed by the World Bank to measure different aspects of governance across the world is very useful in this regard. To facilitate understanding of the role of Government in promoting economic development, the Bank has constructed a series of 'good governance' measures. Currently, there are 20 years of data on these indicators available for a very large number of countries around the world, many of them not democracies.[10] These governance indicators are defined by the Bank as follows:

Voice and accountability – the extent to which a country's citizens are able to participate in selecting their government, as well as freedom of expression, freedom of association and a free media.

Political stability and absence of violence – the likelihood that government will be destabilized or overthrown by unconstitutional or violent means, including politically motivated violence and terrorism.

Government effectiveness – the quality of public services, the quality of the civil service and the degree of its independence from political pressures, the quality of policy formulation and implementation, and the credibility of the government's commitment to such policies.

Regulatory quality – the ability of the government to formulate and implement sound policies and regulations that permit and promote private sector development.

Rule of law – the extent to which agents have confidence in and abide by the rules of society, and in particular the quality of contract enforcement, property rights, the police, and the courts, as well as the likelihood of crime and violence.

Control of corruption – the extent to which public power is exercised for private gain, including both petty and grand forms of corruption, as well as 'capture' of the state by elites and private interests (Kaufmann et al. 2009: 8).

These indicators are constructed from hundreds of sources that represent the views of many different individuals and organizations. The team involved in developing and constructing the indicators use an unobserved components model to create the indicators from the various sources (see Kaufmann et al. 2009). This model is a type of data-reduction technique that extracts latent variables from many different observable variables. The technique produces a set of scales measured in z scores or standard deviations from the overall mean values that are set at zero. This makes them difficult to interpret directly, but the important point is that positive scores indicate above-average performance and negative scores the opposite on each of the scales.

This approach to measuring governance has generated controversies involving both methodological and substantive issues (Apaza 2009). The authors have vigorously defended their approach against critics (Kaufmann et al. 2007) and argue that the indicators provide valuable insights about the performance of political systems across the world, including the evolution of democracy in various countries over time.

With this point in mind we can use these indicators to evaluate the effects of EU membership on the quality of governance in the member states over time, paying particular attention to the UK. Since the first measures appeared in 1996 it is not possible to examine governmental performance prior to the time when many of the EU member states joined the organization. In particular, we cannot examine trends in UK governance prior to 1973. But it is possible to look at trends since 1996 and to see if the governance measures in the EU as a whole are correlated with those in the UK. Such trends and correlations do not establish that changes in the UK governance are the product of EU membership, but they can show if measures of governance in Britain and the EU are converging over time and, in particular, whether they are improving. This is one way of examining if the political project of 'ever closer union' found in the preamble to the 1957 treaty that established the EU has actually worked in practice.

It is possible to go further than this in the case of the 10 eastern European states that joined the EU in 2004, almost half-way through the period for which the good governance indicators are available. For these countries, we can examine the good government measures before and after EU accession to determine if governance has improved since these countries became members. If this is a general pattern for these countries, it suggests that EU membership may have beneficial consequences for the quality of governance.

Has Governance in Britain and the EU Improved Over Time?

The trends in the governance indicators for Britain are illustrated in Figure 8.5. The vertical scale measures how much the governance scores deviate from the overall average and not surprisingly they are positive, since this compares Britain with many developing countries, a number of which have serious problems of governance. That said, Figure 8.5 indicates that several measures for Britain have trended negatively over time. In this regard, Table 8.3 documents the magnitude of these trends: the control of corruption, government effectiveness, political stability and regulatory quality indicators all *decline* over the 20-year period between 1996 and 2015, with the correlations (r) between these indicators and time varying from $-.56$ for regulatory quality to $-.60$ for political stability to $-.85$ for both controlling corruption and government effectiveness. Only rule of law and voice and accountability show positive trends, with the former being $+.53$ and the latter, $+.10$.

Table 8.3 *Over-Time Trend Correlations: Governance Indicators for the UK and the EU, 1996–2015*

Indicator	UK	EU
Regulatory Quality	−.56	+.62
Government Effectiveness	−.85	−.08
Rule of Law	.53	.94
Political Stability	−.60	−.74
Control of Corruption	−.85	−.74
Voice and Accountability	.10	−.17

Note: correlations (*r*) are between good governance indicators and year.

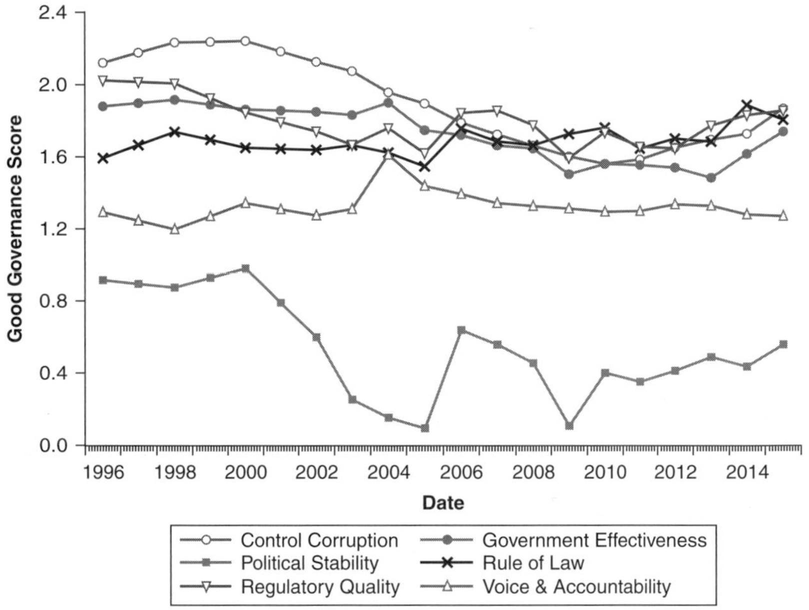

Figure 8.5 Trends in Good Governance Indicators for the UK, 1996–2015. Source: Penn World Tables.

It is instructive to examine changes in the good governance indicators for all 28 EU countries over the same period. These dynamics are displayed in Figure 8.6. When interpreting this figure it should be noted that a number of countries were not EU member states until 2004. However, the EU had considerable influence on governance and regulation before

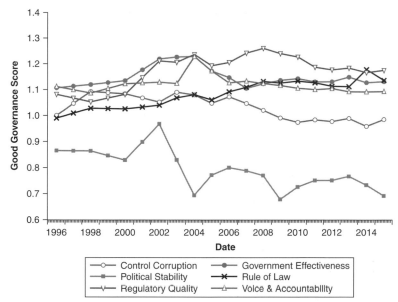

Figure 8.6 Trends in Good Governance Indicators for 28 EU Countries, 1996–2015.
Source: Penn World Tables.

these countries joined since they had to meet the fairly stringent require-ments for accession. Those requirements notwithstanding, trends in a number of the indicators in Figure 7.6 do not suggest that there have been discernible improvements in the quality of governance across the EU as a whole since the mid 1990s. Specifically, the correlations dis-played in Table 8.3 show that although the quality of regulation and rule of law have improved, government effectiveness, political stability, voice and accountability and control of corruption all have deteriorated. Thus, there are similarities in the dynamics of the performance of sev-eral of the good governance indicators for Britain and the European Union over the last 20 years. Both Britain and the European Union as a whole have been successful in improving the rule of law, but both have experienced declining performances in government effectiveness, politi-cal stability and corruption. The exception is the quality of regulation, which has improved in the EU and deteriorated in the UK.

There is an interesting argument in research on European Union that as a political system, the EU can be described as a regulatory

Table 8.4 *Difference of Means Tests of the Governance Indicators in 10 EU Accession Countries, Before and After 2004*

Indicator	Difference of Means in the Accession States	t statistic
Regulatory Quality	.37***	6.2
Government Effectiveness	.14**	2.2
Rule of Law	.17***	9.2
Political Stability	.01	.22
Control of Corruption	.08	1.4
Voice and Accountability	.02	.63

Note: *** = p ≤.001; ** = p ≤ .01; * = − p ≤ .05, one-tailed test.

state (Majone 1994; Moran 2002). This means that it is founded on the principal of providing a level playing field that produces common regulations and standards across Europe and this, in turn, is designed to promote trade and economic growth. The evidence in Table 8.3 is that by and large the quality of regulation has trended upwards over time, something that is also true of the rule of law. The other indicators have negative dynamics, suggesting that governance in both Britain and the European Union has deteriorated over time.

Table 8.4 shows differences between performance on the governance indicators before and after accession of 10 states that joined the EU in 2004. They were Cyprus, the Czech Republic, Estonia, Hungary, Latvia, Lithuania, Malta, Poland, Slovakia and Slovenia. To reiterate an earlier point, changes in the governance indicators for these 10 countries provide stronger evidence of the influence of the EU on governance than trends for states that joined prior to 1996. Table 8.4 indicates that the quality of regulation, the effectiveness of government and the rule of law all improved in these countries after they joined the EU. Most of them became democracies after the collapse of communism in the early 1990s and so they had approximately 15 years to create market economies and prepare for accession to the EU.

It is evident that the rule of law and regulatory quality appear as indicators that improved both for the EU as a whole (Table 8.3) and for the 10 accession countries (Table 8.4). This observation suggests that the EU had a positive impact on these important characteristics of good governance. At the same time, while the effectiveness of government declined across the 28 member states collectively, this did not occur in the accession states. Thus, the EU appears to have had a benign impact on this important aspect of good governance in these emerging democracies even if the same point cannot be made about Britain and other mature EU democracies.

Conclusion: What Price Brexit?

This chapter has taken a broad view of the economic and political consequences of Brexit and several conclusions are important for understanding the long-term implications of the Brexit vote. The EU is a key player in European politics and has entrenched peace as the norm for a continent racked by war for much of the first half of the twentieth century. But regarding growth of the economy it is hard to discern clear positive effects of membership on member states, apart from a handful of ex-communist countries in eastern Europe. This is particularly true of Britain, where there is no evidence to suggest that EU membership has stimulated economic growth over time.

The analysis of net migration to Britain from inside and outside the EU showed that in numerical terms net migration has been growing significantly over time and this is true for both types of migration. However, the argument that if Britain appears unable to restrict immigration from outside the EU then it is unlikely to do this for EU migration after Brexit happens is flawed. We have seen that economic migration into Britain is much more important for EU member states than for non-EU countries. This finding carries the implication that if Britain retains control over immigration from the EU following the negotiations over Brexit, it will be able to curtail economic migration from Europe and bring down the numbers.

Finally, membership of the EU has been associated with only limited improvements in governance, principally in relation to the quality of regulation and the rule of law. As far as political stability, control of corruption and government effectiveness are concerned, member states appear to be converging around declining performance rather than improvement. This conclusion is not really surprising, since if the EU is primarily a regulatory state then we would expect it to do well both in relation to regulation and the laws that support it, but not necessarily with regard to other aspects of democratic governance.

It is clear that membership has not been associated with an improvement in other important aspects of governance. The EU simply lacks the power and authority to do things like improve the efficiency of government, control corruption and improve political stability, apart from in countries that joined in 2004. An illustration of this weakness is provided by the repeated failure of Brussels to get auditors to sign off on the EU budget. This failure shows how weak the EU is in curbing corruption. These trends are unlikely to change in the future unless there is a major drive towards further integration closer to the federalist goal of establishing a United States of Europe.

Much has been made in the debate over Brexit of the problems that Britain will face if it does not have tariff-free access to the single market. However, the evidence suggests that this will have a marginal impact at best on the future prosperity of the UK economy. It is far more important for Britain to exert control over large-scale fluctuations in the value of the pound and, in particular, to avoid a rise in the value of the currency, which can slow growth. This is going to be difficult as long as the pound remains a reserve currency that is sought out as a safe haven in the face of uncertainty in the world economy. This, in turn, suggests that Britain would be better off if the pound was not a reserve currency and was traded much less extensively on currency markets. In this case it would be much easier to avoid these fluctuations, which are essentially a by-product of the City of London being a major financial centre in the world economy.

The process of Britain leaving the EU will take many years, far longer than the two years laid down in the agreements covering this contingency. It has been suggested that the EU will want to make as few concessions as possible to the UK in order to discourage other member countries from following Britain's example. However, one figure it is very relevant in this discussion, namely that in 2015 the EU countries took 44 per cent of British exports, valued at £223 billion, while 53 per cent of British imports, worth £257 billion, came from the EU (Hennig 2016). This trade imbalance of £24 billion is a bargaining chip for Britain, and it may deter any negotiators in Europe who might be tempted to seek a hard line in the settlement. Put simply, the EU would lose more exports in a trade war than Britain would, although in this event both sides in the negotiations would be damaged.

Although the negotiations will be long and complex, it is easy to identify 'redlines' which could prevent a sensible settlement. The UK

Government is unlikely to accept free movement of labour, since this was a key issue in the referendum. In the shadow of the vote even some Labour MPs, perhaps surprised by the scale of public support for leaving the EU in Labour territory, expressed support for limiting free movement and devising an entirely new immigration policy (views that were not shared by the Labour leader Jeremy Corbyn). At the same time, EU negotiators will be very reluctant to allow the UK unlimited access to the single market because it would amount to encouraging member countries to follow suit. But a deal involving a combination of tightening the regulations on free movement of labour in Britain and possibly within the EU as well, accompanied by UK payments for continued access to the single market with minimal barriers may be possible. The alternative is beggar-my-neighbour trade barriers in which both the EU and Britain will lose. If sanity prevails, the latter will be avoided. It will be years before we know the final outcome, but the lesson of this chapter is that Brexit will not necessarily have the grave consequences for the British economy and society that many politicians and pundits have predicted.

9 | *Beyond Brexit*

In this book, we have drawn on more than a decade's worth of survey data to put the 2016 vote for Brexit under the microscope. Aside from examining the campaign, we have probed the drivers of public attitudes towards the European Union during the 11-year period that led up to the referendum, explained why these attitudes have been so volatile, shed light on the factors that have motivated electoral and membership support for UKIP, which has played an integral role in the country's drift towards Brexit, and then investigated what actually motivated the historic vote to leave the EU in the 2016 referendum.

In this chapter, we draw together our findings and arguments before turning to examine some final questions, namely whether the result would have been different had turnout been higher, and will Brexit be a 'one-off' or are there likely to be further countries heading for the exit door, given anti-EU sentiment across the continent? We conclude by discussing the possible implications of Brexit for the British party system and the political system as a whole.

Explaining Brexit: Our Argument

Since the vote for Brexit many observers of British politics have focused their attention on the campaign itself. In the aftermath of the vote a series of books were published on the referendum, most of which talked at great length about the daily dynamics of the campaign, individual personalities in the Remain and Leave camps and suggested that the day-by-day decisions they took were fundamental to the vote for Brexit (e.g. Banks 2016; Bennett 2016; Shipman 2016). Campaigners have rushed to put themselves in the history books and squabbled over the reasons *why* a majority of British people voted to leave the EU. While some traced this decision to public angst over immigration, others have focused on public concerns over a loss of sovereignty to the EU. However, to really make sense of the vote, we need to step back and objectively interrogate the data, as we have done in this book. What do our findings say about these debates?

Let's recall what we have found. First, it is important to recognize that a number of the forces that ultimately led to Brexit were operating for more than a decade before the referendum. As discussed in Chapter 4, there was no one single factor that shaped how people thought about EU membership. Rather, since at least 2004 the public's views about EU membership have been shaped by their assessments of how the governing parties were performing on key issues, especially immigration and, to a lesser extent, the economy and the NHS. People's anxieties about how immigration flows into the country had been managed alongside worries about a perceived loss of economic control to Brussels directly cultivated support for Brexit. While the 2016 campaign may have changed some people's minds and motivated them to cast a ballot, when it came to the fundamental question of whether to vote for Brexit, a number of key attitudes and beliefs were already in place.

We also demonstrated why the rise of the populist right UKIP cannot and should not be seen in isolation from the vote for Brexit. Drawing on survey data gathered from people who became UKIP members, Chapter 5 documented how most of those who joined Nigel Farage's self-anointed 'People's Army' were elderly, white men who mainly became politically active because of their strong desire to leave the EU and reduce immigration. We also showed, however, that far from being confined to the fringe, UKIP members' opposition to large-scale immigration and their populist views are widely shared across the British electorate. Like UKIP members, many voters are concerned not only about immigration but also about rapacious banks, corporate greed, economic inequality, social injustice and the prospect of being 'left behind' by the rapid transformation of the country. Similarly, UKIP members' attitudes towards various minority groups in British society closely resemble those expressed by the general public. Such findings suggest that even after the vote for Brexit there will remain significant potential for populist politics in the UK, even if UKIP is not the beneficiary.

Against this backdrop, in Chapter 6 we considered how two recent elections brought these currents together. The 2014 European Parliament elections and then the 2015 UK general election helped to set the stage for the 2016 vote for Brexit. The results of these contests provided clear signposts for what was about to follow in June 2016. In these two elections we showed how people's support for Euroscepticism was influenced by their negative judgements about how the government of the day had performed on the key valence issues of immigration, the economy and the NHS, all of which had shaped public reactions to the EU since at least 2004. These issues worked to UKIP's advantage. Labour's negative image for managerial incompetence following the Great Recession, and a record surge of immigration into the country, were crucial as well. In addition, there was the fact that the Liberal Democrats had abandoned their traditional role as a 'catch-all' protest party and formed a coalition government with the Conservatives.

People's reactions to Nigel Farage also strongly influenced the likelihood that they would vote for UKIP. Feelings about the UKIP leader helped to mobilize disaffected voters who were exercised about how immigration and other key issues had been managed and felt left behind because their personal financial circumstances had not kept pace with economic conditions in the country as a whole. The 2016 referendum provided Farage and his army of the discontented with a long-awaited opportunity to strike a hard blow at what they believed to be an unresponsive political-economic establishment and to win a long-sought-after referendum on whether the country would remain in the EU.

In Chapter 7 we demonstrated how all of these dynamics came together to shape the Brexit decision. The vote was not governed by any single factor. Rather, we showed how the choices made by voters reflected a complex and cross-cutting mix of calculations, emotions and cues. Some of these factors, such as people's attitudes towards immigration and their national identities, had been 'baked in' long before the referendum was called and the campaign began. Similarly, if people felt as though they had been left behind and economically marginalized then this helped to minimize the likelihood that they would see Brexit as a serious risk to the country's future prosperity.

Emphasizing that risk was the centrepiece of Remain's campaign. As discussed in Chapters 2 and 3, Remain's 'Project Fear' enlisted a star-studded cast of political and economic elites, media commentators, prominent academics and pop-culture celebrities to its cause. Even US President Obama joined the chorus of pro-EU luminaries. Together with Prime Minister David Cameron, Chancellor George Osborne and other Government officials, the Remainers made massive efforts to frighten voters into believing that exiting the EU would cause enormous economic hardship. Attempts also were made to frighten voters about national security by conjuring the spectre of a war in Europe should the UK attempt to leave. Some even talked about the possible end of Western civilization.

Our analyses in Chapter 7 revealed that people who heeded Project Fear's dark warnings were indeed very likely to vote Remain. However, the concerted effort to scare voters to death by raising threats to prosperity and peace that would ensue were the UK to exit the EU was not quite enough to secure a Remain majority. Many people were deeply worried about immigration and concluded that the UK would be better able to control its borders and counter terrorism if the country were outside of the EU. These people opted for Brexit in huge numbers.

We also showed how people's images of the Leave camp's leaders were important factors affecting how people voted. Analyses presented in Chapter 7 demonstrated that feelings about Boris Johnson had particularly strong effects on the probability that voters would opt for Brexit. Although it is not possible to say with certainty that 'it was Boris wot done it', he was considerably more popular than the leader of the Remain campaign, Prime Minister David Cameron. As a very high profile establishment Conservative representing the official Vote Leave campaign, Boris Johnson helped to attract 'polite Eurosceptics' who otherwise might have been put off voting Leave because it involved acknowledging – to themselves, if not others – that they were siding with the highly controversial Nigel Farage and assorted other 'deplorables'.

Although undoubtedly toxic among parts of the electorate, Farage's 'straight out of Clacton' populist appeal was a plus for Leave in other respects. Representing the insurgent Leave.EU and Grassroots Out Leave campaigns, and lavishly bankrolled by business magnate Arron Banks, the plain-speaking Farage attracted enthusiastic high-street crowds in market towns and generated copious, if not always flattering, media coverage as he traversed the country in his purple battle bus. The resulting 'oxygen of publicity' helped Farage to mobilize his 'People's Army' and other discontented voters, including a sizeable number of Labour supporters, who were attracted by his forthright emphasis on the dangers of mass immigration and accompanying argument that Brexit was the only way ordinary people could 'take back control'.

It bears reiteration that fears about immigration mattered. Although arguments about how exiting the EU would help to re-establish national sovereignty and invigorate democracy were prominent themes in the Leave campaign, our analyses indicate that strong public concern over the large number of migrants entering the country was front and centre to Leave securing victory. Controlling and curtailing immigration was seen as a primary benefit of leaving the EU, while voters for whom immigration was seen as a very important issue were very likely to back Brexit. When the official Leave campaign shifted onto this issue in the final month before the balloting, as discussed in Chapter 3, they were very much in tune with a core driver of the vote to exit the EU. Farage had recognized the potency of the immigration issue from the outset of the campaign and, indeed, years earlier (Ford and Goodwin 2014). In this sense, Leave's dual-track campaign organization enabled its two rival armies to leverage the populist power of the immigration issue while simultaneously allowing miscellaneous middle-class Eurosceptics to keep a safe distance from the politically incorrect UKIP chieftain. An inadvertent product of protracted internecine squabbling among sharp-elbowed rivals, Leave's bifurcated campaign became an increasingly potent political weapon in the run-up to the balloting. Its power was demonstrated on 23 June.

Could Things Have Been Different?

In the aftermath of the historic 2016 referendum, there has been continuing speculation about whether the outcome represented the will of the British electorate. This arises in part because the outcome was so close and also because nearly 28 per cent of eligible voters did not participate in the referendum even though the turnout of over 72 per cent was very respectable by the standards of recent UK general elections.

This raises an interesting question – might the result have been different if turnout had been higher? A second and related issue concerns the effects of Brexit on the rest of the European Union. Since the vote, much of the debate in the UK has focused on the negotiations to leave the EU. One of the arguments emerging in discussions of these negotiations is that the UK may face a so-called 'hard Brexit' if EU negotiators are keen to send a message to the remaining member states that leaving will impose real costs on any countries that attempt to follow the UK's example.

The latter point raises another interesting question – how many other EU member states may be tempted to leave the EU in light of the Brexit vote? Is Brexit likely to be a 'one-off' or could it trigger other defections in the future as part of a contagion effect across the continent? In this final chapter we consider these questions. The focus is on whether the result of the referendum could have been different in the UK and whether Brexit will encourage others to think about doing the same thing.

After the referendum some pro-Remain commentators argued that the result would have been different if *all* eligible voters had exercised their franchise. In other words, some observers view turnout as a key factor in explaining the victory for Leave. This carries the implication that Leavers were more motivated to vote than Remainers, which, given the findings in this book, is a plausible idea. We can interrogate this conjecture further by using data gathered in our ECMS pre- and post-referendum panel surveys and some simple arithmetic.

To begin, recall that the shares of the vote for Leave and Remain were 51.89 per cent and 48.11 per cent, respectively, with a 72.21 per cent turnout. These figures imply that 34.73 per cent of the eligible electorate voted to remain. In the post-referendum wave of our ECMS survey, those who said they had *not* voted at the referendum were asked to estimate how they *would* have voted if they had instead exercised their right to vote. Responses to this question indicate that 39.1 per cent of these non-voters would have opted for Remain. Given that 27.79 per cent of the electorate actually failed to turn out, this puts an additional 10.87 per cent (27.79 × .391) in the Remain column if everyone had participated in the referendum.

Another 32.2 per cent of the non-voting ECMS respondents said they 'didn't know' how they would have cast their ballots. This represents 8.95 per cent of the electorate (27.79 × .322). To determine how these people would have voted, we employ a question in the pre-referendum wave of the ECMS survey asking respondents how they were going to vote. Of those who said they 'didn't know' in reply to this question, 53.1 per cent reported in the post-referendum wave of the survey that they opted for Remain. Using this number to estimate how many of the 8.95 per cent of the electorate would have cast a Remain ballot suggests that 4.75 per cent (8.95 × .531) would have done so. Combining the results of these several calculations gives Remain 50.35 per cent (34.73 + 10.87 + 4.75) of the vote, indicating a very narrow win in the referendum. So, on the face of it, the argument that things would have been different if everyone had voted appears to have validity. However, this 50.35 per cent figure is not *conclusive* evidence that Remain had majority support across the entire electorate. This is because we need to take into account the possibility of sampling uncertainty in our survey data. A 95 per cent confidence interval – a standard measure of uncertainty about a survey-based statistic – suggests that Remain's share of the vote could have varied from 48.65 per cent (Remain loses) to 52.05 per cent (Remain wins). Thus, even if everyone who was eligible to vote had gone to the polls, there is a distinct possibility that Remain could still have been defeated.

To provide insight into the probability of a Remain loss, we can simulate the outcome of multiple referendum votes. Imagine conducting 1 million (!) referendums with a random component distributed according to a normal (bell-shaped) distribution about a mean of 50.35 per cent and with a standard deviation of 0.85 per cent – the standard error of our survey estimate of Remain strength. This gives us a picture of the range of possible outcomes that would emerge from running the referendum a million times. The results of this exercise are displayed in Figure 9.1. As illustrated, Remain's total is greater than Leave's in 66.03 per cent of these contests, with Leave winning the remainder. Thus, the odds of a Remain victory would have been substantial (1.94 to one), but not overwhelming, if everyone who was eligible had cast a ballot on 23 June.

Of course, UK voters did not have 1 million chances to express their preference on EU membership. They had one opportunity, and when this arrived a majority of those who cast a ballot voted for Brexit. Recognizing this, an assortment of pro-EU advocates, including the Liberal Democrats, the Greens and miscellaneous pro-Remain enthusiasts, have called for a second referendum. Others, recognizing that a sizeable majority of MPs favour staying in the EU, have called on Parliament to exert its constitutional power and negate the referendum result. The courts are involved as well, with a High Court decision in November 2016 ruling that Parliament must vote on whether the UK Government can invoke Article 50 of the Lisbon Treaty to

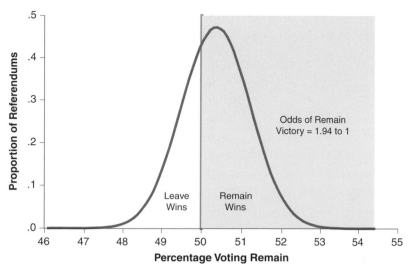

Figure 9.1 Results of 1 Million Simulated EU Referendums.

start the Brexit process. On appeal, the Supreme Court decided that Parliament must be consulted. That has now happened.

Disgruntled Remainers have also suggested that Prime Minister Theresa May and her Conservative Government should 'slow walk' exit negotiations with the EU, that is, fail to invoke Article 50 and generally subvert the referendum decision by means of studied bureaucratic inertia. Although Prime Minister May quietly favoured Remain during the referendum campaign, she has indicated that sabotaging Brexit is not going to happen. Shortly before becoming prime minister, she famously stated that 'Brexit means Brexit', a statement given force by her appointment of prominent Eurosceptics Boris Johnson, David Davis and Liam Fox to important cabinet positions. That said, the 'Brexit means Brexit' mantra remains unclear several months after the referendum, as efforts to negate the result continued. Then, on 17 January 2017, May announced concrete negotiating targets for the kind of Brexit her Government seeks and on 8 February the House of Commons passed a bill providing authority to begin the Brexit process by invoking Article 50.

One type of evidence that might bolster the case of the pro-Remain forces are data from public opinion polls that voters have had a change of heart and many more now want to stay in the EU. However, several

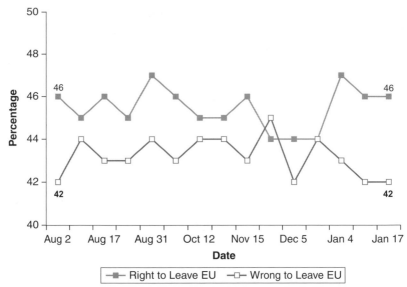

Figure 9.2 Right or Wrong Decision to Leave the EU, August
2016–January 2017.
Source: YouGov Surveys.

months after the referendum, indicators that the electorate is suffering
from a bad case of 'Bremorse' (Brexit remorse) are hard to find. Taking
into account sampling uncertainty, there is little evidence of any real
movement in public opinion. With the exception of a 7 December
2016 Gallup survey showing Remain on 54 per cent and Leave on 46
per cent, surveys by several polling houses including BMG, ComRes,
Survation and YouGov show that the percentages favouring Remain
and Leave vary in a very narrow range from 49 to 51 per cent. Similarly,
since the referendum YouGov has regularly asked voters whether the
vote to leave the EU had been the right or wrong decision. As shown
in Figure 9.2, in early August 2016, less than two months after the
historic vote, 46 per cent of respondents thought that the decision had
been the right one, while 42 per cent thought it had been wrong. Five
months later, in January 2017, these figures were the same, revealing
how there has been little sign of mass regret.

Finally, a survey that we conducted in late September 2016, which
posed the identical question about approval or disapproval of EU
membership that was employed in the other surveys employed

throughout this book, shows that 44 per cent disapprove of continued EU membership, 42 per cent approve and 14 per cent are undecided. These numbers, which again point to a small pro-Leave advantage, are obviously very similar to what happened in the June referendum itself. Taken together, then, evidence from a range of polls that have been conducted in the months since the vote does not indicate that the country has been struck down by a case of Bremorse. On the contrary, the public remains divided but the Leavers continue to hold a slight advantage.

Given this close division, it is conceivable that a second referendum would yield a Remain majority. However, polls provide little encouragement for Remain supporters who have called for a second referendum. For example, YouGov has reported that only 26 per cent believe that it was legitimate to campaign for another referendum, while 59 per cent think otherwise. The polls also show that people are not keen for a referendum to follow the negotiations with the EU to legitimize the terms of Brexit. No more than one third of those who were surveyed by ComRes and Opinium thought that such a follow-up referendum would be desirable.

Further evidence for the idea that another referendum on Europe might not be warmly received by the electorate involves reactions to the 23 June contest. In our post-referendum ECMS survey we presented respondents with a list of five positive words and five negative words and asked them to choose which best described their reactions to the Remain and Leave campaigns. As displayed in Figure 9.3, the words chosen are predominantly negative. Consistent with the evidence on public attitudes towards the campaign presented in Chapter 3, large numbers of voters reacted negatively to the political battle that dominated national politics for the first half of 2016. This is especially the case for the Remain campaign, with fully 64 per cent choosing one or more negative words and only 23 per cent choosing one or more positive words. The balance is somewhat closer for the Leave campaign, with 37 per cent selecting one or more positive words and 52 per cent picking one or more negative ones.

Looking at various pairs of words, we see that negative words outnumber positive ones in every instance for descriptions of the Remain campaign. For example, 27 per cent felt that Remain's campaign was 'frightening' and only 7 per cent found it 'reassuring'. Similarly, 30 per cent described the Remain campaign as 'weak' and only 8 per cent felt

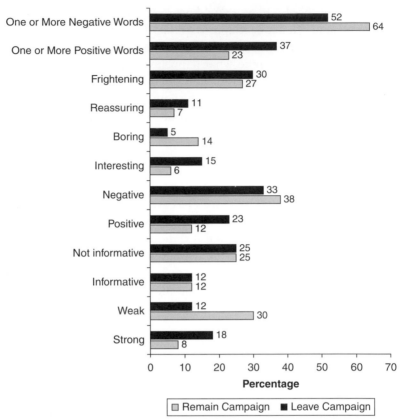

Figure 9.3 Words Used to Describe the Remain and Leave Campaigns.
Source: ECMS Post-Referendum Survey, 2016.

that it had been 'strong'. Comparable results for word pairs describing the Leave campaign are mixed, with 'strong' outnumbering 'weak' and 'interesting' outnumbering 'boring'. However, the other three word pairs are tilted in the negative direction. Thus, 30 per cent felt that the Leave campaign had been 'frightening' and only 12 per cent found it 'reassuring'. Similarly, only 12 per cent said it was 'informative', while 25 per cent said it was 'not informative', and while 23 per cent thought the Leavers had been 'positive' 33 per cent thought they had been 'negative'.

Overall, it is evident that the electorate reacted quite negatively to the Remain and Leave campaigns. Although voters were somewhat more positive about the latter, this is a matter of degree and the overall tenor of reactions to both campaigns was far from sanguine. This negativity, combined with the absence of widespread Brexit remorse, suggests that it is unlikely that Remain irredentists will be able to marshal public opinion to leverage a second referendum. Thus far, voters have precious little enthusiasm for a return engagement.

The lack of public support for a second referendum comports well with economic trends since 23 June. Dire warnings by former Prime Minister Cameron and his colleagues in the Remain camp notwithstanding, the UK economy thus far has not gone into a tailspin. And, as discussed in Chapter 8, our model of long-run economic growth does not suggest impending disaster for a post-EU UK, a conclusion recently echoed in a recent report by a team of prominent Cambridge economists who are highly critical of Remainers' 'doom and gloom' forecasts.[1] Analyses in Chapter 8 also indicated that the quality of democracy in the UK and many other EU countries has not increased over the past two decades. With the exception of some former Warsaw Pact countries, EU membership and progressive increases in good governance have not been synonymous.

Prosperity and penury are opposite ends of a continuum, and there are a variety of political-economic scenarios that may play out in the years ahead. In this regard, it is conceivable that the Remain campaign will ultimately be proven right. Massive economic difficulties will ensue, prompting a large majority of the UK electorate to insist that their Government beg Brussels for re-entry to the EU. However, a mild economic downturn might be viewed quite differently, with voters deciding that modestly degraded economic performance is a price worth paying for 'taking back control'. Although their effects going forward are far from certain, widespread desires to reduce immigration, coupled with substantial populist sentiment to address a longstanding 'democratic deficit' and enhance UK sovereignty, may induce large numbers of voters to discount economic losses and thereby keep Bremorse from engulfing public opinion.

Will Brexit Be a 'One-Off'?

We have seen that people's attitudes to Brexit did not change very much in the six months following the referendum and that a majority felt that the country had made the right decision. Britain is the first major country to vote to leave the EU, which clearly reflects the fact that Britons have been more Eurosceptic than their cousins in Europe in the past. But is Britain that different from the rest of the EU, particularly with respect to attitudes to EU integration? This is an important question that speaks to the likelihood of other countries opting to leave the EU if things go on as they are as this is written.

In Chapter 4, we made the point that during the early years of the EU public opinion actually played a minor role in influencing European integration because of the so-called 'permissive consensus' that existed across Europe at that time. By and large, in earlier years the public were content to leave matters concerning European integration to their national political elites and generally accepted these decisions (Lindbergh and Scheingold 1970). However, this changed as EU membership started to have a bigger impact on the everyday lives of ordinary people.

The Maastricht Treaty of 1992 was a turning point in this process when a vote by the Danes against ratifying the treaty in a referendum held in 1993 awakened decision-makers to the fact that the opinions of ordinary voters did matter when it came to furthering the integration project. The fact that in 1992 the French, who were founding members of the EU, also had nearly rejected the Maastricht Treaty signalled that things had really changed. It was around this point that the 'permissive consensus' gave way to what became known as a 'constraining dissensus' in Europe (Hooghe and Marks 2009). Put simply, public attitudes across Europe were starting to act as a brake on the ambitions of the Euro-federalists. The people could no longer be ignored.

Brexit may well have changed this 'constraining dissensus' further into a 'public veto', in the sense that electorates in a number of EU member states may opt to stop any further integration occurring in the future or to roll back existing agreements. Certainly, the rapid collapse of the Schengen Agreement providing border-free travel inside the EU after the upsurge of immigration from the Middle East and Africa was largely driven by alarmed public opinion. The process of the public becoming more and more important in debates about the future of the EU has grown stronger over time.

But the relevance of this argument depends on public attitudes to EU integration across the continent. If European publics are becoming less supportive of EU integration this veto will grow in importance as electoral and other considerations give rise to further erosion of the federalist ambitions of Brussels bureaucrats and pro-EU politicians in various member states. The rise in support for populist radical right parties across Europe reinforces this point since they are almost uniformly hostile towards the euro single currency, if not the EU itself, and have used anti-EU sentiments among voters to their electoral advantage (Lubbers and Scheepers 2007; Werts et al. 2013). This is one aspect of the growth in populism and the politics of identity that has become so prominent across the world as well as in EU member states. On the other hand, if support for further integration has not really changed very much, with the exception of a few member states such as Britain, this 'public veto' may not matter.

We can investigate trends in attitudes to European integration over time with data from the European Social Surveys (ESS). These are surveys of public attitudes and behaviour in relation to issue perceptions and political participation that have been conducted every other year since 2002.[2] In 2004 and again 10 years later in 2014, the following question was asked: 'Now thinking about the European Union, some say European unification should go further. Others say it has already gone too far. Using this card, what number on the scale best describes your position?' A score of 0 on the scale means that the respondent thinks that European unification has already gone too far, and a score of 10 that unification should go further. Seventeen EU member states were surveyed in both years and so we can see how opinions on EU integration have changed in these countries.

Figure 9.4 compares average scores on the 10-point scales in these countries in 2004 and again 10 years later in 2014, and Figure 9.5 shows the changes in these scores over time. The average score on the scale in all 17 countries was 5.25 in 2004 and 4.85 10 years later in 2014, a fall of –0.40 or about 8 per cent. This is not a large change, although it does show how opinions have been shifting in the EU on this key issue, which is so relevant to its future. In the UK, voters were less enthusiastic about integration in 2004 than was true for all but one of the EU member states, so the UK's reputation as being a Eurosceptic nation, an 'awkward partner' (George 1998), is deserved. That said, the lowest score in 2004 went to Finland, while the Swedes and Austrians were also not that different from UK voters.

However, the average scores conceal large changes in public attitudes to further integration that have occurred over time. It can be seen in Figure 9.5 that support for further integration fell in 12 of

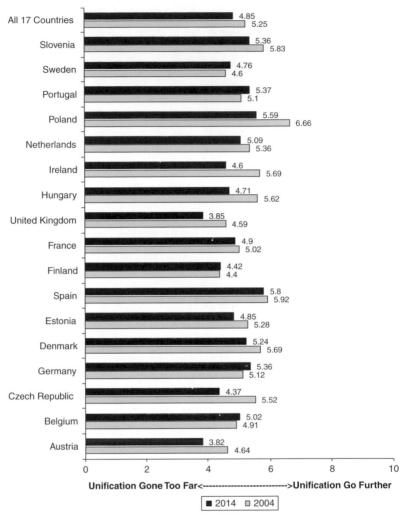

Figure 9.4 Scores on Scale of More or Less EU Integration, 17 Countries, 2004 and 2014.
Source: European Social Surveys, 2004 and 2015.

the countries, increased in 3 and remained essentially unchanged in 1, the already Eurosceptic Finland. Fairly large reductions in support for further integration occurred in a number of these countries. In the UK support fell from 4.59 in 2004 to 3.85 in 2014 or –0.74. But it declined by –1.15 in the Czech Republic, Poland (–1.07), Ireland

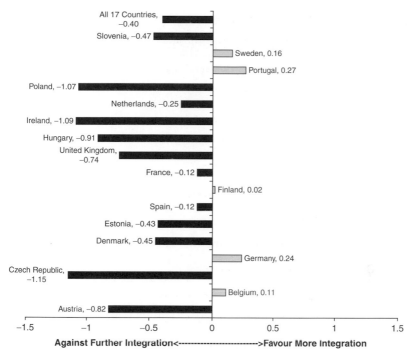

Figure 9.5 Change in Public Attitudes towards Further EU Integration between 2004 and 2014, 17 Countries.
Source: European Social Surveys, 2004 and 2015.

(−1.09), Hungary (−0.91) and Austria (−0.82). In contrast, in the four member states in which support for further integration rose, the changes were all fairly modest, with the largest one being in Portugal (+0.27), closely followed by Germany (+0.24). Thus, the overall conclusion is that a growth in Euroscepticism across the EU is not something confined to the UK.

Another way that we can find out how different the UK is from the rest of Europe is to try to replicate our model of voting to leave the EU (from Chapter 7) across Europe using the ESS data. In this case the objective is to analyse attitudes to EU integration rather than referendum voting. In Chapter 7 several variables were used to predict voting to stay or leave the EU. These included attitudes towards the economy and immigration, perceptions of the risks associated with Brexit, affective attachments to the EU, a sense of feeling left behind, national identities and party and leader cues.

We cannot replicate precisely the same analysis with ESS data, but we can approximate it with indicators that are close to concepts utilized in the EU vote models. We use the latest released version of the ESS from 2014 and this contains variables that are similar to those in the EU referendum voting model. There is a measure of respondent satisfaction with the economy in each of the countries identified using an 11-point scale (0 = extremely dissatisfied and 10 = extremely satisfied). A second variable is based on a question that asks respondents if they think immigration makes their country a better or worse place to live, again using an 11-point scale (0 = worse place to live and 10 = better place to live). These two variables enable us to study the effects of the economy and immigration on attitudes towards European integration.

There is no direct measure in the ESS data of attitudes regarding the risks associated with leaving the EU, but there is a question asking about generalized attitudes to risks as part of a battery of items measuring human values. Respondents are asked about various personality traits, one of which is the importance of 'seeking adventures and having an exciting life'. A generalized risk scale can be constructed from this item. Regarding the concept of relative deprivation, which appeared in the referendum voting model, an ESS question asks: 'Compared to people like yourself who were born in [country], how do you think the government treats those who have recently come to live here from other countries?'[3] The implication is that those who perceive that immigrants receive special treatment are likely to experience a sense of relative deprivation.

The questions about individual politicians, affective attachments to the EU and to political parties in the voting model are replaced by different variables to make comparative analysis possible. First, there is a general question on trust in politicians measured using another 11-point scale (0 = 'No Trust at All', 10 = 'Complete Trust') that we substitute for evaluations of individual political leaders. A second scale asks people about their trust in the European Parliament, which provides a proxy measure of affective evaluations of the EU. An 11-point left–right ideology scale is used to capture the role of individual parties in the different member states. The expectation is that parties on the right are more likely to be Eurosceptic than parties on the left. National identity is measured with a variable that asks respondents how close they feel to their own country, with a high score indicating that they feel very close and really value their national identity.

Table 9.1 *OLS Regression Analysis of Support for European Integration, UK and 18 EU Countries, 2014*

Predictors	18 EU Countries	UK
	ß	ß
Economic Evaluations	−.04***	−.04*
Immigration Evaluations	−.23***	−.21***
Perceptions of Deprivation	.19***	.17***
Generalized Risk Perceptions	−.03***	−.04*
Trust in Politicians	.09***	.06*
Trust in the European Parliament	−.29***	−.39***
Strength of National Identity	.05***	.08*
Left–Right Ideology Scale	.02***	.11***
Satisfaction with Democracy	−.03***	.06**
Gender	−.03	.33***
Age	.003***	.005*
Education	−.14***	.13
Income	.01	.05***
Constant	6.644***	6.118***
N	34,654	2,263
Adjusted R²	.18	.32

*** = p ≤ .001; ** = p ≤ .01; * = p ≤ .05, one-tailed test.

Source: European Social Survey, 2014.

Variables measuring socio-demographic characteristics (age, education, gender, income) are included as well.

The results of analysing predictors of attitudes to EU integration appear in Table 9.1. In this table, the first model pools the data from the 18 EU member states represented in the 2014 ESS, and the second models is for the UK alone. It is apparent that there are close similarities between the drivers of attitudes to EU integration in the UK and in Europe more generally. In both models, if respondents think the local economy is doing well, immigration is improving the country and that the European Parliament appears trustworthy, then they are more likely to support European integration. They are also more likely to do this if they are risk-averse as opposed to risk-seeking, which is an illustration of LeDuc's law referred to in our analysis of voting in the UK's 2016 EU referendum in Chapter 7. In contrast, if people distrust politicians, feel a sense of deprivation in relation to immigrants, have a strong sense of English identity and are ideologically right wing, then they are more likely to be Eurosceptic.

There are a few differences between the two models. Satisfaction with democracy reduces Euroscepticism in the EU member states while it increases it in the UK. Gender appears to make no difference in Europe, but men are distinctly more Eurosceptic than women in the UK. Finally, in Europe as a whole university graduate status makes respondents more supportive of integration but it appears to have no effect in the UK when all other variables are controlled. Overall, this evidence suggests that Britain is not that much different from other countries in the EU when it comes to explaining the sources of Euroscepticism and that the roots of Brexit are clearly visible elsewhere.

One thing that really stands out in the analyses in Table 9.1 is the importance of immigration as a driver of Euroscepticism, both in Europe and in the UK. It influences attitudes directly via the immigration variable and also via the deprivation variable, both of which have strong effects. In contrast, while evaluations of economic conditions are statistically significant, their effects are distinctly weaker than those for immigration. Fortunately, the 2014 ESS asked people across the continent a wide range of questions about immigration. This allows us to probe the impact of the free movement of people inside the EU and also of asylum seekers and immigration from outside of the EU.

Are Immigration Attitudes Different in Britain?

The 2014 ESS survey asked people about two aspects of immigration. First, it asked about the ethnic dimension of immigration, that is, whether respondents favoured immigration from the same race/ethnic group as themselves as opposed to different ethnic groups. Second, respondents were asked about immigration from poorer countries in Europe and countries outside Europe. These questions allow us to study the effects of ethnicity and poverty on attitudes towards immigration.

The evidence presented in Chapter 7 has already shown how public concerns over immigration played a major role in influencing the outcome of the 2016 referendum in the UK. The analyses summarized in

Table 9.1 suggest that feelings about immigration also have a strong influence on public attitudes towards European integration in various countries on the continent. This raises an interesting question: did the UK vote to leave the EU because it is more hostile towards immigration than the rest of Europe? Or are the views of Britons similar to those in Europe?

Figure 9.6 displays evidence of the influence of ethnicity on public attitudes to immigration in EU member states surveyed in 2014. Each bar in the figure shows the percentage of respondents in a particular country who said that they would accept no immigrants or a few immigrants from these groups. On average, across all of these countries 30 per cent would accept 'none' or 'a few' immigrants from the same ethnic group as themselves. The UK comes sixth in these anti-immigrant rankings with a score of 35 per cent. However, anti-immigrant feelings were much stronger in the Czech Republic (57 per cent) and Hungary (48 per cent), and slightly greater in Spain than in the UK (36 per cent), Finland (36 per cent), the Irish Republic (37 per cent) and Portugal (36 per cent). These percentages document how the UK is far from being an exceptional case.

The second bar for each country identifies anti-immigrant feelings in relation to people from ethnic groups that are different from that of the respondent. In this case the average score across the several countries is much greater – the percentage who would accept 'none' or only 'a few' migrants from a different ethnic group stands at 43 per cent. The UK's score was actually below average in relation to this at 41 per cent and is ranked tenth in anti-immigrant feelings. Once again, there are some striking findings in Central and Eastern Europe. No less than 71 per cent of Czechs and 79 per cent of Hungarians refused to accept any or only a few immigrants from a different ethnic group. These large percentages very likely reflect these countries' positions on the front line of the migration flows of refugees attempting to escape the deadly conflicts in Syria and elsewhere in the Middle East.

Figure 9.7 captures the second aspect of attitudes to immigration, which relates to the migration of poor people from within and outside Europe. An average of 41 per cent of respondents said that they would refuse to take any or only a few poor immigrants from Europe. In this case, Britain ranked sixth with a score of 47 per cent, behind Austria (51 per cent), Estonia (52 per cent), Finland (57 per cent), Hungary (79 per cent) and Lithuania (49 per cent).[4] Feelings about

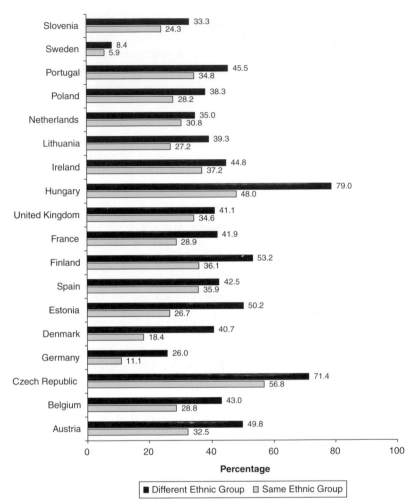

Figure 9.6 Percentages Willing to Accept Few or No Immigrants by Ethnicity, 18 Countries, 2014.
Source: European Social Surveys, 2004 and 2014.

the immigration of poor people from outside Europe, which speaks directly to the migration crisis in southern Europe, were even stronger, with 52 per cent refusing to take any or only a few migrants. In this case, Britain ranked a joint seventh with Austria with a score of 55 per cent. Denmark (57 per cent) Estonia (66 per cent), Finland (65 per cent), Hungary (83 per cent), the Czech Republic (73 per cent) and Lithuania (56 per cent) all had higher scores.

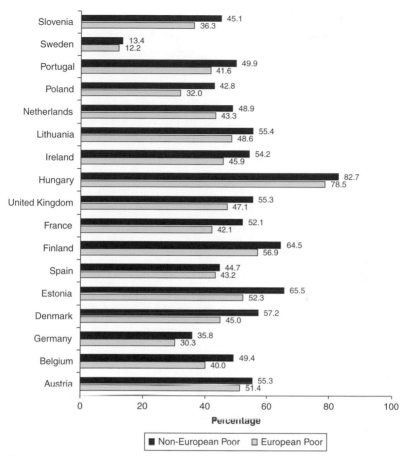

Figure 9.7 Percentages Willing to Accept Few or No Poor Immigrants from Inside and Outside Europe, 17 Countries, 2014.
Source: European Social Surveys, 2004 and 2014.

These data highlight two important conclusions. First, Britain is not unusual by EU standards when it comes to attitudes regarding immigration. In general, Europeans prefer immigrants from their own ethnic groups and they prefer poor immigrants from Europe to immigrants who come from elsewhere. People are most strongly opposed to poor migrants from different ethnic groups who come from outside of Europe, which explains why Europeans reacted so strongly to the flood of immigrants coming from Africa and the Middle East following the announcement by Chancellor Merkel in 2015 that Germany would open its borders to all. This decision led to the collapse of the Schengen Agreement, a policy of open borders across Europe, and it appears to have triggered growing support for right-wing populist parties across Europe.

Since the eruption of the refugee crisis, evidence of the increasing strength of the populist right in the EU has been clearly visible. Aside from UKIP assuming a central role in the vote for Brexit, numerous other populist right parties have imposed themselves on the political systems of Europe. Most notably, in 2016 the candidate from the Freedom Party of Austria polled 46 per cent of the national vote in a rerun of the country's presidential election (although in some states of Austria, notably the eastern and southern states of Burgenland, Carinthia and Styria, the populist right surpassed 50 per cent of the vote). In France, Marine Le Pen and the National Front have become a significant force and are likely to have a major impact on the presidential elections in 2017. Elsewhere, parties like the Northern League in Italy, the Party for Freedom in the Netherlands, Jobbik in Hungary, True Finns in Finland, the Danish People's Party and Golden Dawn in Greece continue to recruit significant support.

Merkel's policy announcement was welcomed by many in Germany as a generous humanitarian gesture but it was made possible, as Figures 9.6 and 9.7 show, because Germans along with Swedes are both outliers in relation to their attitudes about immigration into Europe. They are much less opposed to immigration, whether from inside or outside Europe, and whether immigrants are rich or poor, than the rest of the EU. However, even Germany and Sweden, two countries that long were more open towards immigration, have witnessed a stronger populist right in recent years.

In Germany, the populist right Alternative for Germany (AfD) had already, in 2013, only narrowly failed to meet the 5 per cent threshold that was required to win representation in the Bundestag. The next year the AfD won seats in the European Parliament, as well as seats in 10 of the 16 state parliaments in Germany. By 2017 the AfD had become the third most popular party in the polls and will soon try again to obtain seats in the Bundestag. Meanwhile, in Sweden, the historically unsuccessful populist right (Rydgren 2002) has enjoyed an electoral comeback. By 2017 the Sweden Democrats had become the third most successful political party in Swedish politics after polling nearly 13 per cent of the vote in the 2014 national elections, winning

49 seats in the Swedish parliament and nearly 10 per cent of the vote and 2 seats at the European Parliament elections in the same year.

The conclusion is that when Chancellor Angela Merkel announced her open-door immigration policy it was initially popular in Germany but had the effect of striking a major blow at European integration, and might even have tipped the balance in the 2016 referendum in the UK by invigorating already potent anti-immigration sentiments. With major elections in France, Germany and the Netherlands scheduled for 2017, and further such contests across Europe in the near future, both the ongoing effect of Merkel's decision and the status of Brexit as an isolated case will be under the microscope. With Brexit negotiations also in the offing, the future contours of the European Union are uncertain.

The nature of those deliberations is now coming into focus. On 17 January 2017 UK Prime Minister Theresa May delivered a major speech outlining her Government's negotiating targets for Brexit. The bottom line is that she will seek what commentators have called a 'hard Brexit'. Key provisions include leaving the single market, leaving the customs union, restoring control over immigration by ending the free movement of labour from EU states and terminating the jurisdiction of the European Court of Justice in the UK. Prime Minister May has said that notice to leave the EU under Article 50 of the Lisbon Treaty would be served by the end of March 2017, at which time negotiations would begin.

Although the outcome of these negotiations will not be known for some time, initial public reactions to May's Brexit plan have been quite positive and this may give her Government significant leverage in talks with the EU. For example, a YouGov poll conducted after the speech indicated that while 55 per cent of respondents believed that the plan would be good for Britain, only 19 per cent thought it would be bad. Majorities also approved of May's specific targets; for example, 57 per cent thought it is right to negotiate a new trade deal and fully 74 per cent endorsed May's assertion that the UK should have control of immigration. And, most important, as shown in Figure 9.2, 46 per cent approve leaving the EU and 42 per cent disapprove. The former figure represents 53 per cent of those expressing an opinion.

Public support may be very important for getting parliamentary approval for a Brexit deal. As discussed in Chapter 7, we estimate that there were pro-Leave majorities in 401 of Britain's 632 constituencies.

This broadly based public support for quitting the EU was sharply at odds with the expressed sentiments of Members of Parliament at the time of the referendum. One day before the vote, 471 MPs had declared for Remain and only 158 for Leave. Fully 218 of 228 Labour MPs with declared preferences said they wanted to stay in the EU. Even among Conservatives, there was a Remain majority, with 185 wishing to stay and 138 wishing to go. These numbers suggest that Prime Minister May might have a tough time selling any Brexit deal she brings before Parliament and strong backing from the public could be crucial for getting the votes needed for approval.

Another consideration she may use to persuade her Conservative colleagues concerns the consequences of failure. Failing to approve a Brexit deal might well split the Conservative Party wide open, cause the Government to fall and precipitate a general election. Many Eurosceptic Conservative voters and MPs, disgusted at the turn of events, might move to UKIP or another populist alternative. Potentially, UKIP also could benefit from the failure of Labour MPs in the Midlands and North to heed the existence of substantial pro-Brexit support in their constituencies. Labour's position is made more difficult by the Liberal Democrats' vigorous advocacy of doing what-ever it takes to stay in the EU. If Labour MPs vote to approve a Brexit deal, pro-Remain Labour voters might demonstrate their disapproval by bolting to the Liberal Democrats in a forthcoming election. Lib Dem leader Tim Farron is currently working assiduously to assure such voters that they would be most welcome.

The larger point is that Brexit has strong potential to destabilize what is already a fragmenting and shaky party system. Over the past several decades, public support for the two main parties in UK poli-tics has decreased sharply (Clarke et al. 2016a: ch. 7). In 2015, less than half (46 per cent) of the eligible electorate went to the polls and voted for either Conservative or Labour. Public disaffection with how a Brexit deal is handled could drive that figure further down-ward while simultaneously boosting UKIP fortunes and reviving those of the Liberal Democrats or smaller parties like the Greens.

The future of the UK polity itself may be at stake as well. Immediately after the 2016 referendum, Nicola Sturgeon, leader of the SNP, started taking soundings about holding a second referen-dum on Scottish independence. Very negative reactions among the Scottish electorate to a Brexit deal that then was approved by the UK

Parliament might embolden Sturgeon and the SNP to try to schedule such a second independence referendum. Although the 2014 referendum saw 55.3 per cent of voters in Scotland opt to remain in the UK, widely publicized polls taken only a week before the vote pushed the political establishment into panic by showing that a majority might actually opt for independence. Whether Scottish opinion will be moved strongly in a pro-independence direction by the forthcoming Brexit negotiations and what ensues thereafter is difficult to forecast. Some observers might argue that the possibility of Scotland voting to leave the UK is real, but remote. However, others might rejoin by reminding us that Brexit seemed unlikely less than a year before the referendum. But that has now happened and the future of the UK's economy and its system of party politics are definitely in play. In a populist era of 'people versus politics', the larger political system is not immune either.

Britain is embarking on a journey of historic proportions by leaving the European Union and it will be many years before the full consequences are known both for the UK and for the EU. The last decade has been the most tumultuous and crisis-ridden for the EU in its history, having gone through a perfect storm of a financial crash, economic stagnation and a largely unwelcome mass immigration. It should be noted that the institutions of the EU, the decision-makers in Brussels and political leaders in the individual member states have not coped well. That said, the EU has reserves of strength and may be able to navigate these troubled waters in the future and recover. Whatever happens, the UK will no longer be at the heart of Europe, since its 44-year experiment with European integration has come to an end.

Notes

1 Brexit Introduced

1 'EU speech at Bloomberg', 23 January 2013. Transcript available online: www.gov.uk/government/speeches/eu-speech-at-bloomberg (accessed 12 December 2016).
2 See Jennings and Fisher (2016).
3 'We still expect the UK to stay in the EU', Economist Intelligence Unit, 29 January 2016.
4 See, e.g., Banks 2016; Bennett 2016; Shipman 2016.

2 Campaign Prologue

1 Data taken from YouGov/*The Times*, 'End of Year' survey', fieldwork 17–18 December 2015. Available from the YouGov online archive. See also the Ipsos MORI Issues Index. Available online: www.ipsos-mori.com/researchpublications/researcharchive/2905/Issues-Index-2012-onwards.aspx?view=wide#2016 (accessed 9 December 2016).
2 YouGov/*The Times*, 5–6 June 2016.
3 The report received widespread coverage. For example, Peter Dominiczak and Peter Spence, 'Mass migration driving down wages offered to British jobseekers', *Daily Telegraph*, 21 December 2015.
4 See, for example, 'Nearly 500,000 refugees and their kids "could flock to Britain from EU by 2020"', *Mirror*, 31 May 2016. Available online: www.mirror.co.uk/news/uk-news/nearly-500000-refugees-kids-could-8085533 (accessed 28 December 2016).
5 On the characteristics of Labour members see Tim Bale, 'Corbyn's Labour: Survey of post-2015 Labour members and supporters', Queen Mary University of London Blog. Available online: www.qmul.ac.uk/media/news/items/178403.html (accessed 29 December 2016).
6 Data taken from the regular YouGov tracker series. Available via the YouGov online archive: https://d25d2506sfb94s.cloudfront.net/cumulus_uploads/document/r9pkroarmk/YG%20Trackers-Leaders%20Approval-160408.xlsx.pdf (accessed 29 December 2016).

7 David Cameron referred to Eurosceptic Conservatives 'banging on about Europe' in his speech to the Conservative Conference in 2006. See http://news.bbc.co.uk/2/hi/uk_news/politics/5396358.stm. The 'mad, swivel-eyed loons' reference was made by a senior Conservative in reference to MPs who wanted an EU referendum included in the May 2013 Queen's Speech. See www.theguardian.com/politics/2013/may/18/david-cameron-ally-activists-loons.

8 The Cabinet ministers were Michael Gove, Lord Chancellor and Secretary State for Justice; Chris Grayling, Lord President of the Council and Leader of the House of Commons; John Whittingdale, Secretary of State for Culture, Media and Sport; Theresa Villiers; Secretary of State for Northern Ireland; and Priti Patel, Minister of State for Employment. Of the 39 peers, 32 were Conservative.

9 Prominent supporters of Labour Leave included the Labour donor John Mills and Labour MPs Kate Hoey, John Mann and Frank Field.

10 Stephen Fisher and Alan Renwick, 'Do people tend to vote against change in referendums?', 22 June 2016, Elections Etc. Blog. Available online: https://electionsetc.com/2016/06/22/do-people-tend-to-vote-against-change-in-referendums/#more-1841 (accessed 17 December 2016). They also note, however, that only at one previous referendum (in Malta) did voters support the change option against the advice of their prime minister.

11 YouGov Eurotrack December poll, fieldwork 16–22 December 2016. The poll also included Norway, which we exclude from the comparison. Majorities in Germany, France, Denmark, Sweden and Finland said they would vote to remain.

12 BMG/*Evening Standard* poll, 26 November 2015. Available online: www.bmgresearch.co.uk/standardbmg-poll-in-out-battle-on-knife-edge-as-eu-referendum-poll-narrows-to-5050/ (accessed 13 December 2016).

13 YouGov survey, 20–24 November 2015. Available online through YouGov's archive.

14 The principles listed in Cameron's letter included recognition that the EU has more than one currency, that there should be no discrimination and no disadvantage for any business on the basis of the currency of their country, that the integrity of the single market be protected, that any changes the eurozone makes, such as the creation of a banking union, must be voluntary (never compulsory) for non-euro countries, that taxpayers in non-euro countries should never be financially liable for operations to support the eurozone as a currency, and that any issues that affect all member states should be discussed and decided by all member states. For the full letter from David Cameron to Donald Tusk

see www.gov.uk/government/uploads/system/uploads/attachment_data/file/475679/Donald_Tusk_letter.pdf (accessed 29 December 2016).

15 Survation poll for Leave.EU, 17 November 2015.

16 John Curtice, 'Did the English Dinner make any difference? First evidence from Survation', What UK Thinks, 21 February 2016. Available online: http://whatukthinks.org/eu/did-the-english-dinner-make-any-difference-first-evidence-from-survation/ (accessed 9 December 2016).

17 Oliver Wright, 'EU referendum: Benefits brake could boost numbers of EU migrants', *Independent*, 7 February 2016; Redwood cited in ' "The deal is not good enough": David Cameron's EU talks on migrant benefits FAIL putting June referendum in doubt', *MailOnline*, 29 January 2016.

18 'Revealed: Just one in ten EU migrants could be affected by David Cameron's "emergency brake"', *MailOnline*, 5 February 2016.

19 YouGov polling. In a subsequent poll by Opinium, 17 per cent of respondents felt that the deal was a 'very' or 'quite good', while 42 per cent thought it was 'quite bad' or 'very bad'.

20 John Curtice 'Is David Cameron now leader of the opposition?', 29 February 2016. What UK Thinks Blog. Available online: http://whatukthinks.org/eu/is-david-cameron-now-leader-of-the-opposition/ (accessed 16 December 2016).

3 Into Battle

1 'EU vote: Where the cabinet and other MPs stand', BBC News, 22 June 2016. Available online: www.bbc.co.uk/news/uk-politics-eu-referendum-35616946 (accessed 30 December 2016).

2 The 10 Labour MPs were Dennis Skinner, Frank Field, Gisela Stuart, Graham Stringer, John Cryer, Kate Hoey, Kelvin Hopkins, Roger Godsiff, Ronnie Campbell and John Mann.

3 The 17 ministers were Mike Penning, John Hayes, James Duddridge, Michael Gove, Dominic Raab, Penny Mordaunt, Julian Brazier, Priti Patel, Justin Tomlinson, Chris Grayling, Desmond Swayne, Theresa Villiers, George Eustice, Mark Francois, James Wharton, John Whittingdale and Andrea Leadsom.

4 Andrew Cooper, personal email to Matthew Goodwin, 20 December 2016.

5 Andrew Cooper, personal email to Matthew Goodwin, 20 December 2016.

6 Andrew Cooper, personal email to Matthew Goodwin, 20 December 2016.

7 Will Straw, personal email to Matthew Goodwin, 1 January 2017.

8 Owen Bennett, 'Nigel Farage: Immigration will be main EU referendum issue and Jeremy Corbyn is a gift to us', *Huffington Post*, 25 September 2015.

9 'Liam Fox: Terrorists could enter Britain among refugees', *Daily Telegraph*, 30 January 2016.

10 'Europe: The real crisis', *Daily Mail*, 20 February 2016.

11 'On the referendum #17: The state of the campaign', Dominic Cummings's Blog, 26 September 2015.

12 Business for Britain Bulletin, 26 September 2015.

13 'Pro-EU group says Brexit would cost London £14bn', City A.M., 8 February 2016.

14 Ipsos MORI 'Captains of Industry' survey, 11 January 2016. Available online: www.ipsos-mori.com/researchpublications/researcharchive/3680/More-than-four-in-five-business-leaders-hope-for-remain-vote-in-EU-referendum.aspx (accessed 21 December 2016).

15 'G20 warns of multibillion pound cost to UK', *Sunday Times*, 28 February 2016.

16 Paul Stephenson, 'How to win a referendum', *Politico Europe*, 9 December 2016. Available online: www.politico.eu/article/how-to-win-a-referendum-brexit-inside-story-vote-leave-campaign/ (accessed 9 December 2016).

17 Will Straw, personal email to Matthew Goodwin, 1 January 2017.

18 John Curtice, 'A lot of polls – but still much uncertainty', What UK Thinks Blog, 8 April 2016. Available online: http://whatukthinks.org/eu/a-lot-of-polls-but-still-much-uncertainty/ (accessed 16 December 2016).

19 Rob Davies, 'Airbus executives write staff letter warning of Brexit dangers', *Guardian*, 4 April 2016.

20 'Brexit backers release list of 50 dangerous EU criminals who entered the UK', *Mirror*, 29 March 2016.

21 'Luxury hotels, private jets, limos and even EU-branded chocolate', *MailOnline*, 14 June 2016.

22 'Liam Fox urges Wales to quit EU and invest cash in schools and hospitals', *Wales Online*, 16 April 2016.

23 'Vote Leave must do better for Britain', *Daily Telegraph*, 25 May 2016.

24 YouGov/*Sunday Times*, 9–10 June 2016.

25 See Chris Giles, 'IMF warns Brexit could wreak "severe" damage in UK and beyond', *Financial Times*, 12 April 2016; Jason Douglas, 'IMF doubles down on "Brexit" warning', *Wall Street Journal*, 13 May 2016.

26 HM Government, 'Why the Government believes that voting to remain in the European Union is the best decision for the UK'. Available online: www.gov.uk/government/uploads/system/uploads/attachment_data/file/515068/why-the-government-believes-that-voting-to-remain-in-the-european-union-is-the-best-decision-for-the-uk.pdf (accessed 12 December 2016).

27 'Brexit poses triple threat to jobs, wages and prices', *Belfast Telegraph*, 27 April 2016.

28 'Cameron says UK exit could put peace at risk', BBC News, 9 May 2016. Available online: www.bbc.co.uk/news/uk-politics-eu-referendum-36243296 (accessed 12 December 2016).

29 'Carney warns Brexit risks causing recession', Bloomberg News, 12 May 2016; 'Brexit vote may spark recession, Mark Carney warns', BBC News, 12 May 2016.

30 'The *Guardian* view on the referendum debate', *Guardian*, 15 May 2016.

31 'Migrants are pushing NHS to breaking point', *Daily Mail*, 9 February 2016.

32 'Eurosceptics warn of EU threat to NHS', *Sunday Telegraph*, 3 April 2016.

33 Andrew Cooper, personal email to Matthew Goodwin, 20 December 2016.

34 *Andrew Marr Show*, BBC One, 22 May 2016. See also 'NHS chief says Brexit would be dangerous for health service', *Guardian*, 22 May 2016; see also 'BMA leader: Leave claim "farcical"', *Argus*, 20 June 2016.

35 'Jeremy Corbyn accused of whitewashing history', *MailOnline*, 5 March 2016.

36 YouGov/*Sunday Times* poll, 16–17 June 2016.

37 YouGov/*Sunday Times*, 16–17 June 2016.

38 David Cameron on *Peston on Sunday*, ITV, 22 May 2016.

39 'Vote Leave must do better for Britain', *Daily Telegraph*, 25 May 2016.

40 Research on how the campaign played out on social media underscored the centrality of immigration to the Leave camp. A study undertaken at the University of Sheffield revealed that in the run-up to the referendum day, Leave voters sent twice as many tweets about borders and immigration as they did about sovereignty, employment, the justice system or the NHS.

41 'Gove: EU immigrant influx will make NHS unsustainable by 2030', *Guardian*, 20 May 2016.

42 'UK will see "bodies washing up" on beaches', *Daily Telegraph*, 4 June 2016.

43 'Immigration focus is turning point in EU campaign, says Farage', BBC News, 3 June 2016.

4 Attitudes to Brexit Over Time

1 For a discussion of the report and broader evidence see Jonathan Portes, 'How small is small? The impact of immigration on UK wages', National Institute of Economic and Social Research Blog, 17 January 2016. Available online: www.niesr.ac.uk/blog/how-small-small-impact-immigration-uk-wages#.WGQjhraLSWh (accessed 28 December 2016).

2 For example, survey data from the 1970–2002 Eurobarometer Trend File show that 60 per cent of the respondents claimed to have exclusive national identities in 1993 and 62 per cent did so in 2002, nearly a decade later. In contrast, 45 per cent of respondents thought that EU membership was a good thing in 1993, but this declined to 32 per cent in 2002.

3 This interpretation of party positions is supported by data from the Comparative Manifesto project. In 2010 positive references to the European Union in the manifesto coding scheme (variable per108) were 1.5 for Labour, 2.21 for the Liberal Democrats and 0.99 for the Conservatives. Negative references (variable per110) were 0.26 for Labour, 0.49 for the Liberal Democrats and 1.44 for the Conservatives. The net scores (positive minus negative) mean that the Liberal Democrats were the most pro-EU of the major three parties, the Conservatives were the least pro-EU and Labour was in the middle. See https://manifesto-project.wzb.eu/.

4 The VEC model can be defined as follows:

$$\Delta Xt = \mu + \sum_{i=1}^{p-1} \Gamma \Delta Xt_{-k} + \alpha\beta' X_{t-1} + \varepsilon_t$$

where

Xt = vector of non-stationary variables with order of integration d
Δ = differencing operator
Γ = matrix of parameters p for short-run effects of variables, 1 to k lags
α = adjustment parameters for r cointegrating vectors
$\beta'Xt\text{-}1$ = $r \times 1$ vector of stationary cointegrating relations
μ = constant
ε_t = stochastic error term $\sim N(0,\sigma2)$.

An earlier version of this type of model known as Vector Autoregression (VAR) was introduced by the Nobel Prize-winning economist Christopher Sims (1980) to deal with what he referred to as the 'incredible' restrictions being placed on large-scale econometric models in order to estimate their parameters.

5 The question is: 'Generally speaking, do you think of yourself as Conservative, Labour, Liberal Democrat or what?'

6 Dickey–Fuller tests are used to test for non-stationarity. See Dickey and Fuller 1979; Becketti 2013: 382–4. Note that the Dickey–Fuller tests are conducted with six lags to control for autocorrelation in the residuals.

The second column in Table 4.1 repeats the test for differenced versions of the variables and in this case they are all clearly stationary. Technically, we say that the variables are integrated of order 1 (I(1)).

7 This involves two steps. One is to determine how many lagged or past values of variables are needed to model current values. The second is to find out if the variables do indeed cointegrate by interacting in a long-term equilibrium relationship with each other over time. The lag tests are done by an iterative process of estimating equations with varying lags and from this inferring the optimal lag lengths. Two model selection statistics, the Akaike (AIC) and Schwartz Bayesian (BIC) information criteria, are utilized in this exercise (Becketti 2013: 306). These statistics trade off model complexity against goodness-of-fit and number of model parameters. Models with several lags naturally tend to fit better than models with fewer lags, but the loss of parsimony engendered by the need to estimate extra parameters is penalized by these statistics (Stock and Watson 2001).

8 With six variables in the system there are many possible cointegrating relationships, and Johansen (1991) showed that this number can be inferred from the rank of the $\alpha\beta'$ matrix in the equation in note 4, above. This rank test is influenced by the number of lags in the system and so as a conservative test we use two lags in the analysis rather than one.

9 The adjustment coefficient of –.22 implies that a shock that changes attitudes towards UK membership by 1 per cent will subsequently be eroded by slightly over one fifth of a per cent in each subsequent month, thereby restoring the cointegrating variables to their dynamic equilibrium in about five months.

10 Diagnostic tests indicate that the model does not suffer from residual autocorrelation.

11 The intuition behind Granger causality tests is that if the goodness-of-fit for a model declines significantly when a predictor is removed that is evidence of Granger causality. Since the variables are non-stationary we use the Toda and Yamamato (1995) procedure for testing this possibility. This involves adding extra lags to the system to control for the asymptotic effects created by the non-stationary variables and testing a limited number of these lags only (Giles 2011). Four lags were used and two were tested for Granger causality.

12 Since the dependent variable is a five-category ordinal scale of attitudes to the UK's EU membership ranging from 'strongly disapprove' to 'strongly approve', model parameters are estimated using an ordinal logit analysis (Raudenbush and Bryk 2002).

13 The aggregate-level contextual variables influence variation in the random intercept term in the individual-level equation. See, e.g., Raudenbush and Bryk 2002.

14 Specifically, the log odds ratio of a person strongly approving of UK membership is 1.03 less than the log odds of them holding a less favourable or hostile opinion about membership.

15 The odds ratios for national economic evaluations are 1.04 and 1.12 for personal financial evaluations using the same five-point scales.

5 *The People's Army*

1 'Local elections: Nigel Farage hails results as "game changer"', BBC News, 3 May 2013.

2 'Nigel Farage's speech at the UKIP 2013 conference', *Spectator*, 20 September 2013.

3 Cited in Goodwin and Milazzo (2015: 40).

4 In 2008 a Conservative MP, Bob Spink, did defect to UKIP although he was never elected to the House of Commons under the UKIP banner and subsequently declared as an Independent. Douglas Carswell was the first candidate to be elected as a UKIP MP when he won the Clacton by-election on 9 October 2014.

5 Iain Johnston, 'Nigel Farage is "snarling, thin-skinned and aggressive", claims Patrick O'Flynn', *Independent*, 14 May 2015.

6 The online survey was conducted using the Qualtric platform. See www.Qualtric.com/Survey.Software.

7 See, e.g., 'Ukip is facing financial ruin', *Mail on Sunday*, 8 November 2015.

8 For studies of local party activists in Britain, see, e.g., Seyd and Whiteley 1992; Seyd et al. 1995; Whiteley and Seyd 2002; Whiteley et al. 2006. See also the study of Canada's right-wing populist Reform Party in Clarke et al. 2000: ch: 7, and the comparative study of local party members in the United States and Canada by Kornberg et al. (1979).

9 For information regarding the construction of the several predictor variables, see the Brexit Measurement Appendix at www.utdallas.edu/epps/hclarke.

10 Since the three factors measuring different kinds of activity are continuous variables (factor scores), we use ordinary least squares regression to estimate model parameters.

6 *The Rise of UKIP*

1 A sizeable literature on support for European right-wing populist parties has appeared over the past two decades. See, e.g., Betz 1993; Swank and Eisinga 1999; Hooghe et al. 2004; Minkenberg and Perrineau 2007; Mudde 2007; Oesch 2008; Arzheimer 2009; Goodwin 2011; Ford and Goodwin 2014. More general studies relevant to understanding

openings for minor parties in the British party system include, *inter alia*, Schofield 1993; Steenbergen and Scott 2004; Van der Eijk and Franklin 2004; Nagel and Wlezien 2010; Stevens 2013. See also Dalton 2013; Lewis-Beck et al. 2013.

2 See www.ukpolitical.info/european-parliament-election-turnout.htm.

3 These judgements are measured as latent variables derived from dynamic factor analyses of multiple indicators of attitudes towards each of the issues. The indicators include cognitive evaluations as well as emotional reactions. The details of the measures appear in the methodological appendix located at www.utdallas.edu/epps/hclarke.

4 Note that 0 denotes 'strongly dislike' and 10 denotes 'strongly like'.

5 Technically the model is an EGARCH process, that is, an exponential generalized autoregressive conditional heteroscedasticity model that allows for an asymmetric response to new information that is negative rather than positive (Enders 2014: ch. 3).

6 The dummy variable scores one if the respondent thought that UKIP could best handle their most important issue, and zero otherwise

7 This is captured with a dummy variable.

8 The analyses are logistic regression models. See, e.g., Long and Freese 2014.

9 There are not enough cases at the aggregate level to determine if Nigel Farage had a greater or lesser impact on voting for UKIP over time.

10 The effect is significant at the .17 level.

11 The effect is significant at the .19 level.

12 The correlation with Liberal Democrat support is also sizeable ($r = -.57$), but the correlation with Labour support is considerably smaller ($r = +.32$).

7 Voting to Leave

1 The Electoral Commission website has the official referendum results. See www.electoralcommission.org.uk.

2 The constituency-level referendum voting percentages were estimated by Chris Hanretty. See https://medium.com/@chrishanretty/the-eu-referendum-how-did-westminster-constituencies-vote-283c85cd20e1#.nvevi8ffx.

3 The survey was conducted by YouGov under the direction of Joe Twyman using funds provided by the ESR's The UK in a Changing Europe programme, directed by Anand Menon.

4 A 95 per cent confidence interval (standard error = 1.2 per cent) for the vote shares reported in the survey easily covers the actual vote percentages for Remain and Leave.

5 See the Brexit Measurement Appendix for descriptions of the survey variables used in various analyses: www.utdallas.edu/epps/hclarke.

6 In equation form, the model is:

$$\text{logit}(E[\text{Vote}]) = B_0 + B_1*\text{Fecinf} + B_2*\text{Fimter} + B_3*\text{Emreac} + B_4*\text{Euiss} +$$

$$B_5-B_8*\text{Leader} + B_9-B_{14}*\text{Partyid} + B_{15}-B_{19}*\text{Natid} +$$

$$B_{20}-B_{21}*\text{Ccamp} + B_{22}-B_{25}*\text{Demos}(1)$$

where: Vote = referendum vote; Fecinf = economy–influence benefit–cost factor; Fimter = immigration–terrorism benefit–cost factor; Emreac = emotional reactions to EU; Euiss = importance of EU issue; Leader = leader images (Cameron, Corbyn, Farage, Johnson); Natid = national identities (British, English, European, Scottish, Welsh, Other); Ccamp = contact by Leave or Remain campaigns; Demos = socio-demographics (age, education, gender, social class).

7 Although some voters were enthusiastic about Farage, his mean score on the 0–10 like-dislike scale was relatively low, 3.2, and only 27 per cent of our survey respondents gave him a score of 6 or greater on the scale. These mediocre numbers and the fact that he was a familiar figure on the political stage, indicate that his presence could not be considered a plausible campaign-period intervention that tipped the balance in favour of Leave. Farage's image was an influential, but longer-term, factor in the set of forces driving referendum voting.

8 The Consequences of Brexit

1 'Chief economist of Bank of England admits errors in Brexit forecasting', *Guardian*, 5 January 2017.

2 See https://nimodel.niesr.ac.uk/.

3 This is the variable is called rgdpna in the dataset and measures growth in $ millions.

4 Capital investment is rkna, employment is emp, the human capital index is hc, exports is csh_x and imports csh_m and the exchange rate is xr in the database.

5 This is the same as the error correction mechanism discussed in Chapter 4.

6 The standard deviation of the index is only 0.43 throughout the entire period, so changes are very small.

7 A short-run pulse version of the EU membership model was not statistically significant either, although it is difficult to untangle the short-run effects of the oil crises from those associated with the UK joining the EU.

8 Smaller values of the Akaike Information Criterion (AIC) and the Bayesian Information Criterion (BIC) indicate superior model performance, taking into account the number of parameters specified. See Burnham and Anderson (2011).

9 Note that some of the immigration data in the early part of the decade were missing and so have been interpolated in the analysis.

10 Note that the series was published every other year from 1996 to 2002 and annually thereafter. In the following analysis data for the missing years have been interpolated.

9 Beyond Brexit

1 www.euronews.com/2017/01/07/have-economists-brexit-forecasts-been-too-negative.

2 See www.europeansocialsurvey.org/.

3 The scale is recoded so that a high value indicates that the respondent thinks that the Government gives immigrants special treatment.

4 There were missing data for the Czech Republic for this question, but some 73.3 per cent of Czechs were refusing to take any poor refugees from outside Europe so they were very anti-immigrant at that time.

References

Acemoglu, Daron. 2009. *Introduction to Modern Economic Growth.* Princeton University Press.

Acemoglu, Daron, Simon Johnson and James A. Robinson. 2001. 'The Colonial Origins of Comparative Development: An Empirical Investigation'. *American Economic Review* 91: 1369–401.

Acock, Alan C. 2013. *Discovering Structural Equation Modeling Using Stata*, rev. edn. College Station, TX: Stata Press.

Aghion, P. and P. Howitt. 1998. *Endogenous Growth Theory.* Cambridge, MA: MIT Press.

Anderson, Christopher J. and M. Shawn Reichert. 1996. 'Economic Benefits and Support for Membership in the E.U.: A Cross-National Analysis'. *Journal of Public Policy* 15: 231–49.

Apaza, Carmen R. 2009. 'Measuring Governance and Corruption through the Worldwide Governance Indicators: Critiques, Responses, and Ongoing Scholarly Discussion'. *PS: Political Science and Politics* 42: 139–43.

Armingeon, Klause and Basir Ceka. 2014. 'The Loss of Trust in the European Union during the Great Recession since 2007: The Role of Heuristics from the National Political System'. *European Union Politics* 15: 82–107.

Arrow, Kenneth and Gerard Debreu. 1954. 'Existence of an Equilibrium for a Competitive Economy'. *Econometrica* 22: 265–90.

Arzheimer, K. 2009. 'Contextual Factors and the Extreme Right Vote in Western Europe, 1980–2002'. *American Journal of Political Science* 53: 259–75.

Bale, Tim. 2016. *The Conservative Party: From Thatcher to Cameron*, 2nd edn. Cambridge: Polity Press.

Banks, Arron. 2016. *Bad Boys of Brexit: Tales of Mischief, Mayhem and Guerrilla Warfare in the EU Referendum Campaign.* London: Biteback Publishing.

Barro, Robert. 1991. 'Economic Growth in a Cross-Section of Countries'. *Quarterly Journal of Economics* 106: 407–33.

1999. 'Determinants of Democracy', *Journal of Political Economy* 107(6.2): S158–S183.

Barro, Robert and J. W. Lee. 1994. 'Sources of Economic Growth'. *Carnegie-Rochester Conference Series on Public Policy* 40(June): 1–46.

Barro, Robert and X. Sala-I-Martin. 2004. *Economic Growth.* New York: McGraw-Hill.

Becketti, Sean. 2013. *Introduction to Time Series Using Stata.* College Station, TX: Stata Press.

Beetham, D., ed. 1994. *Defining and Measuring Democracy.* London: Sage.

Bennett, Owen. 2016. *The Brexit Club: The Inside Story of the Leave Campaign's Shock Victory.* London: Biteback Publishing.

Betz, H.-G. 1993. 'The New Politics of Resentment: Radical Right-Wing Populist Parties in Western Europe'. *Comparative Politics* 25: 413–27.

Bijak J. 2010. *Forecasting International Migration in Europe: A Bayesian View.* Springer Series on Demographic Methods and Population Analysis 24. Dordrecht: Springer.

Blaug, M. 1962. *Economic Theory in Retrospect.* Cambridge University Press.

Bogdanor, Vernon. 2016. 'Europe and the Sovereignty of the People'. *Political Quarterly* 87: 348–51.

Boomgaarden, Hajo G., Andreas R. T. Schuck, Matthijs Elenbaas and Claes H. deVreese. 2011. 'Mapping EU Attitudes: Conceptual and Empirical Dimensions of Euroscepticism and EU Support'. *European Union Politics* 12: 241–66.

Boix, C. 1998. *Political Parties, Growth and Equality: Conservative and Social Democratic Strategies in the World Economy.* Cambridge University Press.

Box, George E. P. and Gwilym M. Jenkins. 1976. *Time Series Analysis: Forecasting and Control.* San Francisco: Holden-Day.

Burnham, Kenneth P. and David R. Anderson. 2011. *Model Selection and Multimodel Inference: A Practical Information-Theoretic Approach*, 2nd edn. New York: Springer-Verlag.

Butler, David and Uwe W. Kitzinger. 1996. *The 1975 Referendum*, 2nd edn. London: Macmillan.

Butler, David and Austin Ranney, eds. 1994. *Referendums around the World: The Growing Use of Direct Democracy.* London: Macmillan.

Butler, David and David E. Stokes. 1969. *Political Change in Britain: Forces Shaping Electoral Choice.* New York: St. Martin's Press.

Carey, Sean. 2002. 'Undivided Loyalties: Is National Identity an Obstacle to European Integration?'. *European Union Politics* 3: 387–413.

Castles, F. G. 1982. *The Impact of Parties: Politics and Policies in Democratic Capitalist States.* London: Sage Publications.

Caul, Miki and M. M. Gray. 2000. 'From Platform Declarations to Policy Outcomes: Changing Party Profiles and Partisan Influence over Policy', in R. J. Dalton and M. P. Wattenberg, eds., *Parties without Partisans: Political Change in Advanced Industrial Democracies.* Oxford University Press.

Clarke, Harold D. 2016. 'Neither Loved nor Trusted: British Political Parties', in Philip Cowley, ed., *More Sex, Lies and Politics: Another 50 Things You Need to Know About Elections.* London: Biteback Publishing.

Clarke, Harold D., Allan Kornberg and Peter Wearing. 2000. *A Polity on the Edge: Canada and the Politics of Fragmentation.* University of Toronto Press.

Clarke, Harold D., David Sanders, Marianne C. Stewart and Paul Whiteley. 2004. *Political Choice in Britain.* Oxford University Press.

2009a. *Performance Politics and the British Voter.* Cambridge University Press.

Clarke, Harold D., Allan Kornberg and Thomas J. Scotto. 2009b. *Making Political Choices: Canada and the United States.* University of Toronto Press.

Clarke, Harold D., Peter Kellner, Marianne C. Stewart, Joe Twyman and Paul Whiteley. 2016a. *Austerity and Political Choice in Britain.* London: Palgrave Macmillan.

Clarke, Harold D., Paul Whiteley, Walter Borges, David Sanders and Marianne C. Stewart. 2016b. 'Modelling the Dynamics of Support for a Right-Wing Populist Party: The Case of UKIP'. *Journal of Elections, Public Opinion and Parties* 26: 135–54.

Conservative Party. 2015. *The Conservative Manifesto.* London: Conservative Party.

Cowley, Philip and Dennis Kavanagh. 2016. *The British General Election of 2015.* London: Palgrave Macmillan.

Dahl, Robert. 1954. *A Preface to Democratic Theory.* University of Chicago Press.

1961. *Who Governs?* New Haven, CT: Yale University Press.

Daianu, Daniel, Giorgio Basevi, Carlo D'Adda and Rajeesh Kumar, eds. 2014. *The Eurozone Crisis and the Future of Europe.* London: Palgrave Macmillan.

Dalton, Russell J. 2013. *Citizen Politics: Public Opinion and Political Parties in Advanced Industrial Democracies*, 6th edn. Washington, DC: Congressional Quarterly Press.

Debreu, Gerard. 1974. 'Excess Demand Functions'. *Journal of Mathematical Economics* 1: 15–23.

De Haan, J., S. Lundstrom and J.-E. Sturm. 2004. 'Market-Orientated Institutions and Policies and Economic Growth: A Critical Survey'. *Journal of Economic Surveys* 29: 157–91.

Desai, Meghnad. 1981. *Testing Monetarism*. London: Frances Pinter.

2015. *Hubris: Why Economists Failed to Predict the Crisis and How to Avoid the Next One*. New Haven, CT: Yale University Press.

DeVreese, Claes H. and Hajo G. Boomgaarden. 2005. 'Projecting EU Referendums: Fear of Immigration and Support for European Integration'. *European Union Politics* 6: 59–82.

Dickey, D. and W. Fuller. 1979. 'Distribution of the Estimators for Autoregressive Time Series with a Unit Root'. *Journal of the American Statistical Association* 74(366): 427–31.

Disney, G., A. Wiśniowski, J. J. Forster, P. W. Smith and J. Bijak. 2015. *Evaluation of Existing Migration Forecasting Methods and Models. Report for the Migratory Advisory Committee*. University of Southampton, Centre for Population Change.

Dow, C. 1998. *Major Recessions: Britain and the World 1920 to 1995*. Oxford University Press.

Downs, Anthony. 1957. *An Economic Theory of Democracy*. New York: Harper & Row.

Dustmann, C., T. Frattini and I. P. Preston. 2013. 'The Effect of Immigration along the Distribution of Wages'. *Review of Economic Studies* 80(1): 145–73.

Eichenberg, Richard C. and Russell J. Dalton. 1993. 'Europeans and the European Community: The Dynamics of Public Support for European Integration'. *International Organization* 47: 507–34.

Enders, Walter. 2014. *Applied Econometric Time Series*, 4th edn. New York: John Wiley & Sons.

Featherston, K. and C. M. Radaelli, eds. 2003. *The Politics of Europeanization*. Oxford University Press.

Feenstra, R. C., R. Inklaar and M. P. Timmer. 2015. 'The Next Generation of the Penn World Table'. *American Economic Review* 105: 3150–82.

Fiorina, Morris P. 1981. *Retrospective Voting in American National Elections*. New Haven, CT: Yale University Press.

Ford, Robert. 2010. 'Who Might Vote for the BNP? Survey Evidence on the Electoral Potential of the Extreme Right in Britain', in M. J. Goodwin and R. Eatwell, eds., *The New Extremism in 21st Century Britain*. London and New York: Routledge.

Ford, Robert and Matthew J. Goodwin. 2011. 'Angry White Men: Individual and Contextual Predictors of Support for the British National Party'. *Political Studies* 58: 1–25.

2014. *Revolt on the Right: Explaining Support for the Radical Right in Britain*. London: Routledge.

Franklin, Mark, Michael Marsh and Lauren McLaren. 1994. 'Uncorking the Bottle: Popular Opposition to European Unification in the Wake of Maastricht'. *Journal of Common Market Studies* 32: 455–73.

Franklin, Mark, Cees van der Eijk and Michael Marsh.1995. 'Referendum Outcomes and Trust in Government: Public Support for Europe in the Wake of Maastricht'. *West European Politics* 18: 101–17.

Friedman, M. and A. Schwartz. 1963. *A Monetary History of the United States 1867–1980*. Princeton University Press.

Gabel, Matthew. 1998. Public Support for European Integration: An Empirical Test of Five Theories'. *Journal of Politics* 60: 333–54.

Gabel, Matthew and Harvey Palmer. 1995. 'Understanding Variation in Public Support for European Integration'. *European Journal of Political Research* 27: 3–19.

Gabel, Matthew and Kenneth Scheve. 2007. 'Mixed Messages: Party Dissent and Mass Opinion on European Integration'. *European Union Politics* 8: 37–59.

Gabel, Matthew and Guy D. Whitten. 1997. 'Economic Conditions, Economic Perceptions, and Public Support for European Integration'. *Political Behavior* 19: 81–96.

Garrett, Geoffrey. 1998. *Partisan Politics in the Global Economy*. Cambridge University Press.

Garry, John. 2013. 'Emotions and Voting in EU Referendums'. *European Union Politics* 15: 235–54.

George, Stephen. 1998. *An Awkward Partner: Britain in the European Community*. Oxford University Press.

Gigerenzer, Gerd. 2008. *Rationality for Mortals: How People Cope with Uncertainty*. Oxford University Press.

Giles, David. 2011. 'Testing for Granger Causality'. http://davidgiles.blogspot.co.uk/2011/04/testing_for_granger_causality.html. Accessed 20 March 2014.

Goodwin, Matthew. 2011. *Right Response: Understanding and Countering Populist Extremism in Europe*. London: Chatham House.

Goodwin, Matthew and Caitlin Milazzo. 2015. *UKIP: Inside the Campaign to Redraw the Map of British Politics*. Oxford University Press.

Gudgin, Graham, Ken Coutts and Neil Gibson. 2017. *The Macro-Economic Impact of Brexit Using the CBR Macro-Economic Model of the UK Economy (UKMod)*. Working Paper 483. Centre for Business Research, University of Cambridge.

Haesly, Richard. 2001. 'Euroskeptics, Europhiles and Instrumental Europeans: European Attachment in Scotland and Wales'. *European Union Politics* 2: 81–102.

Hakhverdian, Armen, Erika van Elsas, Wouter van der Brug and Theresa Kuhn. 2013. 'Euroscepticism and Education: A Longitudinal Study of 12 EU Member States, 1973–2010'. *European Union Politics* 14: 522–41.

Hall, R. E. and Jones, C. I. 1999. 'Why Do Some Countries Produce So Much More Output Per Worker Than Others?'. *Quarterly Journal of Economics* 114: 83–116.

Ham, Chris, Beccy Baird, Sarah Gregory, Joni Jabbal and Hugh Alderwick. 2015. *The NHS under the Coalition Government*. London: King's Fund.

Head, K. and T. Mayer. 2013. *Gravity Equations: Workhorse, Toolkit and Cookbook*. Working Paper 2013-27, September. Paris: Centre d'Études Prospectives et d'Information Internationales.

Hellwig, Timothy. 2014. *Globalization and Mass Politics: Retaining the Room to Maneuver*. Cambridge University Press.

Helpman, E. 2004. *The Mystery of Economic Growth*. Cambridge, MA: The Belknap Press of Harvard University Press.

Hennig, B. D. 2016. 'Trade Inside the European Union'. *Political Insight* 7(3): 20–1.

Heston, A., R. Summers and B. Aten. 2006. *Penn World Table Version 6.2*. Philadelphia, PA: Center for International Comparisons of Production, Income, and Prices, University of Pennsylvania.

Hix, Simon. 2004. *The Political System of the European Union*. London: Palgrave Macmillan.

HM Government. 2016. *HM Treasury Analysis: The Long-Term Economic Impact of EU Membership and the Alternatives*. CM 9250, April. London: HM Treasury.

HM Treasury. 2010. *Budget 2010*. London: HM Treasury.

Hobolt, Sara. 2007. 'Taking Cues on Europe? Voter Competence and Party Endorsement in Referendums on EU Integration'. *European Journal of Political Research* 46: 151–82.

Hobolt, Sara and Catherine E. deVries. 2016. 'Public Support for European Integration'. *Annual Review of Political Science* 19: 413–32.

Hobolt, Sara and Christopher Wratil. 2015. 'Public Opinion and the Crisis: The Dynamics of Support for the Euro'. *Journal of European Public Policy* 22: 238–51.

Hooghe, Liesbet and Gary Marks. 2004. 'Does Identity or Economic Rationality Drive Public Opinion on European Integration?'. *PS: Political Science and Politics* 37: 415–20.

2005. 'Calculation, Community and Cues: Public Opinion on European Integration'. *European Union Politics* 6: 419–43.

2009. 'A Postfunctionalist Theory of European Integration: From Permissive Consensus to Constraining Dissensus'. *British Journal of Political Science* 39: 1–23.

Hooghe, Liesbet, Gary Marks and Carole J. Wilson. 2004. 'Does Left/Right Structure Party Positions on European Integration?', in G. Marks and M. R. Steenbergen, eds., *European Integration and Political Conflict*. Cambridge University Press.

Hox, Joop. 2002. *Multilevel Analysis*. Mahwah, NJ: Lawrence Erlbaum Associates.

Huber, E. and J. D. Stephens. 2001. *Development and Crisis of the Welfare State: Parties and Policies in Global Markets*. University of Chicago Press.

Huntingdon, S. P. 1991. *The Third Wave: Democratization in the Late Twentieth Century*. Norman and London: University of Oklahoma Press.

Inglehart, Ronald. 1970. 'Cognitive Mobilization and European Identity'. *Comparative Politics* 3: 45–70.

Jennings, Will and Gerry Stoker. 2016. 'The Bifurcation of Politics: Two Englands'. *Political Quarterly* 87: 372–82.

Johansen, Soren. 1991. 'Estimation and Hypothesis Testing of Cointegration Vectors in Gaussian Vector Autoregressive Models'. *Econometrica* 59: 1551–80.

Johns, Robert, James Mitchell and Christopher J. Carman. 2013. 'Constitution or Competence? The SNP's Re-Election in 2011'. *Political Studies* 61: 158–78.

Juselius, Katerina. 2006. *The Cointegrated VAR Model*. Cambridge University Press.

Kahneman, Daniel. 2011. *Thinking Fast and Slow*. New York: Farrar, Straus and Giroux.

Kaufmann, D., A. Kraay and M. Mastruzzi. 2007. 'Growth and Governance: A Reply'. *Journal of Politics* 69: 555–62.

2009. *Governance Matters VIII: Aggregate and Individual Governance Indicators 1996–2008*. World Bank Policy Research Working Paper 4978. Washington, DC: World Bank.

Kavanagh, Dennis and Philip Cowley. 2010. *The British General Election of 2010*. London: Palgrave Macmillan.

Keegan, William. 2014. *Mr Osborne's Economic Experiment: Austerity 1945–51 and 2010*. London: Searching Finance.

Keman, Hans. 2002. 'Policy Making Capacities of European Party Government', in K. R. Luther and F. Muller-Rommel, eds., *Political Parties in the New Europe*. Oxford University Press: 207–45.

Kennedy, Peter. 2003. *A Guide to Econometrics*. Oxford: Wiley-Blackwell.

Kenny, Michael. 2016. *The Politics of English Nationhood*. Oxford University Press.

Keynes, John Maynard. 1925. *The Economic Consequences of Mr. Churchill*. London: Hogarth Press.

  1936. *The General Theory of Employment, Interest and Money*. London: Macmillan.

Knack, S. and Keefer, P. 1997. 'Does Social Capital Have an Economic Payoff: A Cross Country Investigation'. *Quarterly Journal of Economics* 112: 1251–88.

Kornberg, Allan and Harold D. Clarke. 1992. *Citizens and Community: Political Support in a Democratic Society*. New York: Cambridge University Press.

Kornberg, Allan, Joel Smith and Harold D. Clarke. 1979. *Citizen Politicians – Canada: Party Officials in a Democratic Society*. Durham, NC: Carolina Academic Press.

Krugman, Paul. 2012. *End This Depression Now!* New York: W. W. Norton.

Kurtz, M. and A. Shrank. 2007. 'Growth and Governance: Models, Measures, and Mechanism'. *Journal of Politics* 69: 538–54.

LeDuc, Lawrence. 2003. *The Politics of Direct Democracy: Referendums in Global Perspective*. Toronto: Broadview.

Levine, R. and Renelt, D. 1992. 'A Sensitivity Analysis of Cross-Country Growth Regressions'. *American Economic Review* 82: 942–63.

Lewis-Beck, Michael S. 1988. *Economics and Elections: The Major Western Democracies*. Ann Arbor, MI: University of Michigan Press.

Lewis-Beck, Michael S., Richard Nadeau and Martial Foucault. 2013. 'The Compleat Economic Voter: New Theory and British Evidence'. *British Journal of Political Science* 43: 241–61.

Lijphart, Arend. 1977. *Democracy in Plural Societies: A Comparative Explanation*. New Haven, CT: Yale University Press.

Lindberg, Leon and Stuart Scheingold. 1970. *Europe's Would-Be Polity*. Englewood Cliffs, NJ: Prentice-Hall.

Long, J. Scott and Jeremy Freese. 2014. *Regression Models for Categorical Dependent Variables Using Stata*, 3rd edn. College Station, TX: Stata Press.

Lubbers, M. and P. Scheepers. 2007. 'Euro-Scepticism and Extreme Voting Patterns in Europe. Social Cleavages and Socio-Political Attitudes Determining Voting for the Far Left, the Far Right, and Non-Voting', in G. Loosveldt, M. Swyngedouw and B. Cambré, eds., *Measuring Meaningful Data in Social Research*. Leuven: Acco.

Lutz, W., W. C. Sanderson and S. Scherbov, eds. 2004. *The End of World Population Growth in the 21st Century: New Challenges for Human Capital Formation and Sustainable Development*. London: Earthscan.

McCloskey, Deidre N. 2015. *Bourgeois Equality: How Ideas, Not Capital or Institutions Enriched the World.* University of Chicago Press.

McLaren, Lauren M. 2003. 'Anti-Immigrant Prejudice in Europe: Contact, Threat Perception, and Preferences for the Exclusion of Migrants'. *Social Forces* 81: 909–36.

2012. 'The Cultural Divide in Europe: Migration, Multiculturalism and Political Trust'. *World Politics* 64: 199–241.

McLaren, Lauren and Mark Johnson. 2007. 'Resources, Group Conflict and Symbols: Explaining Anti-Immigration Hostility in Britain'. *Political Studies* 55: 709–32.

Majone, G. 1994. 'The Rise of the Regulatory State in Europe'. *West European Politics* 17: 77–101.

Maier, Jurgen and Berthold Rittberger. 2008. 'Shifting Europe's Boundaries: Mass Media, Public Opinion, and the Enlargement of the EU'. *European Union Politics* 9: 243–67.

Mansbridge, Jane. 1983. *Beyond Adversary Democracy.* University of Chicago Press.

Marcus, George E., W. Russell Neuman and Michael MacKuen. 2000. *Affective Intelligence and Political Judgment.* University of Chicago Press.

Migration Advisory Committee. 2012. *Analysis of the Impacts of Migration.* London: Home Office.

Minkenberg, M. and P. Perrineau. 2007. 'The Radical Right in the European Elections 2004'. *International Political Science Review* 28: 29–55.

Minsky, Hyman P. 1982. *Can 'It' Happen Again?* Armonk, NY: M. E. Sharpe.

1986. *Stabilizing an Unstable Economy.* New Haven, CT: Yale University Press.

Moran, M. 2002. 'Review Article: Understanding the Regulatory State'. *British Journal of Political Science* 32: 391–413.

Mudde, Cas. 2007. *Populist Radical Right Parties in Europe.* Cambridge University Press.

Muller, Edward N. 1979. *Aggressive Political Participation.* Princeton University Press.

Nagel, Jonathan H. and Christopher Wlezien. 2010. 'Centre-Party Strength and Major-Party Divergence in Britain, 1945–2005'. *British Journal of Political Science* 40: 279–304.

Neuman, W. Russell, George E. Marcus, Ann N. Crigler and Michael MacKuen, eds. 2007. *The Affect Effect: Dynamics of Emotion in Political Thinking and Behavior.* University of Chicago Press.

Nicholson, Sir David. 2010. 'Speech to NHS Alliance Conference', Bournemouth International Centre, 18 November.

Norris, Pippa. 2011. *Democratic Deficit: Critical Citizens Revisited.* Cambridge University Press.

North, Douglas C. 1990. *Institutions, Institutional Change, and Economic Performance*. Cambridge University Press.

Oesch, Daniel. 2008. 'Explaining Workers' Support for Right-Wing Populist Parties in Western Europe: Evidence from Austria, Belgium, France, Norway and Switzerland'. *International Political Science Review* 29: 349–73.

Offer, A. and G. Söderberg. 2016. *The Nobel Factor: The Prize in Economics, Social Democracy, and the Market Turn*. Princeton University Press.

Office for National Statistics. 2014. *National Population Projections, 2012-Based Reference Volume*. Titchfield: ONS.

Okun, Arthur M. 1962. *Potential GNP, Its Measurement and Significance*. New Haven, CT: Cowles Foundation, Yale University.

Piris, Jacques-Couvas. 2010. *The Lisbon Treaty: A Legal and Political Analysis*. Cambridge University Press.

Pollard, S. 1982. *The Wasting of the British Economy*. London: Croom Helm.

Rallings, Colin and Michael Thrasher. 2009–15. *Local Elections Handbook*. Plymouth: Elections Centre.

Raudenbush, Stephen W. and Anthony S. Bryk. 2002. *Hierarchical Linear Models: Applications and Data Analysis Methods*, 2nd edn. Thousand Oaks, CA: Sage Publications.

Ray, Leonard. 2003. 'When Parties Matter: The Conditional Influence of Party Positions on Voter Opinions about European Integration'. *Journal of Politics* 65: 978–94.

Reinhart, Christopher M. and Kenneth S. Rogoff. 2009. *This Time is Different: Eight Centuries of Financial Folly*. Princeton University Press.

Romer, David. 1994. 'The Origins of Endogenous Growth'. *Journal of Economic Perspectives* 8: 3–22.

Rose, Richard. 1980. *Do Parties Make a Difference?* New York: Macmillan.

Runciman, William G. 1966. *Relative Deprivation and Social Justice*. Berkeley, CA: University of California Press.

Rydgren, Jens. 2002. 'Radical Right Populism in Sweden: Still a Failure, but for How Long?'. *Scandinavian Political Studies* 25: 27–56.

Sachs, Jeffrey D. and A. M. Warner. 1995. 'Economic Reform and the Process of Economic Integration'. *Brookings Papers on Economic Activity* 1: 1–95.

Schmidt, M. G. 1996. 'When Parties Matter: A Review of the Possibilities and Limits of Partisan Influence on Public Policy'. *European Journal of Political Research* 30: 155–83.

Schofield, Norman. 1993. 'Political Competition and Multiparty Coalition Government'. *European Journal of Political Research* 23: 1–33.

Seyd, Patrick and Paul Whiteley. 1992. *Labour's Grass Roots: The Politics of Party Membership*. Oxford: Clarendon Press.

Seyd, Patrick, Jeremy J. Richardson and Paul Whiteley. 1995. *True Blues: The Politics of Conservative Party Membership*. Oxford University Press.

Shiller, Robert J. 2000. *Irrational Exuberance*. Princeton University Press.

Shipman, Tim. 2016. *All Out War: The Full Story of How Brexit Sank Britain's Political Class*. London: William Collins.

Sims, Christopher. 1980. 'Macroeconomics and Reality'. *Econometrica* 48: 1–48.

Smith, Adam. 1976 [1776]. *The Wealth of Nations*. Indianapolis, IN: Liberty Classics.

Steenbergen, Marco R. and D. J. Scott. 2004. 'Contesting Europe? The Salience of European Integration as a Party Issue', in G. Marks and M. R. Steenbergen, eds., *European Integration and Political Conflict*. Cambridge University Press.

Steenbergen, Marco R., Erica E. Edwards and Catherine E. de Vries. 2007. 'Who's Cueing Whom? Mass–Elite Linkages and the Future of European Integration'. *European Union Politics* 8: 13–35.

Stevens, Daniel. 2013. 'Issue Evolution in Britain: The Debate on European Union Integration, 1964–2010'. *European Journal of Political Research* 53: 536–57.

Stock James H. and Mark W. Watson. 2001. 'Vector Autoregressions'. *Journal of Economic Perspectives* 15: 1010–15.

Stokes, Donald E. 1963. 'Spatial Models of Party Competition'. *American Political Science Review* 57: 368–77.

1992. 'Valence Politics', in Dennis Kavanagh, ed., *Electoral Politics*. Oxford: Clarendon Press.

Swank, D. H. and R. Eisinga. 1999. 'Economic Outcomes and Voting Behavior in a Multi-Party System: An Application to the Netherlands'. *Public Choice* 101: 195–213.

Toda, Hiro and Taku Yamamoto. 1995. 'Statistical Inference in Vector Autoregressions with Possibly Integrated Process'. *Journal of Econometrics* 66: 225–50.

Vandenbussche, J., P. Aghion and C. Meghir. 2006. 'Growth, Distance to Frontier and Composition of Human Capital'. *Journal of Economic Growth* 11(2): 97–127.

Van der Eijk, Cees and Mark N. Franklin. 2004. 'Potential for Contestation on European Matters at National Elections in Europe', in G. Marks and M. R. Steenbergen, eds., *European Integration and Political Conflict*. Cambridge University Press.

Vliegenthart, Rens, Andreas R. T. Schuck, Hajo G. Boomgaarden and Claes H. De Vreese. 2008. 'News Coverage and Support for European Integration 1990–2006'. *International Journal of Public Opinion Research* 20: 415–39.

Vossing, Konstantin. 2015. 'Transforming Public Opinion about European Integration: Elite Influence and Its Limits'. *European Union Politics* 16: 157–75.

Walker, Iain and Heather J. Smith. 2002. 'Fifty Years of Relative Deprivation Research', in I. Walker and H. J. Smith, eds., *Relative Deprivation: Specification, Development and Integration*. Cambridge University Press.

Walker, Iain, N. Wong and K. Kretzschmar. 2002. 'Relative Deprivation and Attribution: From Grievance to Action', in I. Walker and H. Smith, eds., *Relative Deprivation: Specification, Development and Integration*. Cambridge University Press.

Ward, Colleen, Stephen Bochner and Adrian Furnham. 2001. *The Psychology of Culture Shock*. London: Routledge.

Werts, H., Scheepers, P. and Lubbers, M. 2013. 'Euro-Scepticism and Radical Right-Wing Voting in Europe, 2002–2008: Social Cleavages, Socio-Political Attitudes and Contextual Characteristics Determining Voting for the Radical Right'. *European Union Politics* 14: 183–205.

Whitaker, Richard and Philip Lynch. 2011. 'Explaining Support for the UK Independence Party at the 2009 European Parliament Elections'. *Journal of Elections, Public Opinion and Parties* 21: 359–79.

Whiteley, Paul. 2000. 'Economic Growth and Social Capital'. *Political Studies* 48(3): 443–66.

Whiteley, Paul and Patrick Seyd. 2002. *High-Intensity Participation: The Dynamics of Party Activism in Britain*. Ann Arbor, MI: University of Michigan Press.

Whiteley, Paul, Patrick Seyd and Anthony Billinghurst. 2006. *Third-Force Politics: Liberal Democrats at the Grassroots*. Oxford University Press.

Whiteley, Paul, Harold D. Clarke, David Sanders and Marianne C. Stewart. 2013. *Affluence, Austerity and Electoral Change in Britain*. Cambridge University Press.

2015. 'Why Do Voters Lose Trust in Governments: Public Perceptions of Government Honesty and Trustworthiness in Britain 2000–2013'. *British Journal of Politics and International Relations* 18: 234–54.

2016. 'Hunting the Snark: A Reply to "Re-Evaluating Valence Models of Political Choice"'. *Political Science Research and Methods* 4: 221–40.

Wray, L. R. 2016. *Why Minsky Matters: An Introduction to the Work of a Maverick Economist*. Princeton University Press.

Index